Neoliberal power and public management reforms

MANCHESTER
1824

Manchester University Press

SOCIAL AND POLITICAL POWER

Series editor: Mark Haugaard

Power is one of the most fundamental concepts in social science. Yet, despite the undisputed centrality of power to social and political life, few have agreed on exactly what it is or how it manifests itself. Social and Political Power is a book series which provides a forum for this absolutely central, and much debated, social phenomenon. The series is theoretical, in both a social scientific and normative sense, yet also empirical in its orientation. Theoretically it is oriented towards the Anglo-American tradition, including Dahl and Lukes, as well as to the Continental perspectives, influenced either by Foucault and Bourdieu, or by Arendt and the Frankfurt School. Empirically, the series provides an intellectual forum for power research from the disciplines of sociology, political science and the other social sciences, and also for policy-oriented analysis.

Already published

Power, luck and freedom: Collected essays
Keith Dowding

Neoliberal power and public management reforms

Peter Triantafillou

Manchester University Press

Published by Manchester University Press
Altrincham Street, Manchester M1 7JA

www.manchesteruniversitypress.co.uk

British Library Cataloguing-in-Publication Data
A catalogue record for this book is available from the British Library

ISBN 978 1 5261 0374 1 hardback

First published 2017

Typeset by
Servis Filmsetting Ltd, Stockport, Cheshire
Printed in Great Britain
by CPI Group (UK) Ltd, Croydon, CR0 4YY

Contents

Series editor's foreword

Bertrand Russell once argued that power is to social science what energy is to physics (Russell, 1938, p. 10). While power is one of the most important concepts in the social sciences, it is also one of the most complex and elusive to research.

Weber's analysis of power and authority (1947 and 1978) is one of the first social scientific discussions of power and it influenced the US power debates, which developed after the Second World War. In these debates Dahl's careful analysis stands out for its clarity in providing us with a conceptual vocabulary of power (Dahl, 1957 and 1968). This includes an agency-based, exercise and decision-making definition of power; conceptualised in terms of powerful actors (A) making subordinates (B) do something that they would not otherwise do. This exercise of power is distinct from resources (that may or may not be exercised) and it provides powerholders with power of specific scope. However, while providing a new set of conceptual tools to analyse about power relations, Dahl's work was subject to sustained critique from Bachrach and Baratz and others, who argued that power is also exercised through structural biases that are not necessarily reducible to overt decision-making (Bachrach and Baratz, 1962). Lukes followed this critique with his theorisation of the third dimension of power (Lukes, 1974), which concerns the mobilisation of belief and ideology to legitimise power relations of domination. The three-dimensional model was applied in a richly textured empirical study of Appalachian mining communities (Gaventa, 1982). Overall, as the three-dimensional power debates develop, the focus shifts from actions of the dominating actor A to the counter-intuitive and fascinating phenomenon that subordinate actors B often appear to actively acquiesce or participate in their own domination.

In a qualified critique of Lukes, Scott argued that appearances are often deceptive (Scott, 1990). The relationship between public and private discourse renders the working of three-dimensional power more complex than any simplistic images of the oppressed willingly participating in their own domination, or internalising false consciousness. In turn, Scott's work has inspired an ongoing power literature on the complexities of resistance versus acquiescence.

In the 1980s, under the influence of the translation of Foucault's work (for instance, Foucault, 1979 and 1982), the Anglophone power debates shifted towards more epistemic and ontological analysis, which resonated with the shift of emphasis from the powerful to the conditions of the oppressed. This gave rise to fascinating work on the relation between power and discourse; power and truth; the way power influences the ontological formation of social subjects through discipline; and how new modes of governance have changed systemic power relations (including Clegg, 1989; Dean, 2010; Laclau, 2005; Flyvbjerg, 1998 and Hayward, 2000). However, in critique, many have argued that neo-Foucauldians tend to lose sight of the significance of individual agency (Lukes, 2005).

Bridging the intellectual divide between those following the Dahl–Lukes trajectory and the neo-Foucauldians, another important thread to the power debates comes from Giddens (1984) and Bourdieu's (1989) conceptualisations of structure as a verb. This way of thinking provides us with conceptual tools for making sense of how agents both structure and are structured by relations of power.

In international relations, the shift from agency toward systemic, epistemic and ontological perceptions of power took the form of a gradual move from realist focus on resources to a more idealist emphasis upon soft power (Nye, 1990 and 2011). Similarly, in rational choice theory, there emerged an emphasis upon the systemic situatedness of strategic choices.

In *Neoliberal power and public management reforms*, Peter Triantafillou bridges these contemporary theoretical trends in a highly sophisticated manner. This work documents the clash between classical traditions of understanding bureaucracy, as typified by Weber, and perspectives of governance deriving from neoliberal traditions that emphasise the construction of markets, performance indicators and the audit of bureaucratic structures. From these perspectives, systems are considered *sui generis*, yet they are thought to require the ideational control and managed structuration in order to become optimal. Of course, the concept of optimality is not simply an empirical fact but a normative judgement.

The effect of interrogating the social contexts and social ontology of agents has caused many theorists to re-evaluate the nature of power normatively, moving away from the automatic equation between power and domination to a perception of power as a condition of possibility for agency, thus freedom (Morriss, 2002 and 2009). Thus, freedom and power move from being opposing categories to being mutually constitutive. Associated with this normative re-evaluation, power theorists distinguish between power-to, power-with and power-over (Allen, 1998 and 1999; Pansardi, 2012). To begin with, power-over was considered a normative negative, suggesting oppression, while power-to and power-with were the positives. However, some theorists argue power-over can also have emancipatory, as well as the more obvious dominating, aspects (Haugaard, 2012). In *Neoliberal power and public management reforms*, Trianfillou shows us how current attempts to manage the power structures of society are premised upon a neoliberal vision of freedom, which is paradoxically controlling of behaviour while seeking normative justification through the use of discourses that suggest individual emancipation.

Overall, the book series, Social and Political Power, seeks to build upon these rich traditions of power analysis, which currently make the study of social and political power one of the most vibrant fields in the social and political sciences. It also builds upon the success of the *Journal of Political Power*, which provides an important forum for article analysis, while this book series facilitates longer works on social and political power.

The book series is open to any of the multiplicity of traditions of power analysis, and it welcomes research that is theoretically oriented, as well as empirical research on power or practitioner oriented applications.

Mark Haugaard
National University of Ireland, Galway, Ireland

References

Allen, A. (1998). Rethinking power. *Hyptia*, 13.

Allen, A. (1999). *The power of feminist theory: domination, resistance, solidarity*. Boulder, CO: Westview Press.

Bachrach, P., & Baratz, M.S. (1962). The two faces of power. *American Political Science Review*, 56(4), 947–52.

Bourdieu, P. (1989). Social space and symbolic power. *Sociological Theory*, 7(1), 14–25.

Clegg, S. (1989). *Frameworks of power*. London: Sage.

Dahl, R. A. (1957). The concept of power. *Behavioural Science*, 2(3), 201–15.

Dahl, R. A. (1968). Power. In David L. Shills (ed.) *International encyclopedia of the social sciences*, vol. 12, 405–15. New York: Macmillan.

Dean, M. (2010). *Govermentality: power and rule in modern society*, second edition. London: Sage.

Flyvbjerg, B. (1998). *Rationality and power: democracy in practice*. Chicago: The University of Chicago Press.

Foucault, M. (1979). *Discipline and punish: the birth of the prison*. Harmondsworth: Penguin.

Foucault, M. (1982). The subject and power. In H. L. Dreyfus and P. Rabinow (eds), *Michel Foucault: beyond structuralism and hermeneutics*, 208–26. London: Harvester Wheatsheaf.

Gaventa, J. (1982). *Power and powerlessness: quiescence and rebellion in an Appalachian valley*. Oxford: Clarendon Press.

Giddens, A. (1984). *The constitution of society*. Cambridge: Polity Press.

Haugaard, M. (2012). Rethinking the four dimensions of power. *Journal of Political Power* 5(1), 35–54.

Hayward, C. (2000). *De-facing power*. Cambridge: Cambridge University Press.

Laclau E. (2005). *On populist reason*. London: Verso.

Lukes, S. (1974). *Power: a radical view*. London: Macmillan.

Lukes, S. (2005). *Power: a radical view*, second edition. Basingstoke: Palgrave Macmillan.

Morriss, P. (2002). *Power: a philosophical analysis*, second edition. Manchester: Manchester University Press.

Morriss, P. (2009). Power and liberalism. In S. Clegg and M. Haugaard (eds), *The Sage handbook of power*. London: Sage.

Nye, J. S. (1990). Soft power. *Foreign Policy*, 80, 153–72.

Nye, J. S. (2011). Power and foreign policy. *Journal of Political Power*, 4(1), 9–24.

Pansardi, P. (2012). Power to and power over: two distinct concepts? *Journal of Political Power*, 5(1), 73–89.

Russell, B. (1938). *Power: a new social analysis*. London: George Allen & Unwin.

Scott, J. C. (1990). *Domination and the arts of resistance: hidden transcripts*. New Haven: Yale University Press.

Weber, M. (1947) *The theory of social and economic organization*, ed. Talcott Parsons. New York: Free Press.

Weber, M. (1978). *Economy and society: an outline of interpretive sociology*, ed. G. Roth and C. Wittich. 2 vols. Berkeley: University of California Press.

Acknowledgements

This book is indebted to a wide range of intellectual sources and institutional environments. First of all, I want to express my gratitude to Mark Haugaard of the National University of Ireland for inviting me to contribute to the new series on Power with Manchester University Press. My colleagues at the Department of the Social Sciences and Business at Roskilde University in general and the Roskilde School of Governance in particular have provided very important intellectual inspirations. In particular, Jacob Torfing has pushed me to get going and supported me along the way with this book project. Also, Torben Dyrberg and Magnus Paulsen Hansen (at the Copenhagen Business School) have both provided important input to my conceptual discussions of neoliberalism. I am greatly indebted to the Department of Public Administration and Sociology at the Erasmus University for allowing me to stay there for a month in the autumn of 2015 and focus on this project. A particular thanks to Victor Bekkers, Joop Koppenjan and Erik-Hans Klijn. But I am also grateful to the helpful library staff of the Erasmus University. Last but not least I would like to thank the staff of the Manchester University Press for a very constructive dialogue throughout the whole process of conceiving, writing and publishing this book.

1

Introduction

Contemporary mutations of power in public administration and management

Almost half a century ago, the political scientist Philippe Schmitter asked whether Western liberal democracies were still in the age of corporatism (Schmitter, 1974; see also Lembruch & Schmitter, 1982). His answer was affirmative, though he also foresaw that corporatism would probably not last into the twenty-first century due to a number of inbuilt political and social tensions. Today, most scholars seem more concerned with the question of whether we are still in the age of neoliberalism. While such grand questions may be useful in that they may enable a mapping of wider tendencies and shifts in the ways our societies are governed, the task of this book is not to make a diagnosis of entire political systems or societies. Rather, I am trying much more modestly to analyse a few contemporary instances of power in public administration and management and trying to render these intelligible by linking them to neoliberal political rationalities. Thus, I will try to show in this book that neoliberalism is indeed very important for understanding the kind of power exercised through public administration and management in the early twenty-first century. Yet, my claim is not that neoliberalism is the only important political rationality. I will show that neoliberalism is in itself a complex phenomenon that is linked to public administration and management in no straightforward manner.

Over the last two or three decades, the public sectors of many liberal democracies have seen a tremendous surge, if not explosion, of reforms, programmes and policies seeking to promote accountability, credibility and evidence. These reforms include new ways of accounting for the procedures and results of the services produced by the public sector, the adoption of experimental and statistical techniques to provide so-called evidence to support policymaking, the institutionalisation of ever more sophisticated performance-measurement systems and the accreditation of institutions providing key public services. The general ambition of these interventions was to move from a rule-based to a result-based public sector.

Written two decades ago, the diagnosis found in Michael Power's *Audit society* (Power, 1997), appears more relevant than ever. Informed by a number of distinct political values, such as liberal democracy, goal effectiveness, resource efficiency and citizen choice, the attempts to promote accountability, evidence and transparency have proliferated and diversified in ways that go well beyond Power's incisive analysis. Many of the attempts to promote these three factors in the public sector have been analysed under the general notion of New Public Management (NPM). Following Hood's seminal definition (Hood, 1991), a growing body of literature has argued that the public sectors of liberal democracies are seeing the emergence of a new administrative or managerial paradigm focusing on professional management and market-inspired service production and delivery systems (Sahlin-Andersson, 2002; Pollitt & Bouckaert, 2011).

A relatively limited number of studies have tried to understand how contemporary public administration and management reforms, such as the quest for accountability, credibility and evidence, are linked to neoliberal power (du Gay, 1993; Clarke & Newman, 1997; Box et al., 2001; Thomas & Davies, 2005; Miller & Fox, 2007; Catlaw & Sandberg, 2012; Triantafillou, 2012). Notwithstanding insights produced by this literature, at least two important things remain underexplored. First, the intellectual or ideational underpinnings of these reforms are not very well understood. It has been argued that new public-management reforms are caused by, or at least in line with, neoliberal political ideologies favouring market over state provision of services (Dibben et al., 2004; Larner & Craig, 2005; Connell et al., 2009). Yet, the orientation towards market solutions in public-management reforms seems to play a much more limited role in Continental European countries than in the Anglophone countries. This diversity questions the existence of any straightforward relationship between these reforms and a so-called neoliberal ideology. Moreover, the public sectors of most liberal democracies have seen the rise of a number of more or less new practices that have little if anything to do with favouring market-based solution. These include new forms of accountability, evidence-based policymaking and accreditation. Thus, there is a need for a more adequate conceptualisation of the intellectual or ideational underpinning of contemporary public-administration and management reforms.

Secondly, the material underpinnings of contemporary public management reforms are often overlooked. Or, more precisely, only a few studies examine the link between the techniques and mechanisms of the ways in which neoliberal power is exercised through recent public sector reforms.

Studies of the forces behind the emergence and adaptation of NPM reforms have pointed to a mix of ideology, financial pressures, political systemic features and historical traditions (Christensen & Lægreid, 2002; Sahlin-Andersson & Engwall, 2002). In order to explain the emergence of NPM reforms I agree that we need to look into a mix of different country-specific factors. However, I also think that we need to have a better understanding of the ways in which the mechanisms and techniques of these actually work and link up with neoliberalism. However, with some important exceptions (Bäckström, 1999; Vrangbæk, 1999), few studies examine the new forms of power enabled by the techniques and tools of the new forms of public management. In sum, there is a need for more systematic interrogation of the diverse and shifting links between neoliberal political thinking and forms of expert knowledge on the one hand and the many administrative reforms, mechanisms and techniques on the other. This book will look into this by focusing on the contemporary quest for accountability, credibility and evidence in the public administration of some leading liberal democracies.

Aims and assumptions

The primary aim of this book is to examine contemporary public-management reforms and propose a more adequate understanding of contemporary neoliberal forms of power implicated by the quest for accountability, credibility and evidence found in recent public-management reforms. The secondary aim is to provide a critical analysis in the sense of addressing the power relations at stake in the quest for these factors in the public sector. Both aims imply providing an analytical framework grasping both the intellectual and the material underpinnings of the quest for them. These aims also imply discussing how the material and normative space of freedom for public administrations and civil servants is shaped by neoliberal power.

Apart from the dual aim of understanding and critically assessing neoliberal forms of power as they are articulated in public administration and management reforms, the book is driven by three propositions or working hypotheses. The first proposition is that these diverse public-management reforms and programmes constitute a series of distinct practices, each with its own logic, which over the last two or three decades have coalesced in a strategic assemblage attuned to the governing of government. By governing of government, or reflexive government, I am alluding to the ways in which the exercise of public authority is primarily targeting no longer individual citizens and populations but itself (Dean, 1999, pp. 176–7; Triantafillou, 2012, pp. 45–52). What is characteristic of many of these reforms is not only that they promise to provide services to citizens but also that they come with a number of instruments that seek to administer, incentivise and govern those public managers, civil servants, public professionals and frontline workers in order to make these operate in a more effective, efficient and innovative manner. Thus, governing seems to be increasingly targeting those who are engaged in governing the health, wealth and well-being of the citizenry and the population.

Secondly, new forms of knowledge and new ways of producing knowledge constitute a fundamental element in the emergence of the political and managerial reforms of the public sector and public services. The proliferation of computer systems, the internet and software solutions accessible both to the public administration and the populace which it is supposed to serve has enabled new ways of quantifying, calculating, comparing and disseminating knowledge about public-sector activities. This includes, among other things, new ways of objectifying and calculating the unit income and unit costs of public services; internet-based solutions to disseminate quality and performance measures allowing users to act as enlightened consumers of public services; systematic benchmarking of public-sector services; and the comprehensive and systematic reviews of existing knowledge on the effect of particular programmes and policy interventions. These new computational and calculative technologies have not only generated more knowledge and transparency around existing services, they have actively shaped the assessment and making of these services by providing new ways of turning public sector activities into discrete measurable product units.

Thirdly, I assume that neoliberal political thought lends crucial intellectual support to the quest for accountability, credibility and evidence in the public sector. Yet, it does so in a non-straightforward and apparently paradoxical way that calls for further clarification of the notion of neoliberalism. A key tenet of Friedrich Hayek's critique of socialism and comprehensive welfare-state planning was epistemological: since no single (political) actor can ever get to know the diverse wills and preferences of the citizens of a given state, comprehensive state planning and interventions are bound to fail and likely to lead to authoritarianism (Hayek, 1944, 1979). This critique seems to have played an important role in the public-sector reforms launched in Britain and the US during the 1980s, which favoured privatisation and market-based solutions. However, privatisation was never the only instrument used to reform the public sector. The last two decades have seen the emergence of a wide range of managerial systems and techniques that seem to be informed by a far more optimistic view of the state's cognitive capacities. This is particularly clear in the evidence-based policy movement, but also the quest for accountability and credibility appears to be informed by a strong faith in the political benefits of generating systematic knowledge of and insight into the ways in which public-sector activities are conducted.

The persistent faith in the governing potentials of comprehensive knowledge raises both conceptual and political questions. Conceptually, is the quest for accountability, credibility and evidence in the public sector an indication of a change in neoliberal thinking, a mixture of neoliberal and more welfarist rationalities, or do we see the emergence of a wholly new political rationality? This book argues that it still makes sense to use the term 'neoliberalism' about the kind of thinking informing current public-sector reforms. However, because the object of government in the quest for accountability, credibility and evidence is not society but rather government itself, Hayek's critique seems less relevant. Rather, the central part of neoliberalism here is not its epistemological critique but its interventionist or, more precisely, constructivist dimension, namely: how to construe an environment conducive to the self-governing capacities of citizens and, in this case, government itself. By the same token, current reforms seem to be more optimistic regarding the ruler's utilisation of knowledge. Rather than advocating the limitation of intervention because of the ruler's (state's) limited capacity to get to know the desires and needs of civil society, contemporary public management reforms seem to be informed by the belief that it is both necessary and even possible to rule better by the systematic production of more and better knowledge.

Book overview

The book is structured as follows. Chapter 2 accounts for a number of distinct approaches seeking to analyse critically the role of neoliberal power in contemporary public-administration and management reforms. The chapter discusses six analytical approaches, including both political science and sociological strands. It argues that, while all six approaches offer valuable critical insights into contemporary public management reforms, the Foucauldian analytics of government has a certain advantage due to its focus on the at once enabling and critical role that academic discourses on the state in general and neoliberal political rationalities in particular play for the art and practice of contemporary administrative reforms.

Chapter 3 addresses the academic discourses or intellectual underpinnings of the reforms with a particular focus on neoliberal political rationalities. It examines the contours of neoliberal political thinking as it is expressed both in the political philosophy of Hayek and others and in the more mundane theories of public choice, neo-institutional economics and principal-agent theory that have all more or less directly informed public-management reforms. The main point made here is that the political rationalities informing public-management reforms have changed quite substantially over the last three decades from focusing rather narrowly on market solutions to a wider array of schemes focusing on the facilitation of the self-steering capacities of public agencies by way of the unprecedented production of knowledge on the public sector. This change is best understood by addressing neoliberalism as a problematic of government (i.e. a set of questions about how best to govern) rather than an ideological template for intervention (i.e. a set of answers and normative blueprints for intervention).

The next four chapters focus mainly on the material elements of the quest for accountability, credibility and evidence. By material elements, I am referring to the plurality of schemes, procedures and techniques at play in the governing of the public sector. By the intellectual elements, I am referring to the kinds of reasoning and forms of knowledge informing the public-sector reforms. They are based on examples from Anglophone countries (Australia, Britain, New Zealand and the US) and from Continental Western Europe (mainly the Nordic countries, the Netherlands, Germany and France). All are liberal democracies, though they differ in many ways, including the ways in which the pursuit of accountability, credibility and evidence is unfolding. The examples are meant not to be representative but rather exemplary of the most elaborated governing attempts to promote the said virtues in the public sector. In order to examine these reforms, I draw heavily on existing academic studies and expert reports in the area. Moreover, a large number of official and publicly available policy documents issued by governments, public agencies, national audit offices and other public institutions have been compiled and analysed. Finally, a few interviews with top public managers have been made to supplement the information drawn from documentary studies.

Chapter 4 and 5 both examine reforms seeking to promote accountability. Chapter 4 provides an overview of key instruments and reforms adopted to promote accountability in the public sector. It also discusses the key political logics at play in these reforms. The chapter first discusses how to grasp accountability in a way that allows us to map the kind of power it entails. This conceptual clarification points to the historical variation in the practice of accountability and the kinds of power linked to it. I then examine how accountability relates to efforts to democratise sovereign power. This is followed by an analysis of the ways in which accountability links up with the governmentalisation of public administrations and the role played by accountability in the attempts of government to be more attentive to and to mobilise citizens.

Chapter 5 zooms in on the changing role of supreme audit institutions

(SAIs), or national audit offices. It examines how performance auditing of state and other public institutions has become increasingly important in most OECD countries. It explores SAIs' move from a relatively narrow focus on the technical and legal control of public expenditures to a much wider focus including assessments of efficiency and goal-effectiveness. This move testifies to the influence of neoliberal political rationalities overlapping, but not wholly replacing, classical liberal concerns with the abuses of state power. Using examples from the public-health sector, I examine how SAIs conduct performance audits and thereby seek to penetrate domains of professional authority. The chapter shows how the SAI performance audits hinge on standardising and quantifying knowledge and techniques that render complex activities susceptible to external assessment and government interventions.

Chapter 6 turns to the governing technique of accreditation, which seeks to make the production of public services credible. Accreditation may constitute the pinnacle of the wider movement whereby the government reflects upon and governs itself. The chapter examines the ways in which governments and ministries use accreditation in order to try to ensure the credibility and quality of the services produced by hospitals and universities. This includes scrutinising the political arguments around the use of accreditation and the material elements of the accreditation schemes.

Chapter 7 moves on to examine the evidence-based policy movement. It tries to map and understand how and why new experimental and statistical techniques for producing knowledge have spread from medicine to education, crime prevention, employment and other social areas. It examines the somewhat uneasy relationship between evidence-based policymaking (EP) and neoliberal rationalities of government. I explore the ways in which EP promotes experimentation, piecemeal reforms and the constant possibility of refuting the knowledge upon which reforms are based. I argue that, to the extent that EP has gained political credence as a regulative ideal, it entails that the public administration must constantly question itself, test its policy-delivery solutions and see to it that its interactions with citizens in order to better their situation are based on available evidence.

Chapter 8 examines and discusses the implications of the quest for accountability, credibility and evidence for those supposed to carry out these reforms, namely civil servants. The chapter examines general shifts in the regulative ideals informing the making of the bureaucratic persona in liberal democracies from ones emphasising the importance of upholding a strict separation between public and private spheres to ones stressing the need for civil servants to engage in extensive interactions with public and private stakeholders. This chapter explores how this shift links up to a wider change in the political rationalities of government informing the working of the public sectors from classical liberalism to constructivist neoliberalism.

Finally, Chapter 9 sums up and discusses the findings. It draws together the analysis of neoliberal political rationalities conducted in Chapter 3 and the analyses of the concrete reforms and devices employed over the last few decades to promote accountability, credibility and evidence-based policymaking. The chapter essentially concludes that the quest for accountability, credibility and the use of evidence in the public administration are examples of a more or less new form of power. This form of power is in turn informed by what I call constructivist neoliberalism. It is stressed that the administrative reforms and mechanisms examined in this book cannot be reduced to or read off from a single and coherent political rationality (neoliberalism). However, even if other political rationalities and specific events are important to understand contemporary forms of power exercised through public administration and management reforms, these are provided with a certain intellectual and strategic coherence both by recent academic discourses within the disciplines of public administration and management, and by a political rationality seeking to make the public administration turn back upon itself in order to ensure its efficiency and quality.

2

Critical approaches to public administration and management

Introduction

This chapter provides an overview of some of the key approaches available to grasp critically contemporary public-management and governance reforms. By 'critical' I am referring to an examination of the shifting ways in which power is exercised over and through the public sector. My aim is to identify the framework able to render intelligible how and why – by what governing mechanisms, norms of conduct and modes of reasoning – government started more or less systematically to fold back upon itself. This framework should also allow for an exposition and discussion of the new forms of freedom propagated and the forms of freedom excluded by these governing mechanisms, norms of conduct and modes of reasoning.

The overview includes Max Weber's analysis of the modern bureaucracy and its link to liberal democracy. I then move on to account for what I term realist critiques of public administration and policymaking, notably Lindblom's and Wildavsky's studies of liberal democracy and its administrative interventions. Thirdly, I touch on a few works critically addressing the modernist features of the bureaucracy. This is followed by an exploration of Gramscian-inspired discourse analysis applied to recent public-management reforms. Fifthly, I discuss the political-economy-inspired analysis of neoliberalism by key French sociologists. I then explore the ways in which Latour's science-and-technology approach has inspired a limited number of studies of public administration and management. Finally, I briefly account for Foucault's analytics of power–knowledge relations in general and his notion of government and governmentality in particular. I try to explain why I find the latter approach the most adequate one. By implication, Foucault's analytics of government informs the analyses of this book.

Modernity critiques

Scores of publications have been written on Weber's incisive and critical analysis of modern bureaucracy, and it may therefore seem impossible to add much new to our understanding of Weber's analysis. Nevertheless, I think there is a need to highlight Weber's understanding of the link between modern bureaucracy and liberal democracy, as this link is absolutely essential to the problem of this book. In the following I argue that Weber saw modern bureaucracy and the power invested in it as a crucial precondition for liberal democracy but that he was at the same time deeply ambivalent about the moral virtues of modern bureaucracy.

Before moving on to the topic of liberal democracy, it may be useful to recapitulate briefly the essence of Weber's conception of modern bureaucracy. First of all, he linked modern bureaucracy to formal rationality. The bureaucratic administration has a formally and often legally defined structure carefully specifying authority and duties. Thus, formal, general rule is the defining means of the bureaucracy: 'The authority to order certain matters by decree – which has been legally granted to an agency – does not entitle the agency to regulate the matter by individual commands given for each case, but only to regulate the matter abstractly' (Weber, 1978, p. 958).

The formal character of the bureaucratic organisation is also expressed in a distinctive ethos. Devoted to 'impersonal and functional purposes', the bureaucratic official acts in a 'spirit of formalistic impersonality … without hatred or passion, and hence without affection or enthusiasm' (Weber, 1978, pp. 225, 959). As noted by Brubaker, this formalistic and impersonal bureaucratic persona corresponds to the impersonality of market transactions (Brubaker, 1991, p. 21). Whether driven by self-interest as Adam Smith would have it, or by the accumulation of capital as Marx argued, the acts of production, trade and consumption in a capitalist market economy are mediated not by personal relationships but by the impersonalised medium of money. Secondly, Weber saw technical efficiency as another defining feature of the bureaucratic administration, which is why this mode of organisation was about to become the dominant one in both the private and public sectors – at least around the early twentieth century. The bureaucracy owed its superior efficiency to its machine-like character in which material and personal costs of performing a given task are minimised, and the problem is solved in the optimum way (Weber, 1978, p. 973). The strict definition and division of labour enables the bureaucracy to utilise its resources efficiently and allows for a high level of calculability of results. Finally, the bureaucracy is based on expert knowledge in order to provide the most effective solutions to given ends. Weber linked this systematic use of technical expertise to a particular persona or ethos, namely that of *Sachlichkeit* or matter-of-factness. In the bureaucracy, employees are hired on the basis of their merits or, more precisely, their formal education instead of personal relations or status. Thus, the individual civil servant and the bureaucratic organisation owe their superior effectiveness and their power to impersonal and meritocratic character.

Weber linked the formal character of the bureaucracy to the functioning of liberal democracy. The establishment of a modern bureaucracy, the dominant and most effective instrument of power in a territorial state, was seen by Weber to be conducive to what he called mass democracy. By being based on impersonal rules and procedures and merit-based expertise, modern bureaucracy encourages the 'levelling of the governing in face of the governing and bureaucratically articulated group' (Weber, 1978, p. 985). This levelling between the people and their governors (politicians and civil servants) is to be conflated neither with more direct public influence on decision-making nor with a change of balance of power between the people and their governors in favour of the former. Rather, it ensures that all citizens are treated equally in the face of the laws and procedures according to which the bureaucratic administration can exercise power over the people. Thus, the generalised civil and political rights of individual citizens grounded in constitutional law as envisaged by liberalism are importantly supplemented by the rules and procedures disciplining the way in which the state bureaucracy intervenes in society and the life of individual citizens. The taming of state power by means of impersonal rules and expertise correlates with Weber's understanding of freedom as the absence of physical and psychic coercion and allows the individual to pursue rational or meaningful actions (Weber, 1949, pp. 124–5). In brief, Weber seems to regard the formal and impersonal organisation and functioning of modern bureaucracy as functionally conducive to a liberal mode of democracy where the key concern is to ensure the formal rights of citizens and protect them from arbitrary use of (state) power.

If Weber saw the bureaucracy as a mechanism of rule that was functionally conducive to liberal democracy, he also identified some fundamental moral and political problems of bureaucracy. Firstly, modern bureaucracy does not allow for more direct democracy. On the contrary, the impersonal and expert-based form of rule constituting the core of bureaucratic power seems to be directly at odds with more participatory and direct forms of democracy. Accordingly, as already argued, bureaucracy does not change the balance of power between the people and their rulers. Secondly, the cultivation of the bureaucratic ethos must take place within a formal and very limited value sphere that leaves little room for socially meaningful action. By the latter, Weber is referring to actions guided by rational and conscious reflections about how to realise certain substantive ends or values. To be free then is to rationally pursue substantive values (Weber, 1922, p. 192). The extension of bureaucratic power constitutes a significant danger to individuals' free pursuit of substantive values (Brubaker, 1991, pp. 104–5). This limitation of substantive freedom includes not only the civil servants inhabiting bureaucratic organisations but also the citizens governed by the expansion of bureaucratic power, something that Weber sees as a more or less irreversible tendency of modern Western societies (Mommsen, 1974). More generally, Weber envisages formal or instrumentally rational action to expand into and displace existing value spheres. Thus, Weber seems to be suggesting that the kind of formal rationality embodied in bureaucratic power is, on the one hand, a precondition for liberal democracy and its formal equality of citizens, but, on the other hand, undermining the kinds of socially meaningful action committed to the pursuit of ultimate values. It is crucial to understand that Weber is criticising not the state or state power per se but rather the expanding and imperialist ability of generalised, formal reason to exclude other forms of substantive rationality.

Weber's analysis of the expansion of formal, instrumental rationality has – together with Marxist theory and Freud's psychoanalysis – been the key inspiration of the Frankfurt School. In the works of Horkheimer, Adorno (Horkheimer & Adorno, 1972) and, later on, Habermas (Habermas, 1989), we find several incisive and deeply pessimistic assessments of Enlightenment, science and formal, instrumental rationality, which is seen to encroach on personal authenticity and autonomy (for an overview: Jay, 1996). As they locate formal, instrumental rationality not only with the public administration but also – and much more fundamentally – with capitalist market forces, it is perhaps no surprise that few of these works directly address modern bureaucracy. An important exception to this, is Zygmunt Bauman's *Modernity and the Holocaust* (Bauman, 1989), which argues that the Holocaust was made possible by the kind of formal and impersonal rule exercised by the Nazi administration. According to Bauman, the Holocaust cannot be reduced to some perverse, German ideology of a superior *Volk* seeking to protect its purity but must (also) be seen in the light of a generalised feature of modern bureaucracy, namely its impersonal character enabling the strict objectification of the governed even if the latter are human beings.

Another seminal, though less dramatic, work is James Scott's *Seeing like a state* (Scott, 1998), which launches a strong critique against what he terms high-modernist state planning. This is not just a neoliberal crusade against state interventions, though Scott shares with neoliberal and realist critiques the point that the inherent epistemological limitation of the state is a universal hindrance for effective state intervention (see next chapter). Scott however goes further and exposes the role played by various types of scientific expertise in simplifying what are really highly complex natural phenomena and social process with a view to making them amenable to enumeration, taxation and, more generally, to state planning and control. It is these modern forms of objectifying expert knowledge that constitute the gaze of the modern state and tend to wreak havoc among natural environmental and civil societies.

Finally, and more recently, a group of US scholars linked to the Public Administration Theory Network (PAT-Net, 2015) have launched a series of critical studies focusing on the modernist underpinnings of public administration. One of the milestones produced by the members of this group is *Postmodern public administration*, which launches a comprehensive critique of modern representative democracy in general and public administration in particular (Miller & Fox, 2007). It argues that the loop model of representative democracy whereby the governors are held accountable to the sovereign people has little to do with political realities. By the same token, the increasingly painful attempts to control the behaviour of bureaucrats through ever more detailed rules are in vain. It points to the craze for measuring, monitoring and designing incentive systems in the public administration and argues that for public administration today it seems more important to show that you are doing your job than actually to do it. More precisely, Miller and Fox demonstrate that NPM-like reforms are not simply driven by neoliberal ideologues but depend more generally on a series of modern, objectivist forms of knowledge that purport to represent bureaucratic conduct as an accountable and predictable activity. Yet, it is argued that these apparently innocuous forms of expert knowledge are complicit in creating the people as a knowable object, with particular preferences and needs on the one hand, and may be used to legitimise almost any type of (particularistic) political intervention on the other. The critique delivered in *Postmodern public administration* is both compelling and comprehensive. It is compelling in the sense that it points to the depoliticising effects of managerial techniques of bodies of knowledge that present themselves to be merely technical but in reality come with strong biases. It is comprehensive in the sense that it locates this danger not with one particular discourse, such as neoliberalism, but with a multitude of mainstream public-administration theories and with a series of administrative instruments.

Realist critiques

If the modernist analyses often work at a rather general level and try to locate the public administration with the latter's dependence on formal rationality and objectifying expert knowledge, realist critiques focus more directly on the actual working of bureaucratic politics. In particular, they focus on the inability of bureaucratic politics to meet stipulated goals due to a mixture of power struggles and, not least, the state's limited knowledge about the society in which it intervenes.

Like Herbert Simon's before him (Simon, 1946), Lindblom's critique is targeted against the rationalist planning ideal, according to which societal problems and political goals are precisely defined, the costs and benefits of various instruments of solutions are carefully analysed and the optimum one is likely to be chosen (Lindblom, 1959). While this may be a desirable ideal, this is not how politics and policy processes are really played out. Not only does the public administration not have the knowledge or capacity to examine the suitability of all possible means, Lindblom argues, but also the political ends are rarely clearly defined and their internal ranking usually unspecified. Thus, akin to critical neoliberalism (see next chapter), Lindblom argues that because of the impossibility of analysing in depth all the consequences of all possible policy solutions, political decisions and policy implementation cannot be based on comprehensive planning. Moreover, as policy elites tend to differ only marginally on important policy issues, such as employment, social security and infrastructure, it is only relevant to examine a limited array of policy solutions. Finally, according to Lindblom, it is much more important for a society to ensure that all, or at least most, of its major political interests have a 'watchdog', such as was the case in the US during the late 1950s, than to have the public administration trying to examine all possible policy solutions (Lindblom, 1959, p. 85). Such watchdogs are much more likely to provide democratically satisfactory solutions than any kind of comprehensive, rational expertise. While Lindblom would go on to address critically some of the negative effects of market forces at play in liberal democracies, such as spells of mass unemployment and the disproportionate power of business elites (Lindblom, 1977), he maintained that liberal democracy, or polyarchy, is the least inferior type of political system because of its insistence that a society cannot be grasped and therefore cannot be planned in its entirety by the human intellect.

In *Speaking truth to power* (Wildavsky, 1986), Wildavsky is trying to strike a delicate balance on the relationship between truth and power/politics. On the one hand, Wildavsky holds on to the Enlightenment ethos that policy debates should be unfettered by power and that policy decisions should be informed by the best available knowledge. Solid knowledge about a societal problem is likely to result in better solutions than ignorance is. Thus, the art and craft of policy analysis hinges on expert knowledge. On the other hand, he insists that knowledge is prone to error and what we today agree is true we are likely to discard as a folly tomorrow. Accordingly, policymaking should be informed, but not determined, by what we think is true. More precisely, policy advice should be given with the recognition in mind that we are likely to err: 'Error must be the engine of change. Without error there would be one best way to achieve our objectives, which could themselves remain unaltered and unknowable. The original sin, after all, was to eat of the tree of knowledge so as to distinguish between good and evil' (Wildavsky, 1986, p. 404).

Wildavsky's observation of the frailty of human knowledge is likely to be indebted to his and Pressman's now famous study of the implementation of the programmes under the Economic Development Agency (Pressman & Wildavsky, 1973). One of the important but often overlooked points in this book is that implementations fail even in the case of clear policy goals, adequate resources and what – initially – appears to be a solid programme theory. However, the many technical and political obstacles involved in the implementation of any larger policy programme cannot be foreseen. Accordingly, experimental learning is absolutely fundamental to ensure implementation (Pressman & Wildavsky, 1973, chapter 6; Majone & Wildavsky, 1978). Policymaking should avoid epistemological and technological hubris and instead be prepared to conduct step-by-step trial-and-error processes in which the political actors – and policy analysts – show a commitment to modify their assumptions and try out new ways of reaching political goals. This experimental ethos is quite close to Donald T. Campbell's vision of the experimental society, which is discussed in Chapter 7. More generally, Wildavsky's emphasis of the frailty of human knowledge and his warning against letting knowledge determine political action is echoing the core sense of liberal political rationalities. This includes John Stuart Mill's argument in favour of the freedom of speech (Mill, 1974 [1859]) and, much later, the neoliberal warning against (excessive) state intervention because of the essential unknowability of civil society: see next chapter. Thus, while Wildavsky is providing a crucial critique of power exercised by the public administration, he is doing so from within the problem-space defined by liberal political rationalities.

The changes going through public administration in liberal democracies since the 1980s, under the heading of new public management (Hood, 1991), have resulted in a series of new critical studies. These studies criticise the new kind of public management not so much for its excessive trust in scientific knowledge and centralised planning, but – on the contrary

– for its unqualified belief in the blessings of market-based solutions. In order to increase value-for-money or produce better public services for less money, the public sector has seen the widespread use of privatisation, contracting out, internal contracts, performance measurement, total quality management systems and benchmarking. While the critiques of these reforms vary immensely, one of the key strands of critique is the realist one: NPM reforms are problematic, if not outright bad, because they do not deliver what they promise (Newman, 2000; Hasselbladhet al., 2008; Lowe, 2013). Others have pointed to the unintended and negative effects of accountability and performance management in the public sector (Smith, 1995; Bovens, 1998; Bevan & Hood, 2006).

More recently, studies of the US federal administration (Dilulio, 2014) and the UK central government (Hood & Dixon, 2015) suggest that three decades of public management reforms have seen a substantial growth of public expenditures combined with a drop in quality (at least in the UK). Interestingly, the increasing public expenditures are due not to civil servant staff costs, which have been more or less constant if not slightly reduced, but rather to the costs linked to the outsourcing of public service to private companies. My point is not whether this is a correct assessment of the outcome of NPM reforms but that much of this critique is entirely framed within the normative framework set by the NPM reforms themselves, i.e. are these reforms really providing more value for (the same or less) money? Such assessments are of course very important and provide a valuable academic contribution to the political debate over contemporary forms of public administration. Yet, the critique they provide is limited in the sense that they do address the kind of political rationalities and the working of the kinds of power unfolding under these new forms of public administration.

Discourse analysis

Gramscian-inspired discourse analysis has been used to critique recent public-management reforms and the celebration of network governance (Davies, 2011a, 2011b). The twofold argument here is, firstly, that network governance purports to posit itself as a new hegemonic governance discourse and, secondly, that network governance tends to reproduce hierarchical structures and often to continue bureaucratic domination because citizens are either unable or unwilling to become actively engaged in public service design and production. I think both points have certain credence. Network governance is presented, at least among many academics, as a new mode of public governance that supplements and partly supplants classical or Weberian-inspired public administration and new public management (Rhodes, 1994; Osborne, 2010). Moreover, many scholars have pointed out that hierarchical steering has not disappeared and is not likely to do so in a foreseeable future because of both functional reasons and political interests in maintaining control (Pierre & Peters, 2005; Torfing & Triantafillou, 2013). Notwithstanding the plausibility of this kind of Gramscian-inspired ideology critique, it comes with an implicit normative foundation that is remarkably similar to the governance discourses that it criticises. As I have argued elsewhere, if network governance and new public governance discourses have a normative core, it is the desire to empower citizens and, by implication, to reshape public administrations in ways that engage and tap into the resources of civil society (Triantafillou, 2004a, 2012, pp. 84–91). The ideology critique, at least in the version offered by Davies, mainly serves to reproduce this norm of empowerment purporting to create active and responsible citizen-subjects. But as argued succinctly by a number of Foucauldian-inspired scholars, this is also the very normative kernel of neoliberalism (Cruikshank, 1999), at least the kind of constructivist neoliberalism proliferating since the 1970s in many liberal democracies (see Chapter 3).

A closely related but perhaps a bit more sophisticated analysis of state action has evolved around the notion of 'referential' (Jobert & Muller, 1987; Muller, 1995). Inspired by the work of Lucien Nizard (1931–96), professor of political science at Grenoble, Bruno Jobert and Pierre Muller analysed public policies as a more or less coherent system of representation linking together a set of specific values, norms, causalities and connecting images (for an overview see Zittoun & Demongeot, 2010). Like discourse, the referential is not only a mental representation but also something that is expressed through and regulates practice. Also, while actors may manoeuvre strategically around a referential, it cannot be reduced to an instrument used by actors to further pre-given interests. Moreover, in contrast to Gramscian or Laclau-inspired discourse analysis, the notion of referential suggests a local and practical specificity that does not imply the existence of some kind of totalising discourse structuring what can and what cannot be said in a given period. This understanding of the referential as a discursive and regulative disposition that favours particular kinds of policy solutions, while obstructing others, has been used in a number of studies of EU employment policies (Morel et al., 2012b). However, so far, it has apparently not fed into the study of public management reforms (Moini, 2011).

Political economy approaches

Recently, a number of French sociologists have provided a refreshing and sharp critique of neoliberal politics in terms of political economy. Perhaps the most famous is Loïc Wacquant's critical analysis of the neoliberal state (Wacquant, 2009, 2010). Taking his point of departure in the tendency of going tough on crime in many OECD countries since the 1990s, Wacquant argues that neoliberalism is not only about market rule but also about supervisory workfare, a proactive penal state and the generalised elevation of an ethos of individual responsibility (for social misfortunes). While Wacquant is careful not to reduce the increasingly draconian penal laws to the functional needs of the capitalist economy, he argues that there is a clear strategic correlation between the dismantling of social welfare programmes and the stepping up of penal laws and regimes targeting poor people and their petty crimes to make ends meet.

If Wacquant's analysis of neoliberalism is primarily targeting the state, the work of the French sociologists Boltanski and Chiapello on the spirit of capitalism has mainly targeted organisations – private and public (Boltanski & Chiapello, 2005). They show how emancipatory ideals and participatory techniques that were part and parcel of the 1960s anti-establishment movement were taken up and adapted to suit the management theories emerging during the 1980s and 1990s, emphasising flexibility and delegation of responsibility to employees in both the private and the public sectors. This type of analysis implies combining insights from both Marxist and Weberian understandings of the capitalist political economy and its reproduction. Matthew Eagleton-Pierce, for example, has used this framework to examine the 'corporate governance' discourse of 1970s and the 'governance' agenda launched by the World Bank from the late 1980s (Eagleton-Pierce, 2014). This analysis is interesting because it emphasises the manifold and often very critical uses of the term 'governance', a term often applied to contest crude market-oriented management reforms and hierarchical forms of steering. Notwithstanding this attention to the multifarious character of governance discourse, Eagleton-Pierce regards governance as part of a wider cultural ideology that contributes to the constitution of 'a neoliberal spirit of capitalism'.

On the one hand, this analysis is highly thought-provoking and nuanced in its discussion of the role of (public) governance discourses and reforms. These analyses allow us to capture how highly diverse elements, such as management theories, managerial techniques, social welfare reforms, penal reforms and discourses of individual autonomy and responsibility coalesce in unexpected ways to form neoliberal forms of governing. In particular, I agree with the take on neoliberalism as being much more than the faith in market forces: see next chapter. On the other hand, I find that the critical edge of this type of analysis hinges too narrowly on its claim that the function of governance is, at least partly, to legitimise the functioning of capitalism. One could question why such an affiliation should constitute a normative problem – unless capitalism per se is regarded as a bad thing. More fundamentally, this kind of critique assumes that capitalism is a totalising system of material and symbolic production and reproduction. Despite all the incantations offered by Boltanski and Chiapello to convince the reader that it seeks to overcome the economic reductionism of Marxism, they insist on retaining capitalism as a societal system the functioning of which explains or must be explained by various discursive grammars of justification. While it may make sense to talk about capitalist forms of production, I think it implies a level of abstraction from a number of material and technical practices and diverse political and administrative strategies that limits the capacity to address critically such practices and strategies. Moreover, totalising notions such as the capitalist system or, more recently, empire (Hardt & Negri, 2000) may have been remarkably good at instigating all kinds of protests and revolutionary critiques. Yet they risk becoming just as diffuse as the object they intend to criticise. If effective critique implies a mode of analysis providing the reader with an account of how concrete political and administrative practices, knowledges and strategies coalesce to enable or actually generate effects of power, then an analysis evolving around 'the capitalist system' may not be the best starting point.

At the most general level, the political-economy approaches to neoliberalism fail to see that neoliberalism is not only a more or less sophisticated way of governing the state, the public sector, the economy and its citizens but also a critique of political power (Folkers, 2016; Foucault, 2008, p. 319). As we shall see in more detail in the next chapter, neoliberal rationalities of government have a double character in that they seek both to govern more efficiently and to interrogate the need for political interventions. That is, neoliberalism comes with a critical ethos of power and government. Thus, if managerial theories and schemes proliferating since the 1980s seem to have subsumed the 1960s anti-establishment agenda, this may be due less to a more or less sophisticated capitalist co-optation and more to the fact that neoliberalism has emerged and developed as a immanent critique of the dangers of the state power and their infringement on individual liberties and the right of citizens to decide for themselves. By reducing neoliberalism to the expression of the contemporary needs of the political economy, we fail to understand parts of the reason way neoliberal power continues to hold such strong sway on us in spite of all the criticisms launched against it.

Science and technology studies

The work of the French philosopher and sociologist of science Bruno Latour and the British sociologist Steve Woolgar has relatively recently inspired a limited number of interesting analyses of public administration. It may not seem very surprising that studies of science and technology inaugurated by Latour and Woolgar should inspire scholars of public administration. Thus, Latour and Woolgar were originally interested in providing a better understanding of the making, rather than the neutral revelation, of scientific facts (Woolgar & Latour, 1986). To this object Latour and Woolgar applied an anthropological method that entailed following scientists at work in laboratories and exploring how new scientific artefacts were produced by way of experimental methods and more or less sophisticated instruments (Latour, 1987). Subsequently, Latour expanded this study to a new sociology of associations (Latour, 2005). It may be taken as an indication of the analytical utility of the science and technology studies that it has been elevated to a discipline in itself, created its own journals and been applied to a number of social science issues, such as economics (MacKenzie, Muniesa & Siu, 2007). Here the approach has been used to study the production or expression of economic artefacts by way of ideas and techniques enabling us to talk about and ultimately manipulate what we today term 'the economy' (Mitchell, 1998).

However, until recently the science-and-technology-studies (STS) approach has had very little influence in political science and public administration studies. Apart from the usual compartmentalisation of academic disciplines, this may have to do with the not-too-obvious relevance of STS studies to the studies of political power. At least, many STS studies seem happy to limit their critical edge to being able to provide a 'better' account of how objects are produced, compared to mainstream sociology or other social sciences. That is, the success criterion of STS studies seems to be more an epistemological one, in the sense of providing more truthful accounts of how science and technological systems really work, than a political one, in the sense of critically interrogating how scientific discourses link up and enable the working of power relations. In fact, Latour's notion of critique seems quite conventional in that he locates it within the 'difference of potential between the world of delusion and the world of reality' (Latour, 2010, p. 475). In an earlier paper, Latour explains that STS studies seek to unravel how a particular matter of fact becomes a matter of concern in a 'critical situation' of techno-scientific controversies (Latour, 2004). Again, it seems as if Latour is more interested in epistemological and technological disputes than in the ways in which discourses of truth interact with the exercise of power. Of course, Latour does not define the entirety of STS studies and a few scholars do seem acutely attentive to some of the political dimensions of technological systems. Relevant STS studies include the works of Andrew Barry (Barry, 2001, 2012) and an attempt to establish a research agenda addressing the ways in which administrative and political instruments contribute to shaping the kind of political questions and goals that are deemed worth asking and pursuing (Lascoumes & Le Gales, 2007). This has resulted in a limited, but highly interesting set of studies of administrative technologies in diverse policy areas (Palier, 2007; e.g. Muniesa & Linhardt, 2011; Wolff, 2015). However, so far, these studies have not paid much attention to the link between these administrative technologies and the political discourses and rationalities purporting to tell the truth about how best to govern the state, such as neoliberalism.

Foucauldian analytics of government

Inspired by Foucault's notion of 'regime of truth' (Foucault, 1980b), the book focuses on the ways in which the schemes and techniques of power engrained in public management reforms hinge on new ways of producing true knowledge about the object of government. Such forms of knowledge include, on the one hand, rather lofty liberal political philosophy, public choice and principal-agent theorising, and, on the other hand, the 'grey' and petty forms of technical knowledge generated through performance auditing, randomised controlled trials and statistical surveys, and the everyday knowledge produced in accordance with the thousands of guidelines rolled out as part of the comprehensive accreditation of academic and public-health institutions.

In order to analyse the more or (very often) less systematic relationship between power and knowledge, I am inspired by Foucault's notion of dispositive (Foucault, 1980a, pp. 194–5). This entails paying attention to the contingent and the strategic character of power–knowledge relationships. A dispositive (or assemblage) is contingent in the sense that particular techniques of power may be employed for a variety of norms and reasons, and, conversely, that the very same form of reasoning may inform very different forms of power techniques. Thus, there is really no way we can reduce a particular form of power to a particular political logic or mode of reasoning. Notwithstanding this contingency, the notion of dispositive entails that we look for the various kinds of means–ends calculations – often involving multiple intentions – that connect at least tentatively a set of otherwise distinct ideas, practices and techniques. At some point, Foucault argued that power relations should be regarded as 'both intentional and non-subjective' (Foucault, 1978, p. 94) in order to avoid the tendency of reducing political interventions to the realisation of the intentions of one or two powerful actors. In other words, we should regard power like a strategy without a strategist to allow for the possibility that the concrete exercise of power, such as a political programme seeking to make citizens change their conduct, is the result of the interests, interactions and negotiations of a wide number of individuals and organisations. Thus, rather than trying to identify the (single) mastermind of a political programme, we may want to focus on the various rationalities and bodies of knowledge informing the procedures, techniques and practices making of the political intervention.

Power is approached from a nominalist perspective, i.e. as a name for a very diverse set of practices whereby some seek to influence the conduct of others (Foucault, 1978, p. 93). The term is used to address practices that seek to change the conduct of others indirectly, for example by urging individuals or groups to exercise their freedom in a particular way, and practices seeking to change the conduct of other more directly, for example through legally sanctioned coercion and disciplinary techniques. This Foucauldian-inspired notion of power differ fundamentally from behaviouralist and Marxist-inspired understandings. In contrast to the former, the Foucauldian notion of power is attuned to analyse not behaviour but the manifold techniques, routines, systems and norms engaged in the attempt to shape the conduct of others. In contrast to the Marxist notion of power, it does not reduce power to a matter of class relations or positions. Instead, it allows for power to emerge in all kind of social relationships in which one part is trying one way or another to influence the other. In brief, Foucault's analytics entail addressing the *how* of power rather than the who of power (Foucault, 1982). Thus, instead of seeking to identify the actor or class possessing power exercised by way of more or less sophisticated ideological chimeras, we should pay attention to the manifold administrative mechanisms and techniques by which power is exercised. This is essentially what I am trying to do in Chapters 4 to 7 where I explore the administrative devices employed in producing accountability, credibility and evidence.

The functioning of liberal democracies hinge on the exercise of a number of quite distinct forms of power, some of which are very direct and coercive. Yet, the main way of regulating the conduct of both citizens and the public administration (and its civil servants) is more indirect and less coercive.

Thus, it seems that our public administration and its actions are predominantly run by a politics of self-governance (Sørensen & Triantafillou, 2009). Foucault formulated the concept of government to denote the ways in which some try to act upon the actions of others (Foucault, 2008). It is the specific kind of power exercised over individuals, groups or organisations that are free in the sense that they have a certain room to choose the ways in which they conduct themselves. Government then does not imply determining the conduct of those governed or narrowing down their scope of action but facilitating and engendering particular ways in which they conduct themselves.

Finally, one of the key analytical advantages of the Foucauldian analytics of modern forms of power, such as government, is its attention to the role played by expert knowledge. The key point is that the exercise of modern forms of power hinges fundamentally on expert knowledge about the object that is being governed. Expert knowledge on the state and its many challenges, such as the disciplines of economics, sociology, political science, public management and psychology, are not just providing more or less correct mappings of reality, they are rendering that reality in ways that are more or less amenable to political interventions, i.e. power. Thus, the analytical point here is not the epistemological quality of these forms of expert knowledge – are they really telling the truth? – but their *performative* quality. What matters is what can be and is being done on the basis of them. What types of problems are they framing? What kind of technical possibilities and answers do they envisage? And, how are they informing concrete political and managerial programmes through which the conduct of individuals, groups and organisations is shaped? Of particular relevance to these political calculations and reflections, what Foucault called governmentalities (Foucault, 2008), is expert knowledges such as economics, political science and, not least, public administration or public management. It is above all these disciplines that provide input to the political calculations and reflections on how best to govern the state and the public administration.

Thus, I am latching on to an analytical framework that may address the kinds of knowledge and political rationalities informing public administration and management by exploring the problematisations, public-administration reforms and managerial techniques they give rise to in their attempts to make the public administration and its actions more accountable, credible and evidence-based. In the next chapter I am examining the neoliberal political rationalities informing contemporary public administration and management reforms, and in Chapters 4 to 8 I am exploring the more specific bodies of expert knowledge that are informing and being produced by the administrative techniques of accountability, accreditation and evidence-production in policymaking.

Conclusion

This chapter has explored six analytical approaches critically addressing various aspects of power exercised through public administration and management. All the approaches share a concern for the potentially negative effects of power and all provide analytical insights that have significant critical value. Yet, the approaches vary substantially both in terms of the exact object of their analysis and in the kind of research questions, theoretical assumptions and reflections on the role of truthful knowledge.

With regard to the object of analysis, it is clear that Weber, Bauman, Lindblom, Wildavsky and Scott are addressing what we today often label traditional, Weberian-style bureaucracy. That is, the kind of bureaucratic action and organisation based on hierarchical steering, impartiality, *Sachlichkeit* and a strong faith in the planning potential of expert knowledge. In contrast, the PAT-Net scholars, discourse analysis, the political economy approaches, STS studies and much of the Foucauldian-inspired literature are generally more preoccupied with recent public administration modalities launched under the heading of NPM. However, it is not only the various historical forms of bureaucracy that differ between the six approaches. While some focus on very concrete public-management reforms and techniques (e.g. the realist critiques), others (also) focus on wider political ideologies and rationalities (e.g. discourse analysis).

The latter difference has to do with the kind of research questions and theoretical assumptions underpinning the various analytical approaches. Whereas the modernity critique and Foucault shared a concern for the historical specificity of power by and through public administration and the kind of rationalities informing it, the modernist critiques are mainly out to pinpoint the excesses emanating from this kind of power. While I sympathise with the modernity critique I find it is at once both too strong and too weak. It is too strong, or one-sided, in the sense that it exclusively regards formal, instrumental rationality and the objectifying expert discourses as repressive of personal authenticity and autonomy. Thus, it does not see any potential for autonomy and freedom, with administrative systems of power that work by way of objectifying and quantifying that which is governed. However, as I shall try to show in Chapters 4 to 7, the quest for accountability, credibility and evidence hinges on the active participation and freedom of those subjected to these systems. On the other hand, it is also too weak in that it potentially overlooks the kinds of power engaged in the kinds of autonomy and freedom enabled by new forms of administration, such as citizen participation, empowerment and network governance. As I have argued elsewhere, such activating mechanisms of government are replete with power (Triantafillou, 2012, pp. 70–91).

As shown above, political economy and discourse analysis focus more directly (than modernist critiques) on neoliberal state power. Yet, they share with modernist critiques the rather one-sided, negative diagnosis of contemporary power underpinning public-administration and management reforms. Because this power is supported by neoliberal ideologies it is regarded as inherently bad in the sense that contemporary administrative reforms are driven by an unholy coalition of market ideals and customer orientation on the one hand, and on the other a strong state using its coercive powers to ensure a competitive economy and social policies attuned to employability rather than social insurance. Like the modernist critique, I find the political economy and discourse studies examined above too strong and too weak. Here the main problem lies with the two approaches lacking attention to the kind of immanent critique found in the neoliberal rationalities that they attack so vigorously. In order to grasp the ability of neoliberal rationalities to appeal to so many, we need to look not only at obfuscating ideologies or the functional requirements of capitalism but to the actual content of neoliberal rationalities.

While all the approaches explored above hold a strong critical potential in addressing modern power in public administration and management, I find that the Foucauldian-inspired approach is the one that most adequately interrogates the link between this kind of power and the various bodies of knowledge purporting to tell the truth about the best way to govern. The analytical framework will be informed by Michel Foucault's analytics of power–knowledge relations in general, and his notion of government in particular. While Foucault's genealogical analytics of power usually hinges on the critical distance offered by historical excavations, it also allows for critical interrogation of contemporary power struggles (Dean, 1999, pp. 40–59; Lemke, 2002, pp. 57–75). The notion of government, defined by Foucault as the conduct of conduct, seems particularly useful to address contemporary forms of public-management reforms as they seem to rely extensively on indirect forms of regulation and agencification working a distance. However, I will also pay attention to how government and other forms of indirect power may work in tandem with coercive techniques of power, such as legal regulations and various economic and penal sanctions.

3

Neoliberalism: Epistemological finitude or infinite freedom?

Introduction

This chapter addresses the intellectual underpinnings of contemporary reforms in liberal democracies seeking to enhance accountability, credibility and evidence in the conduct of government. The chapter has two overall arguments, a conceptual one and an empirical one. Conceptually, it is argued that we may overcome some of the shortcomings of existing ways of analysing contemporary neoliberalism by analysing it in terms of a particular way of problematising government, rather than as a set of ideas or a more or less coherent ideology. Empirically, it is argued that contemporary neoliberalism is characterised by two distinct and partially conflicting problematisations of government, namely a critical one evolving around the danger of excessive state interventions and a constructivist one evolving around the question of how to facilitate, if not create, freedom.

The first section discusses the principal ways in which neoliberalism has been addressed in political theory. It is argued that we find three principal ways of conceiving it: as a very loose set of ideas, as a more or less coherent political ideology and as particular problematisations of government. For reasons given in the following chapter, the book will utilise this latter understanding of neoliberalism. The chapter then moves on to address neoliberalism as a critical problematisation of government, i.e. the kind of intellectual thinking and debates informed by the questioning of the epistemological capacity of the state and the dangers of excessive state intervention. In the third section, I explore various constructivist problematisations of government or, more precisely, the kind of thinking concerned with the political problematisation of the state's role in facilitating the freedom or self-steering capacities of civil society and of the public administration itself. This implies looking at the EU's social investment strategy, the intellectual rendering of communities and their need to be empowered and made responsible for handling societal problems, and the theories concerned with the capacity of the public administration to co-operate and innovate.

Finally, I sum up and discuss the relationship between the critical and constructivist dimensions of contemporary neoliberalism. It is argued that in order to grasp and critically address contemporary public administration reforms we need to pay attention to both these dimensions.

How to grasp neoliberalism?

This section discusses the principal ways in which neoliberalism has been addressed in political theory. It is argued that we find three principal ways of conceiving neoliberalism: as an ideological expression of contemporary capitalism, as a set of ideas that more or less directly shape state inventions and as particular problematisations of government that inform political power. Of course, it possible to make more detailed distinctions between various conceptions of neoliberalism (e.g. Flew, 2012). However, I do not really think that such further divisions add much new to our understanding of neoliberalism. In fact, it has recently been argued that the term 'neoliberalism' by now is used in so many different ways alluding variously to normative condemnations, empirical descriptions, and explanatory forces that it is essentially useless and should be discarded altogether in the social sciences (Venugopal, 2015). While I agree that the term is used in many, often contradictory, ways, I do not agree that the term is without analytical value as long as we are being clear about what the term implies.

Neoliberalism as the ideological expression of contemporary capitalism

The conception of neoliberalism as an expression of contemporary capitalism essentially conceives of neoliberalism as an ideology that is more or less directly determined by the underlying features of the economic system. While most scholars in this field are adamant that ideologies cannot be simply read off from the economic infrastructure, they do argue that the function of ideology is to legitimise the existing capitalist, economic system. Inspired by Marx's observation in his preface to *A contribution to the critique of political economy* that 'the mode of production of material life conditions the general process of social, political and intellectual life' (Marx, 1994, p. 211), the assumption is that ideologies provide false or at least distorted images of this underlying system in order to cover up its real functioning. More precisely, the emergence of neoliberal ideology must be explained in terms of wider structural changes of the capitalist economy (Overbeek, 1993; Harvey, 2005, pp. 10–11). The demise of social reformism and Keynesian demand management and the rise of neoliberalism and supply-side management can be explained by the shift from a Fordist mode of mass production and consumption to a post-Fordist mode of flexible production and specialised consumer patterns (N. Brenner & Theodore, 2010; Overbeek & Van Appeldoorn, 2012). From the 1980s onwards new short-term (precarious) employment relations, the dwindling purchasing power of regularly employed labour, the rise of rapidly shifting technologies and the opening of international competition in the manufacturing and, increasingly, in the service sectors have meant that the former contract, however uneasy, between capital and labour has been broken.

The emergence of a new ideology, neoliberalism, which has argued that the rolling back of the state, curbing the bargaining power of trade unions and reducing social-welfare programmes are necessary for competitiveness and for the wealth and welfare of all, has served to legitimise this shift in the capitalist economic system. On the one hand, it has served to make the labouring classes accept that they have to restrain their demands and accept inferior salary levels and employment conditions. On the other, it has enabled the further enrichment of the financial capital classes (Harvey, 2005, pp. 16–19, 152; Peck, 2010, p. 9).

This Marxist-inspired analysis is refreshing inasmuch as it addresses some fundamental economic problems linked to neoliberalism, notably growing economic inequality and the limited imagination of policymakers seeking to address one economic and financial crisis after another. However, the approach also has at least two fundamental problems, namely economic reductionism and intellectual arrogance. Firstly, the standard objection to Marxist-inspired analysis also applies here: It simply does not seem plausible to reduce ideas or strands of thought to the structural features of the economic infrastructure – whether in the first or the last instance. Such a reduction is problematic not only because neoliberal ideologies vary immensely over time and between countries but also because, if this argument is taken to its logical extreme, there is really little reason to examine such variations, as they are bound to be levelled out in line with the changing needs of capital. Secondly, the false consciousness implied by assuming that neoliberal ideology distorts some apparently more truthful account of (capitalist) reality, which can be grasped by the Marxist analytical apparatus only, is arrogant and not very convincing. True, our policymakers and public media are replete with stories that do more to confuse than to enlighten us on the machinations of financial capitalism, excelling in explanations like 'greedy' capitalist or 'welfare-dependent' citizens etc. Yet, by assuming that the only valid account of neoliberalism is one that explains this in term of the economic infrastructure and objective class positions, such explanation is bound to dismiss all other accounts at best as inadequate and at worst as being caught within the veil of neoliberal ideology and thereby unwittingly serving to reproduce contemporary patterns of exploitation.

Neoliberalism as ideas

In contrast to the conception of neoliberalism as an ideological expression of contemporary capitalism, the conception of neoliberalism as ideas works with almost the reverse causality. The starting point here is neither the economic infrastructure nor class relations, but ideas. It is ideas that are regarded as influential in shaping shape state interventions, which in turn may shape the functioning of markets. The analysis of neoliberalism in terms of ideas hinge on quite distinct sources of intellectual inspiration, ranging from the early work of Michel Foucault and Ernesto Laclau's discourse theory (Brown, 2006; Springer, 2012) to various strands of neo-institutional theory (Hall, 1993; Schmidt & Radaelli, 2004). However, they share the assumption that neoliberalism comes with a particular value system (free markets are good) that endorses a general set of political interventions (reduce market distortions by minimising social security systems, and enhance choice by way of privatisation and contracting out). Thus neoliberal ideas offer a more or less consistent worldview and provide a more or (often) less consistent blueprint of political interventions and non-interventions.

Some scholars have a broad conception of the ideas deserving the term 'neoliberalism'. For example, Vivien Schmidt and Mark Thatcher argue that neoliberalism is defined by core set of ideas about the market and the state's role in such markets, namely a 'belief in competitive markets enhanced by global free trade and capital mobility, backed up by a pro-market, limited state that promotes labour market flexibility and seeks to reduce welfare dependency while marketising the provision of public goods' (Schmidt & Thatcher, 2013, p. 5). While this is already a fairly broad set of ideas, the authors immediately move on to argue that neoliberalism is even broader and include at least three distinct strands, namely laissez-faire (favouring a strong but limited state), hyper-neoliberalism (wanting to dismantling the state in favour of the market) and social market neoliberalism (in which the state is actively supporting the functioning of the market) (ibid., p. 4). While the authors acknowledge that this wide set of ideas constitutes a conceptual problem for the attempt to pin down neoliberalism, they argue that it is this very diversity of neoliberalism that has been crucial for its – or rather their – resilience (ibid., p. 27). The generality, diversity and mutability of neoliberalism have meant that it has been able to latch on to quite diverse national political traditions and varying interests of business leaders and political elites.

Other scholars have a more exclusive conception of neoliberal ideas.

For example, Maurizio Ferrera distinguishes between two contemporary ideologies: neoliberalism and liberal new-welfarism (Ferrera, 2013). The former is defined by its faith in the self-regulating capacities of free markets and free trade to maximise wealth (nationally and internationally) and its concomitant attempts at cutting social security systems, collective labour organisation and reducing barriers to the circulation of goods (Ferrera, 2013, pp. 80–2), labour power and capital. In contrast, liberal new-welfarism is a label for an emerging ideology underpinned by a dual commitment to welfare – in the sense of striving to provide equal life chances – and to liberty – in the sense of allowing for self-development and ensure non-discrimination (ibid., pp. 96–7). While it is argued that such ideologies do not determine the choice of specific political programmes, an ideology is nevertheless regarded as a 'blueprint for welfare-state modernization' (ibid., p. 79).

Grasping neoliberalism as a set of ideas comes with several merits. First of all, these ideas cannot be reduced to the interests of a particular class as the Marxist-inspired account would have it. Thus, the approach allows for a nuanced analysis of how neoliberal ideas are appropriated by different political and social groups for quite distinct purposes. By the same token, this approach also tends to reject reducing neoliberalism to the writings of the Mont Pelerin society members (Mirowski and Plehwe, 2009). Instead the approach has enabled nuanced analysis of the many sources engaged in the formulation, dissemination and adaptation of neoliberal idea in a variety of political and societal settings. However, conceiving neoliberalism in terms of ideas (only) is not without problems. First, the approach does not offer much in terms of explaining why exactly these ideas emerged in the first place and why they were able to gain such credence. Most accounts list the usual circumstantial suspects, i.e. the long-term economic downturn starting with the oil crisis in the early 1970s, the inability of Keynesian demand regulation to provide adequate answers and a general sense of alienation vis-à-vis a growing welfare state. While these circumstances no doubt provided a fertile environment for the making of new political ideas, it is not easy to see why they had to be neoliberal. Secondly, both the more inclusive and the more exclusive understandings of neoliberalism as a set of ideas assume these ideas amount to a more or less precise political blueprint. Or at least, they assume that neoliberalism ascribes to a certain epistemological and normative worldview that shapes a more or less well circumscribed set of political actions. Thus the understanding of neoliberalism as a set of ideas adopts a kind of descending analytical approach in which we start from abstract worldviews, move down to more concrete ideological orientations and preferences and end up with concrete political programmes. Thus, if the Marxist-inspired understanding of neoliberalism implied an ascending analysis from the economic infrastructure up to the political superstructure, the neoliberalism-as-ideas conception seems to work with a descending analysis, in which neoliberal ideas translate more or less easily into particular state interventions. Yet, political actions are rarely if ever guided by one (or more) consistent worldviews or by programmatic blueprints. Even in hard-core dictatorships like the former Soviet Union or contemporary North Korea, which relied or rely heavily on relatively clearly demarcated political ideologies, it is fairly easy to point out political interventions that have little to do with Marxism-Leninism or the Juche philosophy.

One of the most sophisticated accounts of neoliberalism is provided by Jamie Peck, who squarely rejects seeing neoliberalism as a set of ideas favouring a particular political blueprint. He argues that the wide diversity of neoliberalism may be attributed to the quest for one single goal: market rule. It is the 'very *unattainability* of its fundamental goal – frictionless market rule' (Peck, 2010, p. 16, italics in original) that makes way for a 'permanent revolution' (ibid., p. 7) of constantly shifting and therefore highly variable government interventions and regulations seeking to fix market failures. This is a tempting conception inasmuch as it allows for the obvious diversity of neoliberalism while holding on to a core feature. However, I think the dialectics invoked in explaining the advance of neoliberalism as a self-generating machine feeding on its own failures smacks a bit too much of Kantian metaphysics. Moreover, while I agree that neoliberalism never came with a ready-made blueprint and that it encapsulates a wide range of highly diverse political interventions, I think that the relationship between these interventions may be understood more adequately by two general forms of problematisations than by a single overarching goal (market rule).

Neoliberal problematics of government

Much has been written about the immense diversity of political phenomena that have been encapsulated by scholars as neoliberal. While this has made some propose to regard the terms as too all-encompassing, devoid of analytical value and therefore best avoided, I agree with those who think it still has a certain use. The analytical challenge is of course to provide some analytical coherence to a concept that covers an apparently completely incoherent phenomenon. Rather than starting from the bottom up (from the economic infrastructure to ideology) or from the top down (from a kernel of political ideas or goals to political action), I suggest a lateral analysis or one-level surface analysis in which neoliberalism is understood as historically distinct problematisations of government that link up with particular bodies of knowledge about the state, and particular technologies for governing the wealth and welfare of the state and its citizens. The lateral approach simply assumes that the problematisations, knowledges and technologies work interconnectedly in more or less strongly linked strategic assemblages. In these assemblages no element has a superior status in the sense of being able to shape let alone determine the selection of other elements. Thus, in order to understand the exercise of government or neoliberal power we really need to address all three elements in their specific interaction. The remainder of this chapter focuses mainly on the problematisations and knowledge, whereas the governmental technologies are the topic of the following chapters.

The term 'problematisation' refers to the way in which an issue or social phenomenon is framed as a problem in need of political intervention. Most importantly, to analyse a problematisation entails examining when, where and how – through what forms of knowledge and by what techniques – certain aspects of human conduct or governmental conduct are rendered problematic (Foucault, 1989; Triantafillou, 2012, pp. 20–1). Classical liberalism, for example, may be characterised by its problematisation of the dangers of excessive state intervention. Thus, according to Foucault and others, the key problem informing liberal rule is how to exercise state power without destroying the self-governing processes of civil society (Foucault, 2008, pp. 27–50). Or, put more economically, 'why rule?' (Rose, 1996, p. 47).

Following Foucault and Burchell, neoliberalism is characterised less by its immanent critique of state intervention and more by a constructivist element (Burchell, 1996, pp. 27–9; Foucault, 2008, pp. 120–1, 259–61). Neoliberal thinkers agree with the classical political economists that markets are key to the effective allocation of resources because of their unique ability to communicate individual wills and preferences. Yet, whereas the Scottish moral philosophers like Adam Smith and Ferguson tended to regard civil society as a naturally given sphere with its own logic, most if not all contemporary liberal thinkers seem not to take the existence of markets for granted. Markets have to be developed, facilitated and regulated to avoid monopolies, cartel structures and other phenomena reducing free competition. State interventions are needed not to limit or direct markets but to ensure their proper functioning. In sum, the constructivist element of neoliberalism is based on the following general problematisation: if markets, competition and entrepreneurial conduct cannot be assumed to exist spontaneously as assumed by the classical liberalist, then how do we construct these? In particular, how do we construct entrepreneurial forms of conduct in the public sector, which is widely regarded as an environment not conductive to such conduct?

While I agree with Foucault, Burchell and others on this conception of neoliberalism, I find that the constructivist problematic may be too general to grasp important nuances in neoliberalism. It seems to be more than a matter of emphasis when the thinkers of the Austrian, Chicago and Virginia schools constantly hammer out the limited cognitive and planning abilities of the state as the key problem of government, whereas others take the stimulation of and governing through freedom as their major problem. While the two problematisations of government are interlinked and even co-exist within concrete political actions, they are not simply the same, and they give rise to a number of conflicts between various proponents of political reforms.

Accordingly, in the remainder of this chapter, I explore neoliberalism first in terms of a critical problematisation of government and then in terms of a constructivist problematisation. This implies addressing the kind of problem or problems that neoliberal thinking and knowledge are trying to answer. It amounts to exploring the kind of problem-space that neoliberal knowledge is articulating in the sense of formulating what they regard as the major concerns and problems that need to be addressed in order to govern a state territory and a society in a morally desirable and technically efficient manner. Such problematisations are informed by and inscribed within various bodies of knowledge about the state and how to govern it best. Some of this knowledge is relatively abstract and taught in various economics, political science and political philosophy departments. Other bodies of knowledge, which inform this problematisation, are more concrete and mundane and are produced in the field of public administration as part of the everyday attempt to find ways of securing the efficiency and quality of public services. These more mundane forms of knowledge, related to the production of accountability, credibility and evidence, will be addressed in the following chapters.

At any rate, to grasp neoliberalism as particular ways of problematising government entails that it cannot ever be reduced to a more or less precise blueprint of political programmes. Nor can it be reduced to a set of lofty, political philosophical principles, such as faith in free markets. Neoliberalism understood as a problematising activity implies, on the one hand, that it is possible to pinpoint a set of key problems or questions of how best to govern that is specific to neoliberalism. On the other hand, it implies that we should allow for a wide set of political interventions and programmes, each seeking in its own way to provide an answer to the formulated problem(s). Accordingly, I think that one of the major reasons for the conceptual confusion of the term 'neoliberalism' is exactly the search for a common core of political programmes. Here I agree with the ideational approach when it argues that such a commonality is not to be expected.

However, the reason for this lack of a common core of political programmes is not (only) the existence of a wide array of political ideas and principles but rather that the problems or questions raised by neoliberalism give rise to many different answers.

In the following, I try to show that we currently find at least two distinct, yet often interrelated and partially conflicting problematisations of government that deserve the term 'neoliberalism' in neoliberal thinking, namely a critical one evolving around the state's limited epistemological capacities and a constructivist one evolving around the question of how to facilitate freedom.

Critical problematisation of state intervention: Epistemological finitude

As is now well rehearsed, the early 1970s saw the end of more than two decades of substantial economic growth, more or less full employment, a rapid increase in material living standards and unprecedented growth of public welfare programmes. Following dramatic increases in energy prices, most OECD countries would for the next two decades experience more or less permanent public-budget deficits, high levels of unemployment, low economic growth, negative trade balances and increasing calls for controlling public expenditures.

Intellectually, the state came under fire both from an increasingly anti-authoritarian left, which saw the state as an alienating instrument of the capitalist class, and from the emergence of neoliberal thinkers, such as the Austrian School (Ludwig von Mises and Friedrich Hayek). According to von Mises (von Mises, 1944, 1990, 1996) and Hayek (Hayek, 1944, 1979), the problem with socialism and the social-democratic welfare state is that the state will never be able to get to know the diverse wills and preferences of its citizens and groups. Only the market can communicate this knowledge effectively through price mechanisms. The critical component of neoliberalism thus amounts to the assumption that the actions of the state and of any other actor are always inhibited by epistemological finitude. Similarly, the Chicago School (Milton Friedman) saw state planning and macroeconomic interventions as detrimental to individual freedom and societal wealth. While neither of these strands of state criticisms believed that the economy and society could do without a state equipped with sovereign powers, they both problematised, albeit in very different ways, the state's ambitions of intervening in economic and social life with a view to ensuring the welfare of each and all. For both these critiques, a basic problem was how to reform the state in a way that attuned it to facilitating and maximising the desires, interests and resources of citizens. Both schools are starkly against the social welfarist (if not social-democratic) ideal according to which the state would map in detail the objective needs of citizens and the state would employ an army of public-service experts working to determine the supposedly objective needs of citizens and subsequently provide the services they found necessary to meet these needs.

The critical problematisation of state intervention implies an immanent scepticism towards most, though as we shall see below not all, forms of state intervention. Any attempt to plan and intervene in society will therefore always be based on inadequate knowledge, which in turn will produce all kinds of unintended and negative effects. At the general level, it is morally undesirable because it does not allow citizens to pursue their desires freely, and it is technically inefficient because it will allocate resources in ways that are not societally optimal. Or, in the preferred economic terms of neoliberalism, state inventions in favour of some particular interests or needs are bound to be neither Pareto-improving (making at least one individual better off without making any other individual worse) nor Pareto-optimal (the state of allocation of resources in which it is impossible to make any one individual better off without making at least one individual worse off). The key problem then becomes: how and to what extent should the state intervene in society when any state intervention will always produce some kind of harmful effect? As we shall see below, there are slightly different ways of articulating this problem and, more importantly, there are very different ways even within the Austrian and Chicago Schools of trying to answer this question.

The role of sovereign state power

If neoliberal thinking is inherently critical of state intervention because of the inability to grasp fully the manifold subjective desires and needs of individual citizens, then what role is envisaged for the exercise of sovereign state power? Neoliberalism's general answer to this is that sovereign power should above all take the form of constitutional law – in the shape of general, procedural rules – ensuring citizens' freedom from coercion and thereby the functioning of the market. Most neoliberals also allow for state interventions in order to provide public goods and to ensure equal opportunities, though it is highly contested to what extent the state should engage in such matters.

Political thinkers such as Ludwig von Mises, Friedrich Hayek, James Buchanan and Robert Nozick all regard the rule of law, or *Rechtstaat* principles, as absolutely fundamental for the functioning of any liberal democracy by ensuring freedom from coercion (the following account is indebted to Plant, 2009, chapter 2). This in turn is a precondition for the functioning of markets, which in turn is the most effective way of ensuring both individual and national prosperity. Inspired by the British philosopher Michael Oakeshott, Hayek and other neoliberal thinkers distinguish between constitutional, or nomocratic, law and purpose-oriented, or telocratic, law. Notwithstanding the difficulties of applying this ideal-type distinction to the real world, neoliberal thinkers argue that constitutional law is a sine qua non for ensuring individual desires (freedom) and general prosperity (Hayek, 1976). This general legal framework will allow citizens to pursue their own private ends because it provides – according to neoliberal thinkers – a set of apolitical rules that will protect citizens and their private spheres from intrusions by other civil society actors and by the state. In contrast, laws promoting substantial and particular purposes (telocratic law) should be avoided as they assume that someone, such as the sovereign or welfare experts, are better judges of individual needs than the individuals themselves. Similarly, Buchanan argues that because the public good or the good society can be meaningfully defined only on the basis of the subjective preferences of the individual members of society, any attempt to determine the public good and frame legislation by reference to some external, objective standards is bound to lead to Leviathan, i.e. some kind of authoritarian rule (Buchanan, 1975, pp. 163–4). The constitutional law should basically ensure that the pursuit of the interests of one individual does not inhibit the pursuit of interests by any other individual. In order to ensure this, the state may have to resort to coercion. Because people are regarded as driven by their own subjective desires, all societies will inevitably see conflicts over positions and resources. If not controlled, these conflicts are more than likely to result in the stronger trying to coerce the weaker into abiding by the former's will. Accordingly, it is both necessary and legitimate for the state to use its coercive powers to form constitutional frameworks able to defend individual citizens from coercion by other citizens (Hayek, 1960, p. 21; Buchanan & Brennan, 1985).

Critical neoliberalism's emphasis on the importance of constitutional law and its scepticism against teleocratic or substantive law do not imply a total rejection of the latter. Above all, substantive law may be necessary to ensure the functioning of markets. Such interventions may include: the provision of institutions for money, markets and information where these 'can never be adequately provided by private enterprise' (Hayek, 1944, p. 38); the making and enforcement of a legal system designed to make competition work as beneficially as possible, and to define and protect property rights (Hayek, 1944, p. 81); control of weights and measures to prevent fraud; surveying, land registration and the propagation of reliable statistics (Hayek, 1960, p. 223). Finally, Hayek also cautiously allows for state interventions seeking to control corporate monopolies, though he does prefer to leave it to private actors to use the legal system to appeal for relief (Paul, 2004). Obviously, neoliberal thinkers are against substantive law or interventions seeking to ensure equality in terms of outcome. This would be unjust not only in meritocratic terms but also in terms of infringement of individual freedom on the part of those who have done well. More interestingly, and in strong contrast to a liberal thinker like Rawls, all the key critical neoliberalist are also against the state trying to ensure equality of opportunity. They resist such a state pursuit either because it involves forcing some individuals to give away some of their money (Nozick, 1974, p. 235) or because the costs suffered by a majority of citizens and society at large would significantly exceed the benefits enjoyed by a few fortunate ones (Hayek, 1960, pp. 387–8). In brief, on the one hand, critical neoliberalists envisage a quite active role for the state in order to ensure the functioning of markets, though with the proviso that the possible debilitating effects of such interventions should always be carefully measured against their advantages. On the other hand, they reject any attempt to ensure equality in terms both of result and of opportunity.

Ludwig von Mises, Friedrich Hayek, James Buchanan and Robert Nozick's scepticism towards state interventions could be taken to imply that critical neoliberalism rejects public interventions in the areas of skills and social security. However, this is not correct. Some do allow for interventions in these areas in order to ensure neither equality nor even equality of opportunity, but to ensure the functioning of the market or, more precisely, the ability of citizens to participate in the market. Hayek proposed that particularly gifted students with too little funding to pay for it be granted a public grant, though he clearly questioned the desirability of free education for all (Hayek, 1960, p. 388). Not surprisingly, Milton Friedman was generally sceptical of public support of education. Nevertheless, he did allow both for some restricted level of public support and for a financial scheme orchestrated by the state. Thus, basic education for children should be publicly financed because it promotes 'a stable and democratic society' (Friedman, 1962, p. 86). In contrast, specialised education (college and university) should be financed by equity investment systems where either the state or a private investor would provide the student with a basic monthly living allowance under the condition that the student would pay back the investor a certain percentage of their future income.

An even more comprehensive role for the state in the area of education was developed by a series of other University of Chicago economists under the heading of human capital development. The Nobel Prize winner Theodore W. Schultz (Schultz, 1961), Gary Becker (Becker, 1964) and one of his students and subsequently a professor at Columbia University, Jacob Mincer (Mincer, 1974) all in various ways asked how citizens could augment their accumulated life income by investing in their own education – both during school age and after. While they agreed with classical economists like David Ricardo that capital enables the development of future income, they would focus not only on land, financial capital and labour time but also on human capital, i.e. the kind of personal skills or competences available to the development of income. Accordingly, capital is regarded as something possessed not just by capitalists and landowners but by all individuals, though in different kinds and levels. To ensure their future wealth, the rational citizens will nurture and develop their human capital, they argued, by investing in themselves, through various kinds of education and training. The notion of human capital has implications not only for individual behaviour but also for state intervention. Thus, if it is true that a state's economic growth depends not only on land, work-hours and financial capital but also on the collective sum of the human capital of its population, and Schultz is quite clear that he believes this to be the case, then it is obvious to suggest that the state should intervene in ways that support the availability of educational services to its citizens either by direct subsidies to schools or by various tax deductions to spur private investments in school or continued education (Schultz, 1961, pp. 14–16). Becker proposes that public investment in education should be determined by a careful calculation of the ratio between the social costs of such public investments and their returns, i.e. how they contribute to national income (Becker, 1964, pp. 117–20). Thus, in the same way that the rational citizen should base their private investment in education by calculating the ratio between private costs and extra life income, the state should invest in education if a rational calculation of the social costs show that they are outweighed by the benefits of such investments on the national economy. It is debatable whether the human capital line of thinking belongs to critical neoliberalism inasmuch as they believed in the possibility that the state could actually calculate the social benefits and costs of education, something questioned by Milton Friedman (Friedman, 1962, p. 105). At least, it seems clear that the human-capital line of thinking is relatively optimistic about the possibility of providing a usable estimate of the social benefits and costs of education. Moreover, while the human capital scholars provide neither a political-justice argument (à la Rawls) nor a psychological-developmental anthropology, they do seem to resonate quite well with the constructivist neoliberal problematic: How can the state intervene to spur the developmental and self-steering capacities of citizens? At any rate, this strand of neoliberalism seems more optimistic about the potential of state intervention in the area of education than people like Hayek and Friedman.

In the area of social security or, more precisely, poverty alleviation, Hayek would allow for assistance to individuals afflicted by sickness or accidents with no or little means (Hayek, 1944, pp. 120–1). Later on a more elaborate answer to the problem of poverty was given in the form of the negative income tax. This idea was discussed in the US in the early

1960s by Milton Friedman (Friedman, 1962) and later on in France by president Giscard d'Estaing and one of his technical advisers Lionel Stoléru (Stoléru, 1974). Milton Friedman suggested that a specified proportion of unused deductions or allowances would be refunded to the taxpayer. If, for a family of four, the amount of allowances came out to $10,000, and the subsidy rate was 50 per cent, and the family earned $6,000, the family would receive $2,000, because it left $4,000 of allowances unused. In this way, there is no longer need for minimum wages and other social protection:

> Like any other measures to alleviate poverty, it reduces the incentives of those helped to help themselves, but it does not eliminate that incentive entirely, as a system of supplementing incomes up to some fixed minimum would. An extra dollar earned always means more money available for expenditure. (Friedman, 1962, p. 192)

As argued by Foucault, the key idea of both Friedman's and Stoléru's proposals for negative income tax was to ensure a 'rule of non-exclusion' in the sense of ensuring that all citizens remained players in the market economy (Foucault, 2008, p. 202). It would avoid the situation in which citizens were so deprived of material means that they would not react to economic incentives. The same logic of ensuring market participation can be used to support affordable health services. In sum, even if critical neoliberalists are essentially sceptical of telocratic, substantive laws, they do think these may be legitimate in cases where they contribute to the functioning of the market by ensuring that all citizens may participate in it (negative income tax and health) and where they may contribute to the national economy (education and health).

Critical problematisations of the public administration

In tandem with the macro-level critique and problematisation of state intervention, public-choice theories, which critically addressed the behaviour of public organisations and their employees, gained credence. From around the 1960s, a number of intellectual works started to evolve at the University of Virginia around the application of economic theories to political systems and public administrations.[1] Works like *Social choice and individual values* (Arrow, 1951), *The calculus of consent* (Buchanan & Tullock, 1962) and *The logic of collective action* (Olson, 1965) questioned the ability of democratic systems to produce economically optimum solutions. Starting from the assumption that politicians and voters alike are driven by narrow self-interests (power and material goods), they go on to argue that voters in democratic systems are likely to support policies that favour themselves or that do not create a socially optimum level of wealth.

This style of analysis was subsequently taken up by scholars with an interest in the public administration and resulted, first, in the budget-maximisation thesis (Niskanen, 1971; Dunleavy, 1985) and, following the advent of new public management and budget controls, the bureau-shaping thesis (Dunleavy, 1991). In the former case, public managers – with the support of regular public-sector employees – would exploit the administrative ignorance of politicians to argue for expanded budgets in order to meet public service needs. In the second case, where more or less strict budget controls have been implemented, public managers would use their discretion to hive off non-prestigious day-to-day operational activities on the one hand and retain and develop new managerial and strategic functions with little obvious public value on the other. In both cases, public managers are driven by self-interest, and in both cases the result is the implementation of policies and tasks that produce suboptimal social results. The managerial implications of the essentially self-interested civil servant were further developed by the American economist Kenneth Arrow, who together with John Hicks won the Nobel Prize in 1972 for their contributions to general economic-equilibrium theory and welfare theory. Arrow approached welfare problems in terms of the social outcomes of the aggregation of individual preferences. It was, however, his work on the problem of imperfect or rather asymmetric information between buyer and seller engaging in contractual relation in a market that would prove to have particular importance for public administration (for an early formulation of this problem, see Jensen & Meckling, 1976; Arrow, 1985). Under the heading of principal-agency theory, this rendering of the contractual relationship in terms of asymmetric information would subsequently be taken up by British and American economists from the late 1980s to point out the moral dangers incurred by an agent (such as a frontline worker) having more information about the actual costs involved in the implementation of a political programme than the principal in charge of allocating resources for its execution (Rees, 1985; Holmstrom & Milgrom, 1991). In the absence of control systems or appropriate incentives, the self-interested agent would be expected either to not do the job as agreed or to claim more resources than necessary for completing it.

Notwithstanding the diversity of the public choice and principal-agent literatures, their analyses informed the articulation of the following problematisation of the art of governing in general and the machinations of the public sector in particular: How to monitor and penetrate the authority of essentially self-serving professional groups paid to provide crucial public services? (Rose, 1999, p. 153). If we cannot do without doctors, teachers, lawyers, academics and engineers to provide public services, then how can we direct their self-interest in a way that will enhance the efficiency of the public sector, rather than undermining it? Following the protracted economic downturn of the industrial countries during the 1970s and 1980s, it is this broad problematisation that informs first the liberal Anglophone countries, such as the US, the UK and the Antipodes, and subsequently in various ways and degrees the countries of Continental Western Europe. Spurred by the OECD, ministries of finance and many economists and political scientists, governments in liberal democracies are increasingly pushed to ask themselves this question: how to ensure they are made accountable for the kind of results and performance of their work, which increasingly is couched in terms of products or, even more refined, services? The answers to this question, some of which will be examined in the next chapter, turned out to be quite diverse. Before that, we need to address another significant element of neoliberalism, namely its constructivist problematisation of government.

Constructivist problematisations: How to stimulate freedom?

In the following I first explore the emergence of social investment rationalities in the context of making the EU a competitive knowledge economy. Secondly, the attempts to govern through communities by invoking the freedom and responsibilities of these are analysed. Finally, I examine recent attempts to mobilise the self-steering capacities of public administrations in order to increase their performance and their ability to tap into the resources of the societies they serve.

Social investment strategies: reconciling the economy and the social

The social-investment rationality as articulated since the 1990s essentially regards the current economic problems of many liberal democracies as a question of inadequate competition, which in turn calls for a reorientation of social-security systems from a system of compensation to a system of investment in the development of human resources. The key problem for the social-investment rationality is neither the fact that the state cannot get to know the preferences and processes constituting civil society nor the dangers of excessive state intervention. Rather, the problem is how to harness the human resources in ways that engender national competitiveness. The role of the state then is not to limit itself and its steering ambitions but to attune taxation systems to favour investments, expand educational systems to ensure better and lifelong learning, improve day-care services to enhance employment and not least reform social-security systems in ways that will activate and enhance the employability of the unemployed. Since the 1990s, this strategy has in various forms been found in New Labour's Third Way and its investment in education, in the active labour market policies of the Nordic countries and the Netherlands, in Germany's labour-market (Hartz IV) reforms and in the family policies of Belgium and France (Morel et al., 2012b).

This activist role envisaged for the state is not entirely new to neoliberal thinking. The German Ordo-liberalen of the 1930s and 1940s came to inspire the making of the West German social market economy following the Second World War and also envisaged a very active role for the state. Following the horrible experience of the Nazi regime, it became pertinent to imagine a role for the state that would confine and control its horrific powers (Foucault, 2008, pp. 101–57). The economists Walter Eucken and Wilhelm Röpke and the jurist Franz Böhm were some of the key thinkers involved in the formulation and to some extent the implementation of the new role for the West German state following the Second World War. They were envisioning not a minimal state but a state bound by strong judicial and regulatory controls on the one hand and building its legitimacy on its capacity to ensure the effective functioning of a market economy on the other. The state was clearly not supposed to intervene directly in order to ensure the wealth and welfare of its citizens, something the Nazi regime experience squarely forbade. Instead it was supposed to nurture an independent sphere of freedom and wealth creation, namely the market or, more precisely, the conditions of competition. Thus, the state's interventions in the market aimed neither to ensure equilibrium between supply and demand (as the neoclassicals took as a given, and Keynes struggled for) nor to stabilise the exchange of commodities (as the neoclassical liberals thought of) but to ensure the functioning of the mechanisms of competition.

Notwithstanding certain similarities between the social-market economy and the social-investment strategies of the 1990s, the latter seems to be less inspired by the German social-market model and more by a sociological recasting of John Rawls's thinking on social justice. The problem that the state interventions were to answer would not be how to ensure competition but rather how to ensure competitiveness in a socially beneficial manner. This sociological recasting took place by way of an intense political-intellectual debate on how to ensure economic growth and social welfare in the EU. This debate entailed the objectification of the so-called Nordic Model as *both a descriptive and a normative model* of societal regulation.

As Magnus Hansen and I have tried to show, the so-called Nordic Model was formulated by figures like the former head of the EU Commission Jacques Delors and the Danish sociologist Gøsta Esping-Andersen as a viable policy-regime model to ensure the competiveness of the EU (Hansen & Triantafillou, 2011; see also Morel et al., 2012a). The project of constructing a European social model was first and foremost formulated in the late 1980s by the then-President of the European Commission, Jacques Delors, and a group of intellectuals working in his cabinet. Delors's idea was that the internal market had to be completed if Europe was to regain competitiveness vis-à-vis the US and Japan. While further European economic integration would lead to growing pressure on individual welfare states and ultimately cause social dumping, it would also generate a need for more Europe-wide social integration. Thus the vision was to create an 'organized European space' (Ross, 1995, p. 9), from wherein the process of social integration and a 'European social model' could emerge and counterbalance the completion of the internal market. Thus, until the beginning of the 1990s, the debates over how to secure welfare in the EU were widely informed by an essentially antagonistic understanding of the relation between the economy and the social. One position criticised the EU for suffering from 'Eurosclerosis' and spoke in favour of trimming down the welfare states by means of deregulation and privatisation, thus making way for flexibility in the market. Another position regarded the expansion of social rights as a dialectical and necessary objective in order to offset the negative effects produced by economic liberalisation and market expansion.

In 2000, the Lisbon Strategy was adopted by the EU to ensure its economic growth, international competitiveness and social cohesion. Accordingly, the overall goal of the Lisbon Strategy was to turn the EU into 'the most competitive and dynamic knowledge-based economy in the world capable of sustainable economic growth with more and better jobs and greater social cohesion' (Council of the European Union, 2000, §27). Instead of trying to agree on common social rights, as suggested by Jacques Delors in the late 1980s, the Lisbon Strategy would build on broadly shared European values, which in turn would respect national diversity and sovereignty. The new message of the Lisbon Strategy was that, in order to become the world's most competitive knowledge economy, the so-called European social model would have to be modernised by investing in human resources because '[p]eople are Europe's main asset and should be the focal point of the Union's policies' (Council of the European Union, 2000).

Yet the Lisbon Strategy did not provide a sustained intellectual answer to the problem: how to spur economic growth and competitiveness in the EU without producing high social costs? A first answer to this question was delivered by the famous Danish sociologist Gøsta Esping-Andersen. He had become famous for his publication *The three worlds of welfare capitalism* (Esping-Andersen, 1990). Here he distinguished between three general types of welfare-state systems by using the concept of 'decommodification'. Defined as the ability to provide security and insurance by the means of social rights founded upon citizenship rather than performance, decommodification was the *raison d'être* of the welfare state. Decommodification entailed an essentially conflictual conception of the welfare state as straddling the need for economic growth and wealth on the one hand and curbing the negative social effects of capitalism on the other by means of pensions systems, unemployment insurance and so on. A decade later, Gøsta Esping-Andersen would completely abandon this conflictual view of the welfare state engaged in balancing two incompatible concerns. Instead, the key role of the state was instead to engage in the investment in human resources in support of economic competitiveness and wealth. In the report *A welfare state for the 21st century?*, prepared for the EU Council's meeting, Esping-Andersen argued that 'a knowledge-intensive society must maximise its future human potential in order to be competitive' (Esping-Andersen, 2000, p. 12). Investments in the development of human resources must be accompanied by reform of the social-welfare systems: 'a basic principle of any win–win strategy must be to favour social investments over passive maintenance'. Esping-Andersen argued that instead of aiming for Paretian efficiency, which would lead to increased social inequality, the EU should pursue a Rawlsian principle of justice (Rawls, 1972). Rawls's difference principle, according to which social inequalities can be justified only if they turn out to promote the greatest advantage to the worst off, was taken by Esping-Andersen as a call for ensuring that the greatest advantage of efficiency gains should accrue to the weakest and poorest (Esping-Andersen, 2000, p. 22). In brief, Esping-Andersen's Rawlsian-inspired political approach did not ignore social problems but addressed them by investing in the resources of the weak and poor to the benefit of as many citizens as possible and to the benefit of the general economy.

Similar kinds of arguments for the need of reorienting social expenditures from a logic of compensation to one of investment in human resources attuned to spur (national and/or EU) competitiveness were made by the Belgian economist, Socialist party politician and former Minister of Employment and Pensions Frank Vandenbroucke, who promoted important debates at the EU level during the Belgian presidency in 2001 (Vandenbroucke, 2001; Ferrera, 2013, pp. 90–1).

This social investment strategy was propagated and reinforced by the Open Method of Co-ordination, which had been established under the Amsterdam Treaty in 1998 to co-ordinate, compare and disseminate best practice with employment policy. In the ensuing normalising comparisons, it would turn out that the Nordic countries, the UK and the Netherlands would display relatively high levels of employment combined – except in the case of the UK – with active labour-market policies in the sense of attuning social security and educational policies to increase the employability of the unemployed. Thus, this new regime of truth seemed only to testify to the validity of the social investment strategy and the viability of the so-called Nordic Model. Thus, from around 2000 and onwards, social concerns were no longer about the right to be economically compensated but about being the target of investments seeking to develop the human potential of each and every person. By latching on to Rawls's principle of justice, it became possible to envisage the so-called Nordic welfare model as a desirable approach due to its combination of social equity, in the sense of greater life chances for all, with economic efficiency in terms of higher levels of national competitiveness.

Governing through the community: Empowering rather than protecting civil society

If the social-investment strategies essentially dealt with the problem of how to reconcile the conflicting logics of the economy and the social, the governing of communities involved a shift from the protection to the empowerment of communities. Whereas civil society in the classical liberal rendition is the source of spontaneous and more or less self-regulating processes that the state needs to protect, the community has more recently been invoked as the site of governmental intervention. The problem has been neither that of how to protect it nor how to strike down on unruly elements of civil society, but how to create a sphere that lends itself more easily to the ambition of unleashing its self-governing potentials. Since the 1990s, the general answer to this problem has been the community. The historical processes shaping the governmental role to be played by the community are quite complex and beyond the scope of this book. It may be noted, however, that the US has a long tradition of more or less systematic attempts by government to mobilise the resources of local communities in handling various economic and social problems. A crucial element in this tradition was the 'war on poverty' launched during the 1960s (Cruikshank, 1999). It may also be noted that the collapse of the socialist countries and the bipolar world order provided a fertile ground in the 1990s for thinking about government in ways that did not require direct state interventions.

At the same time, a number of highly influential scholars were in various ways preoccupied with the problem of how to govern economic and social activities in areas where neither sovereign-state power nor market transactions seemed to provide the obvious solutions. In 2009 Elinor Ostrom received the Nobel Prize in Economics for her work during the 1990s on economic governance, especially the commons, which refer to the common areas of resources. Together with a group of scholars at Indiana University, Elinor Ostrom developed what would become New Institutional

Economics, a strand of economic inquiry that would revolve around the problem of how to ensure the pursuit of collective interests in an environment inhabited by individual utility maximisers (Ostrom, 1990). The main object of attention by Elinor and Vincent Ostrom and their research associates was common pool resources in areas hard or impossible to limit access, such as livestock breeding in the commons, fisheries at sea or water-well depletion. Obviously, the market cannot function in a situation without clearly defined (and enforced) property rights. Moreover, if the state cannot or will not enforce the use or exploitation of such resources, then how should it produce effective rules governing the conduct of essentially self-interested actors whose short-term interest is to exploit such resources and violate any rules that are not linked up to coercive state sanctions? In such a situation, it should be impossible to use natural resources in a sustainable fashion. On the basis of existing systems in some developing countries, Ostrom argued that it is actually possible under certain conditions. Above all, the persons using the resources must stay in the area for a longer period of time and have a strong interest in the long-term preservation of the resource, they must be able to exclude people from outside the community from use and there must be a fairly well developed monitoring system and an explicit system of sanctions in case of rule violation. Of course, to assume the existence of such conditions in developing countries may not be very realistic (Thompson, 2000; Agrawal, 2001). However, the main point here is not how realistic the community approach is but its contribution to assuming the existence of a (self-) governing entity: the community. This entity is taken to exist as a subject that should and – under the right conditions – can govern itself (Mosse, 1997).

If the state is actually working, as it is in developing countries, it should work not to take over the regulation of the use of resources or 'community' issues but assist such communities in their own efforts to handle their own problems. In tandem with Ostrom's work on the self-regulating capacities of communities in developing countries, the community is increasingly singled out as a site of intervention in the Anglophone countries, notably the US. There, the works of the sociologist Amitai Etzioni (Etzioni, 1993, 1997) and other influential US scholars (Selznick, 1994; Barber, 1998) outlined an image of the decline of the core moral values of US society from the 1960s onwards. Notions of deviance were relaxed, and commitment to marital conjugation declined together with the respect for public authorities. Moreover, the loss of industrial workplaces and the growth of urban sprawl and inner-city slums have all contributed, Etzioni argues, to a general sensation of individual alienation from society and its norms. Together with William Galston, formerly a professor and dean at the School of Public Policy at the University of Maryland and a founding member of the Board of the National Campaign to Prevent Teen Pregnancy and chair of the Campaign's Task Force on Religion and Public Values, Etzioni formed the Communitarian Network in 1993. This network has organised dialogues, developed Communitarian position papers, conducted public meetings and advised legislatures and community groups on moral and social questions. Of particular concern to the communitarian movement is the apparent surge of individual self-interest at the expense of responsibilities to the community. This diagnosis of decay of social norms and bonds was further detailed by the sociologist Robert Putnam, who in the article 'Bowling alone: America's declining social capital', argued that the civic commitments which used to characterise the modern American state have dwindled substantially over the last few decades (Putnam, 1995a). It is not only that Americans are increasingly bowling alone; it is also that political participation has been reduced, religious sentiments are increasingly individualised, labour union membership is dwindling and volunteering is down (Putnam, 1995b). Thus, during the 1990s, these and other influential US sociologists seemed largely to agree that a number of the societal problems existing in the US and possibly other liberal democracies were linked to a rapid loss of social capital or community commitments.

This intellectual diagnosis of societal problems, which regards the reinvigoration of the community as the general solution to these problems, was not simply an abstract story of the self-governing powers of civil society. Rather, it informed the concrete activities of sociological and ethnographic experts, social workers and resourceful citizens who worked to single out and governmentalise communities, i.e. pin down local areas, institutions and citizens who are supposed to share some kind of common identity and/or destiny and who supposedly have a common interest in protecting and developing their so-called community (Rose, 1999, pp. 175–6). Crime, delinquency, poor housing, teenage pregnancy, low levels of education, obesity and other phenomena hitherto seen above all as 'social' problems calling for state laws and interventions are increasingly defined as community challenges, requiring the mobilisation of community initiatives and resources (Fung, 2004; OECD, 2009a). In short, what we see is not so much a colonisation of communities by state power as the invention of the community as a site of government and self-government. In brief, the community is invented as a site for intervention not only from outside (the state) but also from those subjectified as belonging to a particular community. On the one hand, then, the community is increasingly held responsible for addressing and handling all kinds of societal problems. On the other hand, the state is expected to ensure and nurture the capacity of communities to handle their problems. No longer must the state plan for citizens and their so-called communities. The public administration should use its expertise not to determine and alleviate the needs of society but to help unleash the self-governing resources of the community. This is the topic of the next section.

Constructivist problematisations of the public administration

In this section, I explore two general constructivist problematisations of public administration, namely: how to create competition and how to create collaboration.

Firstly, since the 1980s, one of the key problematisations of public administration has pointed to its *lack of competition*. Based on the universal anthropological assumption that public administrators are by individual self-interested utility-maximisers, public choice theories have identified the non-competitive environment of the public administration as a fundamental societal problem (Dunleavy, 1985, 1991). In the private sector, characterised by competition between companies in pursuit of profit and between company employees in search of advancement and salary rises, private interest is generally conducive to company profits and to the advancement of the most talented employees. In the public sector, however, where there is no clear link between organisational and individual performance on the one hand and payment or career advancement on the other, there is no incentive to improve performance or innovate. Moreover, as explained above, public managers – tacitly supported by regular employees – will engage in unproductive manoeuvres such as budget maximisation and, where this is not possible, in bureau shaping. The fundamental problem according to public choice thinking then is not that public sector employees are driven by self-interest but that the incentive structures characterising the public sector are likely to render these drives societally suboptimal.

The solutions to inadequate competition are manifold. Thus, many of the administrative schemes and techniques launched under the heading of new public management are in some way trying to provide an answer to the problematisation of competition (Christensen & Lægreid, 2002). Yet, at the most general level, we have seen two strategies, namely privatisation and the making of quasi-markets. Since the 1980s, most OECD countries have seen extensive privatisation of state-owned organisations, such as railways, telecommunication, energy and various manufacturing entities (Larner & Walters, 2000; OECD, 2009c). While the timing and scope of privatisation varies significantly between OECD countries, very few countries have escaped privatisation reforms as a way to encourage what is taken as a more competitive mode of producing public services. Notwithstanding the importance of privatisation, the provision of services by the public sector has continued to be a key characteristic of most OECD countries. To those hostile to an all-out privatisation and to those having a political desire to retain control over the public sector, quasi-markets seem to provide a much more palatable solution. The establishment of quasi-markets in the public sector has been undertaken, on the one hand, by tendering and contracting out in order to generate competition between public and private providers by legal contracts (Eardley, 1997). On the other hand, quasi-markets have been established through soft contracts and benchmarking with a view to creating internal competition between public service providers (Triantafillou, 2007; Bruno, 2009).

Secondly, we find an increasingly elaborate problematisation of the *lack of collaboration* in the public administration. From around the late 1990s, we have seen the emergence of a number of works variously labelled governance, network governance, new public governance or participatory planning. Notwithstanding important differences within this emerging field, they tend all to articulate the need for a more participatory form of public administration in the twenty-first century. Most scholars affiliating their work with this label are adamant that new public governance is an analytical-descriptive term and not a normative one (Osborne, 2010, pp. 6ff; Torfing & Triantafillou, 2013). Public administrators, it is argued, are facing a new reality that poses a number of challenges both for the traditional Weberian-style bureaucracy and for NPM. The general societal diagnosis informing the research of many, though not all, scholars in the field of new public governance tends to regard society as increasingly complex (Kooiman, 1993) and saturated with so-called wicked problems (E. Weber & Khademian, 2008). Simultaneously, the state is regarded as being under increasing fiscal pressures and pressure on its sovereignty from both global regimes and local governments. Above all, citizens, private companies, NGOs and other third-sector organisations are increasingly demanding influence on policies directly affecting them. Accordingly, the key challenges facing public administration today are to latch on to the knowledge and resources of other public agencies and above all private actors (J. Koppenjan & Klijn, 2004). In Chapter 8, I examine how this problematisation endorses a new kind of civil-servant ethos attuned to empowering civil society and links up with a series of techniques of empowerment.

Conclusion

In this chapter, I have argued that neoliberalism may be understood as particular ways of problematising the art of governing. Instead of regarding neoliberalism as an ideology veiling and legitimising more substantial, material interests or as a discourse providing a more or less coherent blueprint for political and administrative reforms, I find it both more convincing and more adequate to grasp neoliberalism as particular problematisations of governing a territorial state, its population and, increasingly, itself, i.e. public administration. It seems more convincing to me in that it does not imply the conspiracy tendencies found in treating neoliberalism as an ideology. We do not need to look for a master plan orchestrated by a particular capitalist class or political agent in order to illuminate the strategic character and epistemological consistency of neoliberalism. The understanding of neoliberalism as a problematisation of government is more adequate in that it does not limit our critical interrogation to a particular class or elite or to a discourse providing a particular political programme. As I argued above, neoliberal ideas did not come with blueprints for political action. Accordingly, it seems more adequate to address neoliberalism as an intellectually informed governmental activity. By doing so, we are encouraged to pay attention both to the more or less coherent problematisations of government and to the manifold administrative schemes, procedures and techniques that inform and seek to answer this problematisation.

On the basis of this understanding of neoliberalism, I identified two general types of neoliberalism: a critical and a constructivist problematisation of the art of governing. The former is akin to classical liberalism in that it is generally sceptical about the possibility and the benefits of state intervention due to the state's limited ability to be cognisant of the processes and needs of individual citizens and groups. Thus, like classical liberalism, the key problem for critical neoliberalism is how the state can and should govern in a situation of epistemological finitude without infringing on individual freedom. However, in contrast to classical liberalism, which saw civil society as a sphere of spontaneous order (the invisible hand) that need to be protected by the state from the state itself, critical neoliberalism takes the market as a mechanism of information exchange that needs to be not only protected from the state but also to some extent constructed by way of a constitutional framework. It is the recognition that the market is a thoroughly human artefact, a technical device of information distribution, rather than a more or less given sphere of freedom, that make some, but not all, critical neoliberalists argue in favour of more extensive state interventions in order to secure the functioning of the market. For constructivist neoliberalism, the key problematisation is not how the state can govern in a situation of ignorance and at the same time protect individual liberties but rather how the state can augment freedoms in ways that are instrumental to wider political and societal goals. Accordingly, instead of a critical ethos seeking to find the appropriate limits to state intervention, constructivist liberalism adopts an enabling ethos that interrogates not the need for state intervention but the efficacy with which these facilitate and mobilise the resources of civil society and public administration itself.

If it is correct that both problematisations are informing contemporary public administration reforms, then what is the relationship between these two forms of neoliberalism? I would say that they are agonistic, but not antagonistic. That is, they are clearly in conflict but they share certain basic premises that circumscribe the nature of their conflict. On the one hand, their relation is conflictual in that critical neoliberalism is highly sceptical about state interventions outside the making and upholding of a general constitutional framework ensuring the rights of citizens and freedom from coercion. The Austrian, Chicago and Virginia schools of neoliberalism all denounce positive conceptions of freedom and, by implication, abhor an activist and enabling role for the state. On the other hand, the *raison d'être* of both critical and constructivist neoliberalism is freedom – from state intervention in the former case and by state intervention in the latter. Thus, even the most activist modes of constructivist neoliberalism reject the idea of state dirigisme, i.e. of the state and its experts planning *for* society. If state interventions are necessary and legitimate, it is because they are able to unleash problem-solving and self-steering capacities in society, not because the state should or could handle societal problems by itself. Conversely, even the strongest critics of state interventions argue that it may be necessary and legitimate for the state to intervene in matters ensuring the functioning of markets and in the (limited) provision of certain public goods.

Note

1 The public choice centre, a label acquired in 1969, was established as the Thomas Jefferson Center for Studies in Political Economy at the University of Virginia in 1957.

4

Accountability: The reflection and expansion of government?

Introduction

In 2012, the US General Accountability Office[1] was awarded the (spoof) Ignobel Prize in Literature for its report on the costs of reports in the US defence system (GAO, 2012a). As stated by the Prize Committee, the GAO was awarded the prize 'for issuing a report about reports about reports that recommends the preparation of a report about the report about reports about reports' (Improbable Research, 2012).

Of course, this prize is meant as a joke and should not be taken too seriously. Yet, it does seem to point to a wider trend that was pointed out two decades ago by Michael Power (Power, 1997) and subsequently a number of other academics, namely the growing and apparently insatiable desire to account for public-sector activities (Salamon, 2002; Hood, 2006b). The proliferation of accountability systems and monitory and regulatory bodies is not a trend confined to the public sector. Similar if not even stronger tendencies can be observed in the realm of private and commercial activities, where the number of both public and private agencies seeking to enhance accountability has grown to the point of some scholars invoking 'the rise of the regulatory state' (Majone, 1994). While the trends in these sectors are likely to be related, the focus here is on accountability mechanisms targeting the public sector.

I make two general arguments. First, the attempt to hinder the abuse of power is enabled by a hitherto unseen expansion of power, namely the governing of government. Much attention has been devoted to the democratic control of sovereign power, and this is an important element of the intensified quest for accountability. Yet, another at least as important element is the manifold attempts to govern the activities of the public sector more efficiently, i.e. to make government fold back upon itself with a view to constantly reflect upon how it may improve its efficacy. Second, accountability hinges on making activities visible not by the market – as Hayek would prefer – but by a whole range of new information and calculative technologies employed in the public sector. By implication, partly due to the rapid spread of electronic computer systems, the quest for accountability seems to lead not to less government but to more, by making public administrations constantly account for and reflect upon the ways in which they may improve their services.

The chapter first discusses how to grasp accountability in a way that allows us to map the kind of power it entails. This conceptual clarification points to the historical variation in the practice of accountability and the kinds of power linked to it. This conceptual discussion informs the structuration of the rest of the chapter. The first section examines how accountability relates to efforts to democratise sovereign power. I then move on to analyse the ways in which accountability links up with the governmentalisation of public administrations. This is followed by a section exploring the role played by accountability in the attempts of government to be more attentive to and mobilise citizens. Finally, I sum up by discussing the key political logics at play in contemporary accountability reforms and some of the political implications they have.

Accountability and power: A conceptual clarification

As the quests for accounting multiply and spread to quite diverse settings, it is not surprising that we find important variations in the conception of accountability. Notwithstanding these variations, there seems to be a widespread consensus across social science disciplines that accountability entails that one party X is obliged to produce an account to another party Y, who may in turn impose some kind of sanction on X if the account turns out to be unsatisfactory (Bovens et al., 2014, pp. 4–6). I find this rather minimalist understanding quite useful (for a critique of expanding the concept, see Mulgan, 2000).

Yet even if this understanding explicitly addresses the issue of power, which is crucial for my purpose, I think it misses out at least three important points by focusing too narrowly on actors. Firstly, it misses out the *problematisation* that accountability seeks to provide an answer to. Thus, to what administrative, political or societal problem(s) is accountability seen to be the solution? Mulgan argues convincingly that accountability should not be conflated with, for example, control or responsiveness. Yet today accountability is often taken to provide the solution, whether right or wrong, to inadequate control of responsiveness. If only we can design more effective and precise mechanisms of accounting, so the argument goes, it will be possible to provide better control or responsiveness. Secondly, and closely related to the first point, we need to address the kind of *knowledge* produced by the accounting process in order to grasp what kind problem and values are made visible and which (potential) ones are excluded. My Foucauldian-inspired argument here is that the exercise of modern forms of power, such as the requirement and actual provision of account making, hinge on particular forms of knowledge. Finally, in order to grasp the how of power, we need to address what I would call the *technical* dimension of accountability, i.e. the means or technical device by which accountability is to be achieved. I agree that accountability involves a 'process' of account giving. Yet it also provides one or more administrative or technical devices that materially enable the production of an account that renders the practice conducted by the public agency amenable to inspection and ultimately governing by one or more (external) accountants or other political authorities.

Of course, this quite general conception of accountability and the kind of power it entails cannot be detached from the historically specific form it takes and the political context in which it operates. While accountability has a long and complex history in Western societies, a few general points may be worth pointing out. First of all, accountability is linked to the invention of techniques of accounting – whether of persons, money or performance (Bovens et al., 2014, pp. 2–3). Secondly, it is possible to distinguish between the invention of double-entry bookkeeping in the twelfth century and the decidedly modern form of accounting emerging as a written and disciplinary form of examination emerging from the end of the eighteenth century in a number of penal institutions (Foucault, 1977) and educational institutions, such as Cambridge University, the *Grand Ecoles* and West Point Academy (Hoskin & Macve, 1994). Until around 1800 formal examination in education had been oral and ungraded. With the advent of written and quantifiable examinations, accounting was transformed from a technology measuring and recording transactions and flows of commodities and money to one putting a quantifiable value on persons and their actions (ibid., p. 70). This historical mutation of the technology of accounting enabled a new form of disciplinary and normalising power based on individualising, written and quantifiable accounts. These accounts enabled a systematic comparison of persons and their actions, which could now be translated into simple quantifiable performance indicators. Moreover, they would allow the calculation of normal performance, those below and above it. Finally, it would allow political authorities – without any expertise in education or whatever field was subjected to this new technology – to govern those persons and organisations subjected to accounting in new ways. It would now be possible on a national scale for political authorities to reward those who performed well according to the new quantifiable measures and punish those who did not.

If accounting in Western societies went through important transformations in the twelfth and late eighteenth centuries, it seems that it undertook another crucial mutation by the end of the twentieth century. With the large-scale use of electronic computer systems in the public sector, it became possible to construct and calculate performance indicators and knowledge on a hitherto unseen scale (Traunmuller & Lenk, 1996). In particular, the transition of computer systems based mainly on stand-alone mainframes to personal computers connected to internal networks during the 1980s and the rapid development of the internet from the 1990s allowed performance accounts to be disseminated and made available to public managers and employees (Brown, 1999) and to citizens interacting with the public sector (Homburg & Bekkers, 2005) in something increasingly resembling real time. Whereas the mainframe computer systems introduced in the 1960s enhanced routine operations, such as tax and old-age-pension calculation and the digitalisation of large registers, such as land, population and car databases, the new electronic computer systems emerging from the 1990s enabled the rapid development and diffusion of assessment systems, procedural guidelines, organisational standards, and performance indicators in the public sector.

In some cases, the new way of assessing performance enabled the spread of existing management techniques into new areas. For example, in the effort to engage NGOs and various voluntary organisations in the (co-) production of public services, these organisations were increasingly requested to account for their performance in terms of the new performance standards and indicators. As we shall see below, the new accountability systems enabled public authorities keen to mobilise the resources of citizens and NGOs to govern these at a distance by making them account for the results of their performance in novel ways. Unsurprisingly, the new information technologies and the new public management technologies enabled the production of new forms of knowledge. With the quantification of hitherto complex, qualitative knowledge that made little sense to anyone other than experts and/or those producing the account, we see the production of quantifiable and standardised accounts of organisational performance enabling benchmarking, i.e. a systematic comparison rendering visible the relative performance. Once the relative differences in (quantified) performance are made visible, we see the emergence of new ways of assessing the quality of public services and of delegating responsibility (Kouzmin et al., 1999; Triantafillou, 2007). For example, an oncology department that displays relatively long waiting time for diagnostics or low levels of curing for a particular form of cancer – compared to other oncology departments – will now be made responsible for improving the so-called quality of its services. Quality then is now operationalised as the relative position in a neatly quantified objectification of complex medical practices.

In brief, if the mutation of accounting in educational institutions at the end of the eighteenth century served to produce an account of individual performance with a view to disciplining it and enhancing its productivity, the mutation of accounting over the last few decades has made way for an ongoing account of organisational efficiency that not only enables superior political authorities to govern these organisations more regularly and rigorously but also encourages the organisation to constantly scrutinise its own performance and govern itself in line with prevailing accountability standards. As we shall see below, the increasing technical possibilities for enhancing performance accountability did not seem to quell the thirst for accounts but rather did the opposite. But before turning to the governmentalisation of government, we need to address the way in which accountability has been implicated in the democratisation of sovereign power.

Legalisation and democratisation of sovereignty

With the establishment of liberal democracies during the nineteenth and early twentieth centuries, the exercise of sovereign power was displaced from the monarch or the nobility to a variety of democratic institutions purporting to represent the interests of the people acknowledged as citizens of a state's territory. The regulative ideals of these institutions were not to dispose of the use of sovereign power but to ensure that its exercise took place in the interests of the people and, as far as possible, by the people itself. By the time this transformation took place, territorial states had been in place in Europe and the Americas for quite some time, which made any modality of direct democratic rule impractical. Instead, these states saw the emergence of a variety of indirect democracy, in which legislative assemblies were to represent the interest and well-being of the populace through fair and regular elections. Notwithstanding the immense procedural and institutional variations, these legislative assemblies would then proceed to appoint a government.

While elections remain an essential element of the democratisation of sovereign rule, liberal democracies saw the development of a number of other mechanisms seeking to hold the exercise of sovereign power to account. By requiring government to account for its exercise of power, the hope was that it would be possible to identify possible illegal and other improper uses of sovereign power and if so eventually hold the government responsible for its actions. On the basis of who is in charge of the act of accountability, we may distinguish here between two forms of democratic control of sovereign power: legislative and civic control.

Legislative controls

In liberal democracies legislative control mechanisms are available to elected politicians outside the government and to the judiciary to hold the government accountable for its actions. Of course, control mechanisms available to the judiciary are usually not strictly speaking democratic controls. In most countries judges (with some states in the US as important exceptions) are not directly elected by a democratic constituency but appointed by an independent commission, by the legislature or, more commonly, by the government (Akkas, 2004). Moreover, legislative controls were in place in many countries a long time before these countries became democratic. Accordingly, until the nineteenth century – and in many countries until the early twentieth – legislative controls aimed not to ensure the democratisation of sovereignty but rather to contribute to maintaining a certain balance of power between various political elites and to be able to govern the affairs and ensure the creation of wealth in a state territory more effectively. It is only with the democratic reforms that legislative controls also come to take on the task of controlling sovereign state power and ensuring individual political liberties.

During the nineteenth and twentieth centuries, the legislative style controls expanded to include a number of different techniques available not only to the judiciary but also – and more frequently – to the government opposition. Thus, today, legislative controls in liberal democracies include judicial reviews, formal questioning of ministers, committee inquiries and government auditors (see next chapter). Judicial reviews and hearings through the courts force the government to disclose its actions and the information supporting such actions (Mulgan, 2003, pp. 75–83). Compared to the US, the formal capacity of the judiciary to force governments in parliamentary systems to account for their actions is often limited. Here the legislature, in practice the government opposition, is supposed to be the key force in holding the government to account. Yet even in parliamentary systems, the general trend seems to be to grant the judiciary or court-like bodies such as tribunals wider powers to hold governments to account (Mulgan, 2003, p. 76).

Secondly, ministerial responsibility, which is found in most parliamentary systems, enables the legislature to make a minister accountable for the actions taken within her jurisdiction regardless of whether that decision is taken by a civil servant way down the line of bureaucratic command (Mulgan, 2003, pp. 48–52). Even if a few political systems, such as the Swedish, operate with collective rather than individual responsibility (Öberg, 2003), individual ministers are still required to report to other ministerial colleagues and to parliament. Accordingly, in many parliamentary systems, ministerial responsibility constitutes one of the most important avenues for making the government account for its actions. However, the ministerial obligation to account and take responsibility for actions does not apply to statutory bodies. This is an important limitation as the number of statutory bodies or agencies with a wide room for discretion for the choice of policy instruments has risen substantially over the last decades (see below for the phenomenon of agentification).

This leads us to the final general instrument of legislative control: inquiries by legislative committees. Made up by a mixture of government and opposition party members of the legislature, though not ministers, legislative committees play a particularly strong role in the US, with its highly developed system of congressional committees (Aberbach, 1990). Over the last decades, such committees have come to play an increasingly important role too in Westminster-style and other Continental European political systems (Mulgan, 2003, p. 53). One of the comparative advantages of this instrument is that it allows parliament to hold statutory bodies, which are designed to remain outside direct ministerial control, to account (Mulgan, 2003, p. 55). More generally, legislative committees can question both politicians (on broader policy issues) and leading civil servants (on more narrow administrative actions and procedures), though the formal and actual scope of account giving may actually be rather narrow. Thus, in most systems ministers can order civil servants not to disclose certain types of information. Moreover, in some parliamentary systems, it takes a majority in the legislator to inaugurate an inquiry (Mattson & Strøm, 1995).

Civic controls

Civil control mechanisms available to the citizens at large include complaints, information rights and various forms of public ombudsmen. In most democracies, individual citizens have various rights to complain about decisions directly affecting them. This right provides citizens with grievances the opportunity to seek a remedy, which may result in consequences for the person complained against. In most cases, the complaints are targeting the decision or service of a particular public agency, which will then have specific procedures to deal with the complaint. In cases where such channels have been tried, the citizen may be entitled to complain to an external body – whether judicial or, more likely, some statutory body with the right to pass decisions in complaint cases within a certain jurisdiction. For example, we find Health Service Commissioners and Police Complaints Commissions that are supposed to handle complaints issued over particular incidents or practices (Smith, 2009).

Citizens' rights to information include public access to information about the citizen making the inquiry but also to information that may be considered of public relevance (Mulgan, 2003, pp. 98–103). The former may include personal information on health conditions, social status, tax payments etc. The citizen's interest in the knowledge that authorities have about them is not only to ensure that this information is correct, which may be used to file a complaint over an agency decision or service. It may also be used to hold government agencies to account for illegal registration of personal information. Citizens' rights to information revolving around public affairs may include policy briefs, background reports and expert documents informing government decisions. Such information has a direct bearing on the ability of citizens to hold governments to account for their decisions – or non-decisions – in areas of public interest, such as public health, environment or education policies. This information is often also used by the media (newspapers and television) to hold government politicians and public agencies accountable for imprudent if not illegal use of taxpayers' money, problematic individual social-care decisions and illegal decisions on immigrants and data collection on potential terrorists, which in the post-9/11 period seems to include most of us.

Public ombudsmen are an investigative institution usually appointed by the legislature with the authority to conduct investigations into specific government processes based on the complaint of an individual citizen or some kind of private organisation (Mulgan, 2003, pp. 90–100; Kostadinova, 2015). The Ombudsman or Parliamentary Commissioner for Administration has by now been introduced in most liberal democracies with a view to conducting impartial investigations and thereby providing ordinary citizens with more clout to hold governments accountable. The main focus in most countries is on individual cases of administrative malpractice rather than on general policy decisions (Mulgan, 2003, pp. 92–3). As in the case of juridical review, the origin of the ombudsman institution is not really a democratic one. Thus the Swedish Office of Supreme Ombudsman (later Chancellor of Justice) was established by King Charles XII in 1713 in order to ensure that judges and civil servants acted in accordance with the laws and their duties during his exile in Turkey (Justitieombudsmännen, 2015). It was only in 1809 that a parliamentary ombudsman was established by the Swedish parliament as a parallel institution to the still-present Chancellor of Justice. And it was only during the 1970s that the Swedish Ombudsman was deprived of the legal powers to prosecute incidents of illegal practice and took on a more supervisory and counselling role with a view to preventing malpractices. Apart from the ombudsman, we find government inspectors (in the British systems) and inspectors general (in the US) with the task of monitoring and promoting efficiency in government departments, such as defence, security and taxation (Mulgan, 2003, p. 91). Common to all these institutions is that, while they have the right of access to all the information used by governments in order to scrutinise these, they lack the power to change administrative decisions.

In sum, accountability is part of a wider technical response to the process of democratising the exercise of sovereign power. Some of the accountability instruments have a long history and emerged long before the advent of democratic rule and therefore served different purposes. Today, however, the overall rationale serving most of these instruments is the democratisation of sovereignty, though the division of sovereignty between government, judiciary and legislature seems to constitute an additional rationale for the instruments of judicial review and committee inquiries.[2] Thus, from the end of the nineteenth century classical liberalism was one, but certainly not the only, rationality informing the attempt to hold the exercise of sovereign power accountable.

The governmentalisation of government

Starting in the 1980s, most if not all OECD countries have in varying extent and form seen an avalanche of reforms seeking to spur the efficiency of the public sector (OECD, 1995; Pollitt & Bouckaert, 2011). Usually encapsulated under the heading of New Public Management (Hood, 1991), these reforms include performance-management systems, contracting out, public–private partnerships, total-quality management, lean-style management, etc. that all in various ways seek to improve value-for-money, i.e. economic efficiency of the making of public services. While these performance-management systems clearly do not work only by way of account giving, the promise of more efficient and better-quality public services hinge crucially on the translation of these activities into a form of knowledge, an account, by which non-specialists, such as politicians, public managers and the wider public, may assess, debate and make decisions about the future of these services. These reforms can in general terms be read as an attempt by government to fold back upon itself, i.e. to govern itself in order to improve the ways in which it works and attend to the needs of the population it purports to serve (Dean, 1999; Triantafillou, 2012). In this wider process whereby government folds back upon itself to optimise its functioning, accountability has come to serve as an important logic and technical answer to the problem of how to improve the performance of the public services (Meijer, 2007; Petrakaki et al., 2009; Wallis & Gregory, 2009; Joaquin & Greitens, 2011).

The rise of accountability systems attuned to enhance public-sector performance has been closely linked to two distinct forms of governing, namely central control and agentification. In the first movement, the existing hierarchy of command from the minister to the frontline worker has been reinforced or rather changed in order to ensure that the subordinate levels are working within the political and economic goals stipulated by the superior level. This movement, which seems to have been particularly strong in Britain and New Zealand, has received much attention by academics, professionals and various frontline civil servants who are concerned with what they regard as increasing central control over the ways in which public services are provided and a corresponding erosion of autonomy for professional and frontline workers (Richards & Smith, 2006; Taylor & Kelly, 2006). It is, however, significant that this extension of central control has increasingly taken the form not so much of specific legal regulations as of a variety of internal (non-legal) contracts, framework budgets, agreements, standards, performance targets and benchmarking systems. While such technologies of performance are frequently linked to a wider legislative frame (Dean, 1999, pp. 168–9), their function relies fundamentally on calculative techniques and normalising standards that enable both the central level and those subjected to this kind of power to gauge their performance. Thus, this drive towards enhancing the performance of the production of public services, whether produced by the public or by private sectors, has come with a virtual explosion of accountability mechanisms by which frontline workers, statutory agencies and private contractors are obliged to account not only for the spending of public money but also for the quality of the services they deliver.

In the second movement, which is clearly related to the ambitions of central control, we find a variety of efforts to activate the public administration. Public managers and employees at all levels are increasingly expected not only to assume responsibility to meet the visions and goals of the superior level but also to think constantly about how to improve the efficiency and quality of their services. This second movement, agentification, implies that departments or sections of the public administration are now seen as agents with a certain space of autonomy or instrumental discretion to meet the goals stipulated by superiors or by citizens (Verhoest et al., 2004). Much has been written about the growth of regulatory and statutory bodies that are meant to operate more or less independently of government (ministries). While such bodies clearly are not a new phenomenon (Wettenhall, 2005), they do seem to have proliferated in many OECD countries since the 1980s (Christensen & Lægreid, 2006). The general rationale supporting these organisations is that their relative autonomy from narrow government and short-term electoral concerns will allow them to deal with public issues in a longer-term perspective and provide more efficient and innovative solutions.

Apart from such organisational changes, we also see the proliferation of a range of technologies of agency, i.e. a range of administrative, managerial and psychological schemes and techniques that encourage public-sector employees to be active and constantly reflect on and take initiatives with a view to improving the efficiency and quality of their work (Dean, 1999, pp. 167–8). Such technologies include internal contracts, value-based and trust-based management, transformative and lean-style management and positive psychology. While the rationales, theoretical premises and organisational origins of these technologies vary importantly, they have proved remarkably malleable and useful in the contemporary quest to mobilise the energies and professional resources of public sector employees and harness these into general organisational and political goals (Triantafillou, 2012, pp. 70–91).

In sum, we see a double movement of central control and the spurring of agency that both seek to boost the performance of the public administration. While the central control and centralised establishment of accountability standards and indicators is regarded as a restriction of the professional judgement and operational discretion of local agencies and public sector employees, most academics recognise that the picture of a unilateral decrease of local autonomy is too simple. It is not only that many agencies have been established with the intent of increasing operational autonomy; it is also that public-sector employees in general – even with line ministries – are encouraged to adopt an ethos of activism in place of an ethos of obedience. We thus see the emergence of a new regulated space of freedom in which accountability works not only to monitor and possibly restrict professional judgement and discretion, though this may often be the case, but also encourages or even forces employees to be active, competitive, innovative and service-minded. The making of such a new form of active subjectivity may be at odds with the predominant accountability systems favouring simple calculable indicators. The new forms of subjectivity are not always easily rendered amenable to objectification, calculation and comparison. Hence the recent calls for more qualitative or subjective forms of accountability that are more attuned to (professional) learning than to (political) control (Reeves, 2004; Schillemans, 2008; Zheng & Warner, 2010).

Responding to and mobilising citizens

Accountability is currently at stake in at least two largely distinct logics informing the relationship between government and citizens: the attempt to respond to citizens' needs for various services and the attempt to mobilise the resources of citizens to meet societal challenges. The former is largely associated with the customer-orientation found in NPM reforms since the 1980s. The latter is largely associated with the participatory democracy orientation found in New Public Governance-style reforms since the 2000s.

Responding to citizen needs

As amply described by the literature, most OECD countries have seen a number of more or less radical reforms aiming to make their public administrations cater better to the needs and preferences of citizens. Under the heading of New Public Management, these reforms increasingly regarded citizens as customers whose preferences should heard and as far as possible be met (Aberbach & Christensen, 2005; Brewer, 2007). This customer or consumer focus came with a number of citizens' charters, increasing choice between public-service providers and various information systems allowing an informed choice (Pech, 1997; Dent, 2006; OECD, 2011a). Thus, citizens are regarded less as political subjects with general civil and political rights and duties and more as enlightened, calculating individuals seeking to maximise their own utility and pursue their self-interest. Accountability is here instrumental in the attempt to provide citizens with the knowledge allowing them to make an enlightened choice that will best meet their individual preference. Or, put more sharply, citizens are not only 'free to choose' public services, but 'obliged to be free' (Rose, 1999, pp. 85–9), i.e. to reflect on the choices made available, compile information about these, reflect on their preferences and thereby start acting as consumers. At least, we see a whole range of techniques employed to render visible the price (in case of user fees) and above all the quality of health, education, employment and other public services. These techniques include performance measuring and benchmarking that systematically compare the quality between various public providers of the assumedly same type of service (Kouzmin et al., 1999; Behn, 2014; Hayne & Salterio, 2014).

There has been a substantial debate, both in the academic literature and in the wider public, over the accuracy and utility of the information generated for the purpose of ensuring informed choice of public services. Consumer organisations have lamented the inadequacy of information; professionals and their associations often complain that the kind of accounts of their services produced for the general public are either too simplistic or too complex to be interpreted correctly by the average citizen; and policymakers lament that professionals and frontline workers are unable or unwilling to account for their services in a few simple numbers that allow unambiguous and rapid assessment of the performance of the public sector. A frequent answer, though clearly not a definite solution, to these problems and complaints has been the employment of user-satisfaction surveys (Fountain, 2001; Bouckaert & Walle, 2003). Quantitative surveys used to gauge citizens' satisfaction with a given public service cut through the professional expertise and complex accounts and reduce the quality of service into a simple number (or smiley) that is easy to understand and act upon both for other users and for the responsible policymakers. Of course, such surveys have been criticised too on the grounds of being too simplistic and of citizens lacking sufficient knowledge about the resources available to the public sector to actually produce 'good' services. Yet such criticisms often risk being undermined by their flavour of bad excuses and smacking of academic/professional arrogance. Thus, if users of a service cannot provide a useful account of the quality of these services, then who can? Of course, the very formulation of this question testifies to the erosion of professional authority and the concomitant strength of the consumer-choice rationality. Whether this is a good or bad thing, the prevalence of user satisfaction surveys shows that accountability of public services is linked to new regulative ideals of citizenship, notably that of the enlightened consumer.

Mobilising citizens' resources

Concurrently with the public reforms seeking to cater better to citizens' demands and needs, many liberal democracies have seen the employment of public programmes and reforms seeking to mobilise citizens' resources or, more broadly, civil society (OECD, 2009b, 2011c). These reforms are informed by ideals of citizens' participation and empowerment, rather than the rational, self-interested individual seeking to maximise utility. The attempt to mobilise citizens and their resources is indebted to a form of liberalism for which the key problematisation is not how to protect civil society from excessive state intervention but rather how to harness the capacities of civil society groups in order both to augment the quality of life of individual citizens and to contribute to a thriving society that is better able to ensure the wealth and well-being of its population.

This approach whereby public authorities co-operate with non-profit organisations to provide public services is of course not new but gradually developed in many Western European and North American countries throughout the twentieth century. In fact, the very notion of civil society as a distinct sphere with its own logic and ability to govern itself dates back to the Scottish moral philosophers (Adam Smith and Adam Ferguson) of the late eighteenth century (Foucault, 2008, pp. 295–311). Yet, before we reduce the contemporary political measures seeking to mobilise civil society to vintage-style liberalism in the shape of help to self-help, we need to note both the key role that the state plays in this and the systematic and comprehensive strategies supporting such programmes. Existing comparative surveys suggest that governments in both the developed and developing worlds have been increasingly busy over the last two decades or so to articulate various forms of voluntary or civil-society strategies aiming to mobilise the resources of citizens and groups (Lester et al., 1999). The post-2008 fiscal crisis seems only to have increased the efforts to implement nationwide strategies. Examples are the UK's's Big Society (Smith, 2010; Lowndes & Pratchett, 2012), Germany's National Voluntary Service (Beller & Has, 2014) and Denmark's and Norway's voluntary strategies (Lorentzen & Henriksen, 2014).

These state-orchestrated strategies to mobilise citizen resources are facing inherent problems of ensuring accountability. How does one ensure accountability of participatory activities in which citizens are contributing to the definition of political goals and contribute to the implementation of various programmes? Ideally, full empowerment, whereby citizens are able to articulate and attend to their own needs, implies that citizens become both account givers and account holders (Damgaard & Lewis, 2014, p. 265). Even if the participatory ideal remains just that, a regulative ideal, the governing strategies seeking to mobilise and nurture civil-society resources constantly face the problem of how to do so without encroaching on or even destroying the apparently distinct logics and values of civil society. A common operational device of such voluntary strategies is to allow NGOs and other groups to apply for funding of their activities catering to the provision of public services to various target groups. These activities include assistance to people suffering from abuse problems, neighbourhood renewal projects, elder care, homework support for children of poor parents, sports activities for youth deemed at risk etc. In return for public support, NGOs and other groups have to account for their use of this support. This usually entails reporting on their performance according to a more or less wide range of indicators stipulated by a responsible ministry or municipal council. NGOs must produce annual reports accounting for their progress in terms of the performance indicators. It is also fairly common that such NGOs are expected to establish a board providing strategic advice and perhaps even overseeing progress.

This professionalisation or, more precisely, the governmentalisation of civil society activities has been much lamented not only by voluntary organisations subjected to new and more rigorous accountability measures but also by political parties and governments preaching the moral and self-governing virtues of society. The assumption informing much of this critique of accountability requirements seems to be that it is somehow possible to dissociate empowerment from power. However, as shown by Barbara Cruikshank in a brilliant study of the so-called war on poverty in the 1960s US, the empowerment of the poor entails not simply that the powerless are given power but rather that they are subjected to a form of power (government in Foucault's sense) that works by making the poor govern themselves as democratic subjects (Cruikshank, 1999). Thus, they must exercise their freedom within a quite narrow horizon of citizen norms focusing on self-esteem and self-improvement in order to wrestle free of their poverty, a horizon excluding the problematisation of wider economic inequalities and the use of any form of illegal or violent forms of protest.

The contemporary drive to mobilise civil society by professionalising or, more precisely, governing NGOs essentially follows the same logic. On the one hand, public authorities are obliged – usually by law – to account for the spending of public money and, more recently, to display easily discernible results that induce policymakers to subject civil society projects to more or less rigid mechanisms of accountability. On the other hand, the very rationale informing policymakers' decisions to employ NGOs and other civil society groups is exactly that they are regarded not as mere relays of public support but as propagators of distinct community values and as agents with a superior capacity to empower those in need. The quest for accountability is not the single cause behind this predicament, but it does contribute to it by requiring that the effectiveness of such empowerment programmes is rendered amenable to systematic observation and performance assessment.

Conclusion: The self-perpetuating logic of accountability?

So far, I have explored the emergence and employment of accountability systems in liberal democracies over the last few decades. It has been pointed out that these systems enabled the exercise of new forms of power. In particular, it enables governing at a distance by way of governmentalising those authorities, NGOs and even individual citizens engaged in providing public services and improving the well-being of society. In this final section, I discuss why the quest for accountability seems to be, if not unstoppable, then at least in some sense self-perpetuating. Thus, it is as if the technological possibilities created with the ICT revolution of the late twentieth century combined with neoliberal rationalities of government have given an impetus to constantly develop, improve and disseminate new and more sophisticated ways of accounting for activities linked to the making of public services.

This seemingly unstoppable quest for more and better accountability can be linked to the kind of critique it tends to engender. Basically, much of the critique of accountability seems to spur rather than arrest the proliferation of accountability. Thus, public administration research has identified a number of undesirable administrative and economic effects of the quest for accountability. Under the heading of accountability overload, public administration scholars have pointed out that accountability systems may increase transaction costs and thereby exceed the costs of the errors they were supposed to eliminate or reduce (Halachmi, 2014), discourage innovation by adhering to fixed accountability standards (De Bruijn, 2002), lead to gaming and manipulating indicators (Hood, 2006a), blame game focus instead of remedial action (Behn, 2001) and confuse rather than focus organisational action because of multiple, and at times contradictory, systems of accountability (Lewis & Triantafillou, 2012).

The general conclusion among most public-administration scholars is the sober dictum that, while accountability is necessary and often good, more accountability is not necessarily better. From this flow a number of guidelines and general principles to be observed when designing and implementing accountability systems, such as to consider their purpose, consider the costs of running them, include relevant public-sector employees and affected citizens in the process, and make sure not to monopolise the interpretation of the data produced by the accountability systems. Instead there should be room for dialogical interpretation because the results, whether good or bad, often have quite complex causes (Smith, 1995).

A few other scholars have addressed the effects of the quest for accountability from the boundaries of its normative horizon. For example, it has been argued that the quest for accountability amounts to a 'treadmill' in which accountability deficits and gaps are inevitable and therefore always call for more and/or better forms of accounting (Boström & Garsten, 2008). Accountability, it is argued, is 'never getting to the root of the problem' (ibid., p. 231) because what counts as good accountability to one set of purposes or governance styles is regarded as inadequate or even useless by others (ibid., p. 243). This is akin to Goodhart's Law – that every measure that becomes a target becomes a bad measure. Thus, every attempt to find the right way of accounting for an activity always ends up accounting for it badly and therefore calls for rectification and new accountability measures. This kind of awareness of the political norms and perspective(s) informing any kind of accountability system has been taken further by constructivist-inspired scholars who essentially argue that accountability will always construe and shape its object in a particular way. Human actions are not in themselves auditable, but have to be made so (Power, 1996). Thus, it is not only that political norms about substantive goals and governance styles may contribute to the accountability explosion or treadmill, it is also that the very act of accounting for a certain organisational activity serves to transform the ways in which we assess, debate, govern and – ultimately – carry out that activity (Hoskin, 1996; Dahler-Larsen, 2014).

If contemporary accountability systems seem to be supported by a certain self-perpetuating logic, it may be because they constitute the effective assembling of diverse and reinforcing elements. As mentioned above, the emergence of new computer systems (notably personal computers and the internet) enabled the production of new quantifiable accounts of performance. These technologies evolved in tandem with a relatively recent problematisation of government: how to facilitate the self-governing capacities of the public sector itself and the citizens depending upon it in order to maximise the efficiency and quality of public services? Thus, we see a political pressure to produce accounts of complex services amenable to assessment by politicians and public managers, i.e. non-experts in the various fields of public services. These accounts were almost immediately criticised by the civil servants and professionals working under these systems and by public administration scholars studying them. All tended to lament the reduction of complex activities to a set of simple quantified indicators. This critique of the crudeness and often limited relevance of existing ways of account-producing constituted and constitutes today an important drive for constantly sophisticating accountability systems in order to measure better and to improve the quality of public services. Thus, central public authorities (elected politicians) too are pressuring for 'better' accountability systems in the sense of systems that more adequately facilitate and structure the freedom of public administrations, and citizens involved in the production of public services are mobilised. Despite the often cynical critiques of New Public Management, the point of neoliberal rationalities of government is not to restrict local capacities but to employ accountability systems and indicators in ways that will further encourage public administrations at the front line, NGOs and citizens to freely assume responsibility improving the production of public services. In sum, the interlocking of a system seeking to convert complex activities into more or less simple quantifiable accounts and a political rationality bent on unleashing and controlling the self-steering capacities and resources of public administrations and civil society actors seems to amount to a self-perpetuating quest for new and better forms of accountability.

Notes

1 The General Accounting Office changed its name to General Accountability Office in 2004. The abbreviation GAO is used here for both.

2 The history of non-liberal and non-democratic rationales for the (divided) exercise of sovereign power has been brilliantly traced in Ian Hunter's *Rival enlightenments* (Hunter, 2001). Hunter shows how the legal system was propagated as a key instrument by seventeenth-century German jurists Henning Arnisaeus

and Christian Thomasius in order to secularise the state and make way for a civil order based not on generalised (liberal) rights to pursue individual interests but on constitutionally given freedoms to perform particular 'offices', such as familial, parental, commercial, civil, and administrative duties.

5

Democratic accountability and the institutionalisation of performance auditing

Introduction

This chapter explores the changing role of supreme audit institutions (SAIs), or national audit offices, in the institutionalisation of performance auditing as a part of democratic accountability. It examines how performance auditing of state and other public institutions has become increasingly important in most OECD countries (Posner & Shahan, 2014). Most SAIs seem to have moved from a relatively narrow focus on technical and legal accounting to a wider focus that now also includes performance or value-for-money auditing. It is as if liberal democracies today are no longer content with ensuring democratic accountability by holding governments to account for the legality and technical correctness of their spending of public money; they must also prove that they are doing so efficiently.

Perhaps it not so surprising that SAIs are moving into performance auditing. This could simply be seen as reflecting a wider trend of new public-management reforms, in which SAIs have adopted management ideas emphasising economic efficiency and value-for-money. At least one study suggests just that (Pollitt, 2003). Probably the influence goes both ways. At least in Canada, the Auditor General seems to be an important proponent of performance management systems (Gendron et al., 2001). At any rate, the SAIs' adoption of performance auditing does seem to reflect a mutation in liberal political rationalities. As I argue below, the SAIs have moved from a relatively narrow focus on the technical and legal control of public expenditures to a much wider focus including assessments of efficiency and goal-effectiveness. This move seems to testify to the influence of neoliberal political rationalities overlapping with, but not wholly replacing, classical liberal concerns with the abuses of state power. I will restrict myself to what are vaguely understood as the internationally leading SAIs in the area of performance auditing, at least judged by the most frequently used SAIs in international peer reviews – see below. These are the ones found in the US, the UK, the Netherlands, Australia and the Nordic countries. By being leaders in this area, they are obviously not representative of SAIs globally. Accordingly, what I will try to illuminate is not the average picture of performance auditing but rather the rationalities and technologies of performance auditing when they are most extremely and therefore perhaps most clearly articulated.

The SAIs' new role is also interesting because it is illustrative of a wider predicament of the ways in which neoliberalism spurs the governmentalisation of government. Thus, the turn towards performance auditing can be seen as one particular instance by which government starts folding back upon and interrogates itself in terms of efficiency, quality and effectiveness. As any academic and practitioner of public administration will acknowledge, this governmentalisation of government comes with a fundamental predicament, namely: how to penetrate spheres of professional authority? Or, put slightly differently, how to govern notoriously complex policy areas and the jurisdiction of highly sophisticated professional knowledge? SAIs are not experts in public health, higher learning, taxation or infrastructure. Nevertheless, they publish all the time reports assessing the efficiency with which policies are executed in these areas. Using examples from the public-health sector, the chapter moves on to examine how SAIs conduct performance audits and thereby seek to penetrate domains of professional authority. It will be shown how the SAI performance audits hinge on standardising and quantifying knowledge and techniques that render complex activities susceptible to external assessment and government interventions.

Recently, there has been increasing focus on policy learning. Thus, the performance audits should not only control the efficient spending of public money, they should also enable and spur the auditee to be better at learning from others. More generally, the auditee should be encouraged and empowered to constantly reflect upon and examine how their activities and services can be improved. In order to spur such learning and make their performance audits more relevant, some SAIs design their studies and discuss the results of these in close dialogue with the auditees. As we shall see below, this may pose a challenge to SAI independency and may have contributed to making SAIs reinforce and partly reinvent their ways of maintaining their aura of impartiality.

The move towards performance auditing

National auditing institutions have a long history in Western territorial states. At the most general level, their history can be divided into three periods. First, in the UK, which is probably the country with the longest tradition of formalised public auditing, we find a reference to the Auditor of the Exchequer as far back as 1314 (National Audit Office, 2015a). Similar centralised audit institutions came much later to Continental Europe: France saw the Chambre des Comptes in the fifteenth century (Cour des comptes, 2015); Prussia saw the predecessor to the Bundesrechnungshof during the eighteenth century (Bundesrechnungshof, 2015); and in the Nordic countries such institutions emerged only during the nineteenth century. These centralised national audit institutions essentially functioned as the sovereign's instrument to control the administration, i.e. to make sure that administrative servants were not siphoning money off for their own purpose.

Secondly, with the democratisation of sovereignty and the gradual emergence of liberal democracy, SAIs were increasingly attuned to control of the exercise of sovereign power or, more precisely, the actions of elected governments. This change resonates with classical liberal thinking at the time, emphasising concerns over the dangers of excessive state intervention and the need to control it – either by constitutional or by parliamentary means. From 1834, the British Commissioners for Auditing the Public Accounts worked in tandem with the Comptroller of the Exchequer, who was to control funds to the government. While Parliament had for several centuries been responsible for raising revenue and authorising expenditure, its ability to control and scrutinise public spending remained weak until the 1860s (National Audit Office, 2015a). The 1866 Exchequer and Audit Departments Act required all departments to produce annual accounts known as appropriation accounts. The Act established the position of Comptroller and Auditor General (C&AG) and an Exchequer and Audit Department (E&AD) to provide supporting staff from within the civil service. The C&AG was to authorise the issue of public money to government from the Bank of England, ensuring that this money was within the limits Parliament had voted, and to audit the accounts of all government departments and report to Parliament accordingly. However, it is only with 1921 legislation that the C&AG was required to report to Parliament that money had been spent in accordance with Parliament's wishes. In the US, the 1789 Constitution had spelled out that no public money could be spent by the federal government unless allowed by law. Yet, it was up to the Treasury Department (the Government Controller) to ensure this. As in Britain, it is only with the Budgeting and Accounting Act of 1921 that the GAO is established as a body independent of government with the key task of controlling the use of public funds and reports its findings to Congress. Accordingly, the main activity of the GAO before the Second World War was to check bills and vouchers (Trask, 1991, p. 13).

Thirdly, we see a slow move towards performance auditing after the Second World War , but it took place in most countries only from around the 1980s. The move towards performance seems first to start in the US where the 1945 Government Corporation Control Act authorised GAO audits of wholly owned government corporations and mixed-ownership corporations. This law would carve out a new field of intervention. Under the heading of the 'comprehensive audit programme', the GAO would not only focus on legal control of budgets but also examine the effectiveness of financial and control systems and the suitability of managerial decisions, and ensure that public assets were used efficiently (Trask, 1991, pp. 29–30). The assessment of the many programmes issued under the Economic Opportunity Act of 1964, amounting to what became known as the war on poverty, would constitute one of the first comprehensive GAO evaluation assignments (Trask, 1991, pp. 61–2). After carefully going through hundreds of programmes, the GAO soberly concluded that the many programmes suffered from lack of co-ordination and that the many human resources and training programmes had done little to increase employment and earnings among their participants. Over the next decade, the GAO would significantly step up its activities in programme evaluation based on the development of new methods and standards and engage in evaluation of federal and state programmes ranging from drug abuse treatment, over defence contracts to agricultural subsidies and urban planning (Morse, 1981). Such performance audits included concrete proposals for legislative changes to curb what GAO saw as inefficient spending of public money (ibid., p. 215).

The GAO's move towards performance auditing and the development of new methods and standards for conducting these had quite far-reaching resonance both inside and outside the US. In 1972, the GAO published the *Standardsfor audit of governmental organizations, programs, activities, and functions*, popularly known as the Yellow Book (GAO, 1972). The standards not only pertained to the traditional budget control but also included standards for examining efficiency and economy in resource use and evaluating achievement of programme objectives. While initially only voluntary, the Yellow Book standards quickly gained wide acceptance both nationally and internationally. Within the US, the Single Audit Act of 1984 required auditors to follow the standards when auditing state and local governments receiving federal financial assistance. Outside the US, INTOSAI, the International Organisation of Supreme Audit Institutions, would in 1989 adopt a set of (voluntary) international guidelines that closely mirrored those of the Yellow Book (Trask, 1991, pp. 66–7).[1]

The increased attention to performance auditing did not come without political challenges. Most notoriously, the US Supreme Court in 1986 found the Gramm–Rudman–Hollings law unconstitutional (Trask, 1991, pp. 118–19). This law would have forced the President to comply with GAO plans for reducing spending in federal deficit-running programmes targeted by Congress. While this verdict clearly stated the limits for GAO influence, this did not discourage the GAO from issuing several reports lamenting the rise of federal debt and even more plans on how to remedy this problem, though obviously to little avail as the US federal government today has one of the world's largest debts – even when gauged in proportion to GDP. The GAO also publicised widely debated reports on, for example, the financial management of defence contracts, the regulation of financial capital activities and the social security system. In brief, from the late 1960s, and with particular impetus from around 1980, the GAO engaged in audit activities that went well beyond the traditional scope of legal and technical control of public budgets.

In the UK, the National Audit Act 1983 reflected two important developments. Firstly, it accommodated the call for granting Parliament greater power to control government spending. The C&AG became an officer of the House of Commons and was given the power to report discretionally to Parliament on the economy, efficiency and effectiveness with which government bodies have used public funds. Moreover, the C&AG should be enabled to report discretionally to Parliament on the value for money achieved by government departments. Secondly, it codified that public auditing was not only to include the legal and technical control of government spending but should also address economic efficiency and effectiveness (National Audit Act 1983, section II). While performance auditing was not completely novel in the UK, the National Audit Act 1983 made this a formal task of the new National Audit Office (NAO).

The NAO would subsequently contribute to the 'audit explosion' by conducting and requesting auditees to conduct increasingly detailed value-for-money audits of their own services (Power, 1997; Power, 2003). Thus, the move towards performance auditing did not only include new forms of financial accounting, such as resource (accrual) based accounting and budgeting (cf. the Government Resources and Accounts Act 2000). More strict form of performance assessment and measurement were conducted by the Audit Commission, a Thatcher government invention from 1983, with the task of reviewing the performance of local government services and later also health and social services. In order to save money, it was closed down in spring 2015, and its activities were partly taken over by local authorities, local NHS and policing bodies and private consultancies (cf. the Local Audit and Accountability Act 2014). This Act also stepped up the influence of the NAO by putting the Comptroller and Auditor General – in practice, the NAO's Local Audit Code and Guidance team – in charge of preparing and maintaining the Code of Audit Practice that local auditors are required to follow.

In Canada, performance auditing focusing on the efficient use of public money was legally sanctioned in the late 1970s with the adoption of the federal Auditor General Act, 1977 (Radcliffe, 1998). As early as the 1950s, the Auditor General of Canada began to report instances of 'non-productive' payments. The 1977 Act empowered ihe Auditor General to report cases in which expenditures had been made without due regard to economy and efficiency, and in which appropriate effectiveness reporting was not in place. Influenced by the events at the federal level, all Canadian provincial jurisdictions adopted audit laws that formally established and recognised the practice of efficiency audits by state auditors.

INTOSAI seems to act as a relay for the new rationales and techniques making up performance auditing. Three years before adopting the US GAO Yellow Book standards, the twelfth annual INTOSAI conference was hosted by the Australian National Audit Office (ANAO) in Sydney in 1986. Not without political controversies, the ANAO had gradually started to engage in performance auditing from the late 1970s and seemed eager to push this relatively new activity as a legitimate extension of the public sector audit mandate (Wanna et al., 2001). The 1986 conference resulted in the report *General statement on performance audit, audit of public enterprises, and audit quality*, which was subsequently distributed to all INTOSAI members (INTOSAI, 2004, p. 63). EUROSAI, the European affiliation of INTOSAI, was established in 1990 with the express intent of disseminating good public audit practices to the Central and Eastern European countries divesting themselves of Communist state rule. This included performance auditing, about which an entire congress was held in Hungary in 2002 (INTOSAI, 2004), p. 87). Of course, INTOSAI (and its regional affiliations) can only inspire not force national SAIs to adopt performance auditing. Not surprisingly, even if performance auditing has been promoted as a desirable modality of auditing by INTOSAI at least since the late 1980s, there are great variations both in the extent and ways in which it has been taken up by SAIs.

As noted already, the SAIs of the Anglophone liberal democracies seem to have been first movers and gone the furthest in this area. However, most SAIs of the Western European countries have been conducting performance audits since around the late 1980s or early 1990s. The Nordic countries and the Netherlands, countries with a relatively solid tradition of new public management, seem to have gone the furthest in this direction (Pollitt, 2003). The SAIs of key countries such as France, Germany and Japan, which have been more resistant to NPM reforms, have also to some extent been influenced by performance auditing (Sevillia & Ruffner,

2004). Yet, judging from the audit reports published since 2005 on their respective homepages, it seems that the German Bundesrechnungshof, the French Cour des Comptes, and the Japanese Board of Audit all pay much more attention to the traditional roles of controlling the technical correctness and legality of budget expenditures than to assessing the efficiency of public spending.

In sum, notwithstanding significant variations in timing and form, performance auditing has been taken up by a number of SAIs over the last two or three decades. On top of traditional financial audit control emphasising legality and technical correctness, SAIs have started to audit the economy, efficiency and effectiveness of government institutions. In doing so, SAIs are making assessments that challenge their aura of impartiality for at least two interrelated reasons. First, performance audits question the allocation of public resources, which lies at the very heart of executive power. Such interference will in itself make any government wary and, if such interference can be warded off by accusing the SAI of acting politically, governments may feel more than tempted to do so. Secondly, the standards and criteria supporting performance audits are anything but clear cut. This is particularly clear in the case of efficiency as it requires that the product and its quality of public activities can be easily objectified and quantified. As is well described in the literature and as I indicate in the section below, this certainly cannot be taken for granted.

Auditing the public health sector

Expenses of public-health services make up a sizeable (and in many OECD countries increasing) fraction of public expenditures. For this reason, it is not surprising that SAIs have paid substantial attention to the efficiency of the money spent in the public-health sector. However, the public-health sector also constitutes one of the most complex public sectors, providing services that rely on sophisticated medical expertise. It is inhabited by diligent and self-conscious professionals who for more or less good reasons believe that nobody but themselves is able to assess the quality of their work and therefore look with suspicion on anyone from outside seeking to gauge the so-called value of the health services. It is therefore perhaps also one of the public sectors that prove to be the most resistant and difficult to subject to external performance auditing. Under such difficult circumstances, the question pursued in this section is: how do SAIs manage to penetrate medical professional autonomy and expertise and render health services amenable to performance auditing?

In Norway, Riksrevisjonen, the National Audit Office, recently undertook a major audit of the efficiency of the national health-promotion programme launched by the Norwegian government (Riksrevisjonen, 2015). The implementation of the public-health programme, which was launched 2011, involves all Norwegian counties and most importantly the municipalities (Lov om folkehelsearbeid, 24 June 2011). With effect from 2012, the new public-health law entrusts the municipalities with the responsibility to promote public health and launch preventative and rehabilitation measures cutting across relevant public sectors. The municipalities' and counties' work in this area must be supported by the state, i.e. the Ministry of Health and Care. The audit presented four main findings. Firstly, most municipalities had yet to establish a systematic public-health strategy. Most municipalities had not even conducted a survey of the health status of their inhabitants. Secondly, the existing public-health practices were not sufficiently based on experience and evidence as municipalities have relatively little experience in this area. Accordingly, the Ministry of Health and Care should ensure the dissemination of experience and evidence in the area. Thirdly, the public-health interventions were not adequately integrated with measures taking place in other public sectors. Again, Riksrevisjonen recommended that the Ministry of Health and Care should step up its efforts to work across relevant public sectors at state, county and municipal levels. Fourth and finally, the Ministry of Health and Care needs to step up its support and assessment of the progress of the municipalities' public-health work. This included the making of clear guidelines and the provision of examples of how to undertake good health-promotion strategies and practices.

In 2012/13, the Office of the Auditor General of Canada (OAG) undertook a comprehensive audit of how the Public Health Agency of Canada, Health Canada, and the Canadian Institutes of Health Research have implemented and co-ordinated diabetes prevention and control activities (Office of the Auditor General Canada, 2013). The audit examined three general initiatives and their interrelationship. The renewed Canadian Diabetes Strategy from 2005 was led by the Public Health Agency of Canada and involved several other partners, the Aboriginal Diabetes Initiative within Health Canada and the federally financed research on diabetes taking place under the Canadian Institutes of Health Research. The OAG found many positive elements of collaboration between the three initiatives. However, the management practices for delivering programmes and activities under the Canadian Diabetes Strategy were regarded as weak. Thus the Public Health Agency of Canada had failed to define a clear strategy, priorities, performance measures, deliverables, timelines and expected results to effectively deliver programmes and activities. The Agency also suffered from lack of internal co-ordination of diabetes-control activities. Consequently, the OAG found that the Agency is unable to tell whether its activities have had an impact on the well-being of people who live with diabetes or who are at risk of developing the disease. More generally, the Canadian Diabetes Strategy suffered from insufficient mechanisms ensuring co-ordination and exchange of knowledge between the many partners involved in strategy. For example, a forum established to get advice from diabetes experts did not function as intended and a committee established to co-ordinate activities within the federal health portfolio is no longer active. Moreover, while the Agency aims to deliver evidence-based diabetes policies and programmes, it has established no mechanism for collaborating regularly with the Canadian Institutes of Health Research on its research needs. As a result, federal diabetes activities are fragmented, and the impact of efforts and money spent has not been maximised. In particular, Health Canada and the Agency have made little progress on collaborating to improve the limited diabetes surveillance information on Aboriginal peoples with the result of hampering the Department's ability to gauge the prevalence of Aboriginal diabetes and to determine the impact of its diabetes programmes.

In the Netherlands, the Algemene Rekenkamer (AR) issued a quite critical audit of the quality indicators issued by the Ministry of Health, Welfare and Sports (Algemene Rekenkamer, 2013). The AR found that the indicators had not sufficiently improved the transparency of the quality of care since the late 1990s. As a result, the capacity of patients to make an informed choice of care provider was limited, and it is difficult for the Health Inspectorate to supervise care provision and for care insurers to manage their care procurement adequately. While most care sectors had agreed on a common vision, and all sectors had developed indicator sets around 2012, the AR found that the stability and quality of most indicator sets in measuring quality was limited, few indicators had been developed to measure the outcomes of care, and the practical value of care indicators, which had cost around €31 million to develop, was found disappointing. The AR made no comments as to whether the inadequate quality indicators had any effect on the actual quality of the medical services or if the patients' health had somehow suffered because of this.

The Norwegian, Canadian and Dutch audit analyses contain many of the features found in other SAI performance audits of the public-health sectors in liberal democracies (e.g. ANAO, 2014; Office of the Auditor General Canada, 2011; National Audit Office, 2014b). On the one hand, the audits eschew making substantial assessments of the medical quality or the clinical outcome of public-health programmes. Thus, we are not told whether these programmes really do contribute to improving national public health. In other words, the goal-effectiveness of these programmes if audited at all focuses only on narrow and short-term output measures not on wider long-term outcomes. On the other hand, the audits focus on a series of procedural principles that are supposed to enhance the goal-effectiveness, namely the extent to which there is a solid knowledge base on the purported effects of health interventions made, whether the various interventions are effectively co-ordinated, if the clinical and other effects of such interventions are evaluated in terms of their intended goals and, finally, whether the results of these evaluations are effectively disseminated and applied.

This is not to say that SAI audits completely ignore substantive public health policy goals. For example, in a recent audit of the Medicaid programme, the OAG has explicitly pointed to insufficient access to these programmes by the stipulated target groups, i.e. low-income families and other people with limited financial means (e.g. Office of the Auditor General Canada, 2015). In fact, the GAO at times goes beyond specific programme audits in their assessment of whether general public health objectives are met, such as the availability of treatment for low-income citizens with an abuse or mental health problem (Office of the Auditor General Canada, 2015a). The British NAO has also published a few reports that critically assess the potential of government policies in general to meet (growing) public health-care demands (National Audit Office, 2014a). Notwithstanding this attention to the assessment of substantive policy goals, the SAIs seem careful to avoid assessing the clinical quality of medical services.[2] They also seem to eschew more general and notoriously difficult analyses of the causal links between specific health policies and the health standard of the target population. Such effect studies – with their randomised controlled trial protocols apparel – seem to be left to medical expertise.[3]

It seems then that performance audits more or less systematically pay relatively limited attention to substantial outcomes in favour of an almost manic preoccupation with auditee procedures attuned to promote a solid knowledge base, clear division of labour and co-ordination between relevant partners, evaluation measures and guidelines for disseminating results. On the one hand, this eschewal of assessing substantive policy outputs or outcomes is in line with the narrow jurisdiction given to the Australian NAO during its first inception of performance audit in the late 1970s (Guthrie & Parker, 1999). At the time, it was considered crucial to distinguish between the task of assessing 'administrative efficiency', which could be undertaken by the ANAO, and 'programme effectiveness', the assessment of which were regarded as the proper task of parliament only. On the other hand, the mandate of most contemporary SAIs is to audit all three Es, i.e. economy, efficiency and effectiveness. Seen on this background, it is not obvious why performance audits in the public-health area more or less systematically evade the question of effectiveness, i.e. the biomedical quality or value of the analysed programmes. One could speculate that SAIs are deliberately avoiding making substantial assessment of the medical efficacy and quality of public-health programmes because they know that they do not have adequate expertise in this area. There may be some truth to this explanation. However, another explanation may be that the performance audits are not so much about controlling governing – neither in legal nor in policy-output terms – as about the governing of government. That is, the overall rationale of performance audit is to ensure that government has employed a series of strategies and practices for governing itself in ways that are efficient and are likely to be in support of meeting given policy objectives.

The public-health area is probably an extreme case because of its highly complex subject matter, the workings and quality of which can be assessed only by medical experts. In other less complex areas we do indeed find many instances of the SAIs making assessments of the government's (lacking) realisation of policy goals. Yet, the public-health case may also show performance audit in its purest forms, i.e. in the form where it is more or less exclusively attuned to assess and improve government's governing of itself.

Governing itself: How SAIs work to appear impartial

The introduction of performance auditing since the 1980s has made SAIs work increasingly closely with auditees in conveying the audit results and at times even in designing the audit (Pollitt, 2003, 162). The INTOSAI standards committee recommends that SAIs actively seek to promote good communication with auditees as 'good communication [from] auditors can improve access to information sources and to data and opinions from the audited entity ... it also increases the likelihood that audit recommendations will be implemented' (INTOSAI Professional Standards Committee, 2014).

In the UK, for example, the NAO engages in briefings, governance and ICT reviews, and workshops with the audited government department in order to disseminate its results effectively and make departments take up their recommendations on how to improve efficiency (Lonsdale, 2015). In Norway, Riksrevisjonen regularly invites auditees' opinions about the performance-audit report pertaining to their particular audit (European Court of Auditors, 2010). In the Netherlands, the Algemene Rekenkamer has increasingly opted for a closer interaction with auditees, which involves discussing preliminary results during the performance-audit process and follow-up sessions examining whether SAI recommendations are adopted by the auditee (van der Knaap, 2015). Moreover, under the heading of 'reality checks', the Algemene Rekenkamer started in the late 2000s to conduct interviews with and observation of so-called stakeholders in order to unravel what these groups thought of official policy objectives and criteria and how they actually used the services emanating from these policies. The findings were then reported to both the government and parliament for reactions and with the express intention that politicians were willing to change their choice of policy instruments if they proved ineffective (van der Knaap, 2015, 130). If politics is not only about ideas and visions but also about how – by what methods and instruments – sovereign power is exercised, then it is fairly clear that performance auditing practised as described above is actively engaged in trying to shape politics.

The turn towards performance auditing in general, whereby SAIs have to prove their worth by documenting the amount of taxpayers' money they have saved by identifying slack, and the turn towards closer auditee dialogue, have raised concerns over the ability of SAIs to remain independent from government and from the parliamentary opposition. In the UK, where this concern seems to have been articulated with particular force, Pollitt and Summa (1997) have warned that the NAO may be going too far towards justifying itself in terms of how many of its audit recommendations have been accepted or the amount of savings it has identified. They point out that other SAIs (e.g. in France) do not attempt to prove their worth in such terms but instead stress their constitutional necessity and legitimacy. In the same context, Michael Power (1997, p. 51) has argued that, in reviewing effectiveness, state auditors engaged in performance auditing run the risk of challenging political policies, since it is difficult to distinguish between the effectiveness of achieving a particular policy goal and the question as to whether the policy is worthwhile. A number of other studies of the NAO interactions with the British government in the conduct of performance audits point to the balancing act between providing critical assessments (useful to the opposition and to the wider public) and constructive ones (useful to government) (Humphrey & Owen, 2003; Sharma, 2007). It seems fair to assume that this dual role as public watchdog and constructive consultant will put pressure on SAI independence from the executive. Similarly, it has been pointed out that, following the advent of NPM and increasing reliance on private-sector solutions (by tendering and/or outsourcing of public services), governments, at least in Australia and Britain, have tried in several ways either to withhold information from SAIs or even tried to undermine auditors' independence (from government) (Funnell, 1998).

In the case of Canada, there is apparently a shift in the way in which the state auditor views itself from one preoccupied mainly with legal and budget control to one of contributing to societally relevant problem-solving (Gendron et al., 2001). More precisely, the Auditor General there seems so determined to propagate performance management systems that will presumably improve policy delivery that it may jeopardise their claim to independence. A similar development can be seen in Denmark, where Rigsrevisionen is actively assisting the Ministry of Treasury in promoting accrual-based budget systems in state institutions (Rigsrevisionen, 2013, 9).

My point here is not whether these developments really undermine SAI independence vis-à-vis the executive, something that would require detailed individual case analyses. Rather my claim here is that these general developments amount to a challenge to the image of the SAI as impartial to policymaking. If this claim is correct then SAIs must develop existing ways or find new ways of maintaining their aura of independence. At any rate, the last decade or two has seen the rise of new ways in which SAIs seek to solidify their aura of expertise and, thereby, impartiality. The SAIs' logic seems to be that if only we can substantiate that our actions are driven by expertise and generalised (international) standards of auditing, then our activities are non-political and by the same token not partial to any contemporary political interests – whether those of the government or the parliamentary opposition.

Self-government by means of rules and guidelines

Curiously, whereas we find a number of studies of the dangers of performance auditing and its associated dialogue to (perceived) auditor independence, we find virtually no studies of how SAIs seek to maintain their aura of impartiality under these new circumstances. At the most general level, SAIs have three strategies for pursuing an aura of impartiality: rule-following, internal quality procedures and external reviews. The first is the traditional approach whereby the SAI adhere as closely as possible to existing national laws, regulations and traditional codes of conduct. This is the dominant strategy found in traditional financial audits. However, this strategy is only partially useful, as national laws, regulations and codes of conduct in the area of performance auditing are usually articulated at a very general level. This leaves wide room for interpretation and potential disputes over course of actions taken by the SAI in order to undertake its performance audit in general and to do so in close dialogue with the auditee in particular.

Secondly, most, if not all, SAIs use some form of internal quality-control system including internal consultancy and quality assessments, ensuring board involvement in projects and providing continued professional education for their staff. The US GAO, for example, relies heavily on the procedures stipulated in the so-called Yellow Book, which contains quite detailed guidelines for conducting performance audits, including how to circumscribe the scope of the audit, ensure adequate evidence and report findings (GAO, 2012b). Similarly, the performance audit work of the Dutch Algemene Rekenkamer and the Danish Rigsrevisionen are subjected to an elaborate set of internal guidelines (e.g. Algemene Rekenkamer, 2015, 31; Rigsrevisionen, 2015b). Two things stand out in these internal SAI performance-audit guidelines. First, substantively: they emphasise that the performance audit should always check how the internal control systems of the auditee contribute – or do not contribute – to ensuring efficiency and effectiveness. Thus, it is not only the substantive output and productivity of auditees' actions that are in focus but also the functioning of the auditee's internal control system. It is as if the latter is seen as a proxy of the former. Secondly, procedurally: the SAI performance guidelines are quite specific on how the SAI should communicate with the auditee both in the design and planning of the audit and with regard to the reporting of the findings and the issuing of recommendations to the auditee.

The guidelines adopted by SAIs to ensure the quality of their performance audit are based on a mix of national and, increasingly, international standards. Today, many SAIs are adhering to the International Standards of Supreme Audit Institutions issued by INTOSAI. These standards pertain both to the traditional legal and technical controls and to performance audits. In the area of financial accounting INTOSAI is developing its standards in dialogue with the International Federation of Accountants (IFAC), which is producing standards for the private accounting sector. In the area of performance-audit standards, the INTOSAI's work seems to rely heavily on (the leading) national audit offices. Thus, the international performance-auditing standards (ISSAI 300) issued by a standards committee under INTOSAI are essentially the work of four or five SAIs led by the Danish Rigsrevisionen (Henning & Rasmussen, 2013).

In the 2014 version of the ISSAI 300 standards, it is explained that the objective of performance auditing is 'to provide new information, analysis or insights and, where appropriate recommendations for improvement' in the area of efficient and effective governance (INTOSAI Professional Standards Committee, 2014). The ISSAI 300 envisages that performance audits will undertake one or more of the following three approaches:

1. A system-oriented approach, which examines the proper functioning of management systems, e.g. financial-management systems;
2. A result-oriented approach, which assesses whether outcome or output objectives have been achieved as intended or whether programmes and services are operating as intended;

3. A problem-oriented approach, which examines, verifies and analyses the causes of particular problems or deviations from criteria.

Two of these forms of performance auditing are far removed from the legal and technical world of financial audits in that they require the SAIs to engage in and decide on either strongly normative questions or complicated causal issues, or both. The result-oriented approach may be the simplest one in the sense that it 'only' entails that the SAI should gauge the eventual gap between intended and actual outputs of a programme. Of course, there are many technical discussions about how to measure output and, even more so, outcome and how to control for other factors influencing these. Yet, they remain essentially a technical exercise.

In contrast, in the systems-oriented approach, the SAI has to decide on the norms for the 'proper' functioning of a management system, such as adequate transparency, accrual accounting standards, the linking of budgets to agency objectives etc. While there may be national rules or regulations on state budgeting that the SAI could lean on, these may be very general or even conflictual. In these cases, the SAI will have to take an essentially political stance on deciding on the proper norms.

Finally, the problem-oriented approach catapults the SAI into the role of social science researcher with the task of analysing the complex causes behind a policy problem or the making of a policy output. The problem arising here is that many SAIs are hardly equipped to unravel the causalities of the emergence of a given policy problem or output. Any such analysis is almost certain to give rise to conflicting interpretations by politicians and scientists alike. After all, disputing claims about truth and causality is what science is about. Two other issues are more important. Firstly, as in the systems-oriented approach, normative criteria for objectifying a problem in the area of value-for-money are rarely given in law or regulations. Thus, the SAI will have to make normative assessments of the value or quality of services of which they are likely to have limited expertise. Secondly, the causal analysis invested to identify problems is very likely to put the SAI in the strange position where it will attribute the cause and thereby the responsibility for low levels of performance in a given policy area not to a specific auditee but to a range of other actors and factors. From a scientific point of view this may be a sober result, but from the point of view of controlling auditees' conduct this is hardly very productive.

How and to what extent this problem-oriented approach is actually used by SAIs is not clear. Yet, the very fact that it is endorsed by INTOSAI's standards committee may testify to a more fundamental shift of power, or at least the regulatory ideals of power, by moving from traditional financial to performance audit. This technique is attuned not to assessing and controlling auditees' conduct but to making the auditee reflect on and act in new ways favouring economic efficiency and effectiveness. More generally, performance audits, or the ideals supporting them, seem to imply a move from a classic liberal concern with controlling auditees' behaviour though without the right to make the auditee actually change it, to a governmental form of power in which the auditee must start to reflect on how it can change and govern itself in ways that will make it more efficient and effective.

Self-government by means of external reviews (the auditing of the auditors)

The third strategy, which supplements but does not replace the other two, is for the SAI to subject itself to external review. Within this third strategy, two forms seem to be dominating: external review by experts in public management and evaluation and review by peer SAIs.[4]

External expert reviews seem not to be a very common way for SAIs to ensure their aura of expertise and impartiality. I have managed to find this only in the British and the Danish cases. In the UK, the NAO has been regularly reviewed since 1992 by external reviewers for its performance audits. Initially this was undertaken by Brunel University (led by professor of public management Christopher Pollitt), then London School of Economics, Oxford University Said Business School, then a combination of Oxford University, RAND Europe and Risk Solutions (a consultancy) (Lonsdale, 2015). Until around 2009, they reviewed all the NAO's performance audit reports against ten criteria, including methodology, presentation, recommendations etc. Since then the external reviews have been conducted on a sample and some thematic basis, examining one issue across many reports in detail. On the one hand, this external review process has been highly influential in shaping the NAO's value-for-money (VFM) work. On the other hand, this review process has inspired others such as the Irish NAO and the European Court of Auditors. In Denmark, Rigsrevisionen has used external reviews by leading (Danish) public administration scholars to assess the quality of most of its reports since 2000 (Rigsrevisionen, 2015a).

Starting in the mid-2000s, SAIs have increasingly used *peer reviews* as a way of gauging the quality of their work and by the same token lending credibility to their image of expertise and impartiality. Usually these reviews have a broad scope including both financial and performance-auditing dimensions. In 2004, Canada's Office of Auditor General was apparently the first national audit institution to undergo a peer review by a multinational team of SAIs led by the National Audit Office of the United Kingdom (National Audit Office, 2004). The following year the US GAO underwent a similar assessment by a seven-nation team of national auditors led by the Auditor General of Canada (Office of the Auditor General Canada, 2005).

The regularity with which SAIs subject themselves to peer reviews varies a lot. A few, like the US GAO, subject themselves to international peer review every three years or so (Office of the Auditor General of Norway, 2014). Most other SAIs seem do so on a more irregular basis (Editorial, 2011). The peer review teams are usually made up of three to five SAIs, mainly from countries with a longstanding tradition of liberal democracy but also including other more recently democratised countries. Five SAIs seem particularly popular in the teams conducting peer review of performance audit practices, namely the British NAO, the Dutch Algemene Rekenkamer and the SAIs of the three Nordic countries (Editorial, 2011, 5). This could suggest that these five SAIs are considered particularly advanced by other SAIs in terms of performance auditing. It could of course also reflect a certain European bias in the sense that SAIs of other continents, such as the US GAO, may be assumed to provide recommendations that are not sensitive to the institutions and traditions found in Europe or in the countries formerly colonised by Europe.

It is interesting to note the kind of recommendations issued from the international groups of SAIs to their peers. For example, in the first review of the Canadian Auditor General, the latter was recommended to develop its performance-audit methods to include performance benchmarking (to specify the relative performance of the audited institution), high-level comparisons (of two or more auditee organisations with similar designs which may help identify and disseminate experiences and best practice), case studies (for highlighting good practices and spreading learning among auditees) and focus groups (to help understand the nature of auditees' problems with performance and assist the NAO in formulating practical recommendations) (National Audit Office, 2004, p. 15). There is a double concern at stake here. Firstly, the international team of SAIs is obviously trying to make the Auditor General of Canada improve its way of assessing the efficiency of auditee practices. Secondly, the team is proposing methods that will improve the Auditor's capacity to make auditees adopt more efficient practices. In fact, the case-study and focus-group interviews seem to be more attuned to disseminate new performance practices among auditees than to assess the level of auditees' performance. Moreover, both these methods imply that auditor and auditee engage in close dialogue. Thus, while the peer reviews may serve to bolster the SAI's aura of expertise and impartiality, the international peer reviews paradoxically include recommendations that favour more interaction between auditor and auditee, rather than less.

Conclusion

National audit institutions have existed more or less as long as we have had territorial states in the West. However, their political and administrative role has changed substantially over time. At the most general level, SAIs were inaugurated to essentially consolidate sovereign power, i.e. to ensure the sovereign that his, which was also the state's, money was used the way he intended. With the democratisation of sovereignty during the nineteenth century, it seems that SAIs functions increasingly reflect liberal concern with the excesses of state power and abuse of public money. Accordingly, SAIs become a key element in the constitutional and/or parliamentary control of sovereign power, i.e. executive government. In the decades following the Second World War and with particular force from the 1980s, SAIs are increasingly supplementing their technical and legal control of executive government with performance auditing. Thus, SAIs seem to become part of the wider neoliberal concern of whether government governs itself efficiently. SAIs must address no longer only the liberal concern over the excesses and abuses of state power but also whether government governs itself efficiently. In brief, SAIs becomes an instrument in the wider neoliberal strategy whereby government turns upon itself, i.e. the governmentalisation of government.

My analysis of performance auditing of public health interventions showed that performance audits more or less systematically pay relatively limited attention to substantial outcomes in favour of an almost manic preoccupation with auditee procedures attuned to promote a solid knowledge base, clear division of labour and co-ordination between relevant partners, evaluation measures and guidelines for disseminating results. SAIs may shy away from making substantial assessment of the medical efficacy and quality of public-health programmes because they know that they do not have adequate expertise in this area. Another interpretation is that performance audits are not so much about controlling governing – neither in legal nor in policy output terms – but about the governing of government. Thus, the political rationale informing performance audit is less about controlling and limiting state power but more about ensuring that the latter governs itself, i.e. that it has employed a series of strategies and practices for governing itself in ways that are efficient and are likely to be in support of meeting given policy objectives.

The move into performance auditing has challenged the SAIs' aura of impartiality and expertise. SAIs have responded to that through three general strategies on SAI self-governance to maintain their aura of impartiality when moving into performance auditing: rule-following, internal quality procedures and external reviews. While the first two strategies are fairly logical, the external review strategy may seem paradoxical: If the image of impartiality is the problem, then why opt for a strategy making the SAI more dependent on the outside world? However, the kind of self-government envisaged does not entail insulation from external, political influences, but rather of professionalism. Thus, by subjecting themselves to the critical gaze of university academics and peer organisations, SAIs can bolster their image of expertise and professionalism. This is turn may lend credibility to the assumption that their performance audits are shaped not by narrow political concerns – whether those of the executive government or its parliamentary opposition – but by the more or less universal professional standards reigning within the world of performance audit.

Notes

1 INTOSAI was established in 1953. By 2016 it had 192 members.

2 One of the few exceptions where GAO does engage in assessment of clinical quality is GAO, 2015.

3 An exception to the tendency of avoiding outcome assessments is National Audit Office, 2015b.

4 There are other forms of external review used by the NAOs. The work of the Australian NAO has since the late 1990s been reviewed by the so-called Independent Auditor (Australian National Audit Office, 2015).

6

Accreditation: The ultimate technique for governing government?

Introduction

This chapter analyses the governing technique of accreditation, which may be the pinnacle of the wider movement of making the public sector accountable for its actions. By the term 'accreditation', I refer to the diverse but more or less coherently institutionalised assessment schemes that lead to a formal process of approval of the organisation being assessed. It is carried out by an external organisation that is usually more or less independent from both government and the accredited institution. Moreover, accreditation invariably entails some form of self-evaluation structured by standards set by the external accreditation organisations. As we shall see, the final decision of accreditation may be taken by the accreditation organisation or the government.

The chapter focuses on the use of accreditation in institutions with high levels of professional authority offering complex public services, namely public health (Shaw, 2006; De Walque et al., 2008) and academia (Hoecht, 2006; Skolnik, 2010). More precisely, it examines the ways in which governments and ministries use accreditation in order to try to ensure the credibility and quality of the services produced by hospitals and universities. This includes scrutinising the political arguments around the use of accreditation and the technical elements of the accreditation schemes. In particular, it focuses on the standards imposed on the institutions to produce a form of knowledge that render their activities susceptible to both external and internal assessment, and how these assessments feed into new procedures and routines in the accredited institutions.

As in the case of SAI performance auditing of public-health programmes in the previous chapter, these two sectors have been chosen because they constitute perhaps the most difficult areas to govern because of the high level of complexity and professional expertise necessary to produce these services. Accordingly, it puts the quest for governing public administration and its activities to the ultimate test and may therefore better expose the machinations of power over and through administration. If the medical and the academic sectors share some common features, notably their high level of professional expertise and complexity, they also display some differential political logics. Thus, I have chosen to look at both areas, rather than just one of them, in order to show that there is not one, uniform neoliberal rationality underpinning the introduction of accreditation. Rather, the introduction of accreditation is informed by a historically unique blend of neoliberal rationalities and contingent political events that may have little to do with neoliberalism.

The chapter argues that accreditation of public sector institutions seeks to render these credible. Like many other contemporary public-management systems, accreditation seeks to make institutions conduct and assess themselves in ways that are accessible to the outside world. However, accreditation seems to be an extreme case of the wider quest to spur the public sector to govern itself. Thus, I will try to show that, as a mode of governing, accreditation is above all characterised by its meta-character. On the one hand, to be accredited, the institution must reflect upon itself along certain given standards, document how these reflections take place, take decisions on how to improve its services and account for how these decisions are adhered to in daily procedures and routines. On the other hand, the institutions subjected to accreditation are usually by design given a very wide room on how to translate the given standards into concrete guidelines, procedures and routines. In fact, they are urged – if not forced – to develop their own procedures and guidelines that they find are conducive to improving the quality of their service.

Accreditation of universities

This section explores accreditation of higher education. I first account for the historical developments in the US, because it was here that accreditation emerged first. Secondly, I explore the political forces behind the rather sudden emergence of university accreditation in Europe around 2000. Finally, I zoom in on the British and Dutch cases to see how accreditation actually comes into play. As accreditation of higher learning was completely new for most West European member states except Britain, many countries looked to the latter for inspiration. As an extreme case then of higher-education accreditation within Europe, the British case seems worth examining. However, the advent of accreditation in Britain in many ways reflects the large numbers of institutions within higher education rather than the EU's attempt to install a common market (Schwartz & Westerheijden, 2004). Therefore, I also turn to the Dutch case, which is an early mover within Europe but also reflects wider trends in accreditation in higher education in the Continental EU member states. My focus is mainly on the accreditation of education or teaching. Research accreditation is explored only to the extent that it has been integrated into the general accreditation of higher-education study programmes or institutions.

The United States

The art and practice of assessing the quality of education and teaching can be dated at least back to the late nineteenth century. In the US, it seems that the introduction of electives played an important role in articulating the need for more or less systematic educational evaluation (Kimmell et al., 1998). In 1869, Harvard University introduced a programme of electives that would gradually replace the traditionally accepted and essentially fixed liberal-arts curriculum (Brubacher & Rudy, 1968, pp. 98–118; Resnick, 1987). The replacement of fixed courses and reorganisation of curricula by electives changed higher education in the United States. Academic study groups were organised to address the issue of ensuring and measuring academic performance in the new, less structured setting. In the first decade of the twentieth century, six regional associations covering the whole country were established to evaluate whether secondary schools and, later on, colleges met a set of nationally agreed standards (Selden, 1960; Kimmell et al., 1998). Between the First and Second World Wars, college enrolments remained rather small, and the most common examination forms were essays and oral examinations. Despite the introduction of electives, most students still received a fairly comprehensive liberal-arts education.

The GI Bill introduced after the Second World War not only increased student numbers; it also changed their composition and their educational paths. Many older students were admitted to colleges, and many students became more vocationally oriented. The proportion of students majoring in the liberal arts dropped by half, while business education doubled its share of undergraduate degrees (Kimmell et al., 1998). During the 1960s, accreditation became part and parcel of higher education. Regional accrediting agencies were supplemented by discipline-based accreditation boards. At the time, the accreditation process served the dual purpose of ensuring the quality of higher-education institutions and urging the faculty staff to engage in an on-going process of self-evaluation, research and curricular development (Miller, 1972).

Public dissatisfaction with the quality of higher education began to mount in the early 1980s. Grade point averages were climbing at the same time that average scores on various college admission tests were dropping (Kimmell et al., 1998). Employers increasingly complained about college graduates who were unable to read and write effectively. A series of commissions and study groups called for better accountability and changing the way by which programmes were evaluated. In general, they called for a reduced emphasis on the inputs to the educational process and an increased focus on output measures of student performance (Kimmell et al., 1998). By the early 1990s, all six regional association of colleges and schools were focusing more or less intensively on outcomes assessment (Outcomes Assessment Committee, 1993). Their publication *Criteria for accreditation* provided a series of imperatives to be met by all the over four hundred member colleges. The North Central Region, for example, required that all educational institutions under its purvey 'must have and describe a program for documenting student achievement at the undergraduate and graduate levels ... [and] ... it does expect rigorous assessment of institutional efforts and does require explicit documentation of student academic achievement' (North Central Association of Colleges and Schools, 1993, p. 35). Today, accreditation by one of the six regional associations is important not only to the esteem of an educational institution and its ability to attract students but also to the students and their mobility between universities, because most educational institutions will accept transfer of credits only from accredited institutions (GAO, 2005).

The EU and the Bologna Process

In Europe, very few universities had any systematic accreditation system in place until the turn of the millennium. True, the rapid rise of student population in higher education from the 1970s onwards made many European countries establish various more or less systematic evaluation schemes. However, the European approach to quality assessment of higher education in Europe (with the exception of that of the UK) has been relatively strongly and centrally directed and controlled by the central state. Moreover, there was until recently little emphasis on the role of student choice and the making of a (quasi-) market of higher-education services. Accordingly, systematic attention to quality in higher education and its evaluation and assurance came much later than in the United States and in several countries in Asia (Sebkova, 2002).

Things started to change during the 1990s, when many European countries decided to provide universities with more autonomy but also more responsibility for spending money more efficiently, which usually meant making sure more students graduated for the same amount of public money (Schwartz & Westerheijden, 2007b). It also meant that higher-education institutions were charged with the responsibility of ensuring and reporting the quality of their educational services.

Yet, it is only with the advent of the Bologna Process, launched in the late 1990s by the EU to create a common market for higher-education services, that Western European countries systematically embarked on accreditation of higher education. With the Bologna Declaration of 1999, all EU member states committed themselves to adopt a system of easily readable and comparable degrees, adopt a system based essentially on two levels (undergraduate and graduate), establish a system of credits (the ECTS) and promote student mobility and European co-operation in quality assurance (EU, 1999). While the Bologna Process did not entail the making of a joint European accreditation system, it did force member states to establish an assessment system of their higher-learning institutions attuned to a market-like situation in which universities had to compete for students. As a result of the Bologna Process all member states have established an accreditation system (Schwartz & Westerheijden, 2007b). By the same token, quality assessment has been removed from the central government, typically the ministry of higher education, to a semi-independent body with the sole task of accrediting higher education.

Apart from the rapid development of accreditation systems from around 2000, a number of other common features stand out. With regard to the programmatic characteristics of accreditation there is first of all a tendency to locate responsibility for accreditation within a more or less independent organisation that either takes or prepares the decision for whether accreditation should be given or not (Schwartz & Westerheijden, 2007, p. 21). In contrast, previous and currently competing forms of university evaluation have principally been the responsibility of the ministry (of higher education), the universities themselves or both. We also see a tendency of the assessment criteria to include not so much academic-quality accounts, such as external censor reports, student grades, content of syllabus etc., but more on student/teacher ratios, explicitly defined learning goals, employment prospects for graduates and student evaluation systems, i.e. students evaluating their courses and teachers. Finally, while accreditation has until recently mainly focused on individual study programmes, there seems to be a move towards institutional accreditation, the latter requiring the institution to document that it has internal quality-assurance procedures both for all its study programmes and for the entire institution as such with clear demarcation of responsibilities for enforcing these procedures (Schwartz & Westerheijden, 2007, p. 19). In terms of the reception of accreditation, such schemes are often criticised both by academics who feel the programmes encroach on their autonomy and by employers who find that they ignore relevant student skills, such as entrepreneurship, basic analytical skills and at times even the ability to write correctly. Moreover, academics complain that the time consumed ensuring that everyday practices comply with accreditation standards is taken from teaching and research.

Notwithstanding these common traits, the accreditation systems vary tremendously between the EU member states. This variation obviously reflects the diversity of national higher-education system structures and the political struggles over who should control the quality of education. Accordingly, to get a better grasp of the political rationalities and governing practices at stake I will look closer into two countries, namely Britain and the Netherlands.

United Kingdom

In the UK, accreditation of higher education reflects the fact that universities and colleges are self-governing private organisations. While most depend to a large extent on public funding, almost all have the right to award degrees. Universities are considered autonomous bodies according to their charter or legislation (Watson, 1997). They decide which students to admit, design their own curricula, set their own examinations and confer awards on students who meet their assessment requirements (Jackson & Bohrer, 2010). In brief, there is no national system for higher education managed and controlled by a central statutory authority. Accordingly, colleges and universities have the ultimate responsibility for the quality and standards of their academic programmes and research.

Today, Britain has around 170 institutions of higher education competing for approximately 2.3 million students who pay up to £9,000 in annual tuition fees. Accordingly, the self-governing nature of British higher learning has called for more or less standardised forms of quality assessment. As in most other Western European countries, the demand for higher education grew rapidly during the 1960s and 1970s. This growth was largely facilitated through the creation of new institutions, polytechnics and colleges of higher education. With the Further and Higher Education Act 1992, the Conservative government of the day decided to rationalise funding arrangements and increase UK higher-education participation rates to levels comparable with other industrial competitors. The number of higher-education students in polytechnics started to outstrip those in existing universities (Brown, 2004). The 1992 law also turned polytechnics into universities proper, i.e. legally autonomous organisations with their own degree-awarding powers. The significant growth of student numbers, coupled with a pressure on resources, gave rise to concerns about the standards and quality of the higher education being provided in the UK (Watson & Bowden, 2007, p. 7).

During 1990–91, the Academic Audit Unit was established to undertake the voluntary process of academic audit of quality arrangements within institutions. In 1992, the Academic Audit Unit was incorporated into the new Higher Education Quality Council and was restructured in 1997 to become the Quality Assurance Agency for Higher Education (QAA). The QAA subject-review method was, like audit, based on peer review. Academic subjects offered by UK institutions were grouped into 'units of assessment'. Subject teams were required to conduct self-evaluations, and, on the basis of the evidence provided, a selected number of institutions were visited. Assessors or reviewers were recruited from existing or recently retired academic staff to form review teams, and these teams received information in advance of a week-long visit to the relevant department or school in each of the institutions. Review teams made judgements based on the access to often quite large amounts of data collected by the departments and schools, including primary evidence of student assessments.

In 1995, a programme of universal subject review was implemented. The outcomes involved a numerical scoring system on a scale from 1 to 4 for each of the six topics considered by the review teams. Thus, for each subject, the team reviewed: Curriculum design, content and organisation; Teaching, learning and assessment; Student progression and achievement; Student support and guidance; Learning resources; and Quality management and enhancement. The final score, out of a total of 24, rapidly came to be seen as a quantitative measure of subject quality and fed directly into university league tables, even if the subject review was far more wide-ranging and valuable than the quantitative assessment.

The massive expansion in student uptake during the early 1990s, combined with increasing financial constraints, formed the background for the establishment of a national committee to make recommendations on the purpose, structure, size and funding of higher education (National Committee of Inquiry into Higher Education, 1997). The report contributed importantly to shaping the development of higher education, in particular by influencing the direction of the quality debates emerging in the sector over the past ten years (Jackson & Bohrer, 2010). The report proposed that universities be allowed to retain their autonomy and create financial security in turn for providing accountability for the public funds they received. Accordingly, it was decided to charge tuition fees to full-time undergraduate domestic students (Watson & Bowden, 2007). This in turn led to much more intense external scrutiny of the management of universities.

Notwithstanding these pressures for more intense external scrutiny, the quality review of subjects in English higher-education institutions was brought to an end in 2001. The decision followed complaints from influential institutions concerned about the cost of the review process and the relatively limited value of the outcomes. In an agreement made between the Department for Education and Skills, the Higher Education Funding Council for England, QAA and the representative bodies, the subject-based review was to be replaced by an institution-based review. Institutions were now expected to conduct their own reviews of subjects and QAA was required to conduct institutional-level reviews to check that appropriate systems and procedures were in place and working effectively. Institutions were also expected to produce information about the quality of programmes. The QAA is funded jointly by institutions and by the funding councils who contract with QAA to provide evidence to enable them to deliver their statutory obligations (Jackson & Bohrer, 2010, p. 82). As a consequence, QAA is accountable both to the higher-education sector and, indirectly, to the government, but it is not under the direct control of either. However, the QAA's objectives and methods are clearly influenced by its key stakeholders, and it relies on consensus to secure the willing co-operation of institutions.

The Netherlands

In the Netherlands, all higher education institutions are subject to an accreditation system dating back to the early 1990s (Van Berkel & Wijnen, 2010). The accreditation process is designed by Nederlands-Vlaamse Accreditatie Organisatie (NVAO) and contains seven elements: (1) Selecting the agency undertaking the external review; (2) Writing a self-evaluating report; (3) Forming a visiting committee; (4) Conducting the on-site visit; (5) Grading; (6) Writing a report to procure an accreditation; (7) NVAO making its decision on whether the institution should be approved.

As in the British case, the introduction of accreditation has its background in the existence of more or less self-governing universities operating in a quasi-market, where students are expected to choose between educational services. However, in contrast to the UK, this development is quite recent in the Netherlands. The relationship between the Dutch government and higher-education institutions was restructured in the late 1980s (Van Berkel & Wijnen, 2010). The advent of quality assessment of higher-level education came on the political agenda together with public management ideas of self-regulation, quality improvement and accountability (Enders & Westerheijden, 2014). Spurred by this development, the public universities effectively lobbied for taking up the responsibility to organise external quality assessments by pointing to the precedent of the then-recently started research-evaluation exercises, which were co-ordinated by another but much older intermediary body of the higher education sector, the Royal Netherlands Academy of Arts and Sciences, founded in 1808. In exchange for a greater degree of financial and managerial autonomy, the Higher Education and Research Act 1992 required colleges and universities to account for the quality of their educational services.

The higher education institutions agreed upon a system of quality assurance in which external experts were appointed as members of visiting committees to evaluate the quality of the programmes and to issue recommendations for improvement. The aim of the External Quality Assessment (EQA) was to acquire insight into the quality of education and to contribute to the assurance and improvement of the quality of individual programmes. In this manner, higher educational institutions could demonstrate their accountability concerning the quality of the education they were providing. In addition, EQA contributed to the augmentation of the social recognition of the programmes, to the qualifications obtained and to the public-information facilities. During the first 15 years, the Dutch quality-assurance system was mainly based on internal assessments conducted by the educational institutions themselves. Although there was an external review committee and a meta-evaluation by the inspectorate, there were no formal sanctions linked to the review. Nevertheless, the system had a certain effect in that the self-evaluation reports were made public and there was a growing awareness about the quality of educational programmes.

Following the Bologna Declaration, Dutch policymakers started arguing in the early 2000s that accreditation was needed for the European and international recognition of Dutch university degrees (Enders & Westerheijden, 2014). Hitherto, quality assessments had revolved around programme goals and targets and the attainment of satisfaction by the peer community. In contrast, accreditation centralised and formalised quality judgements by introducing an accreditation framework to which all evaluations had to conform. In 2003, accreditation became obligatory to gain recognition of degrees, to give students rights to governmental grants and loans, and – for public higher-education institutions – to get the programme funded by the government. The change from external quality assessment to accreditation had as a practical consequence in the study programmes that the demands on documenting quality of education provision became much more serious. In the period from 2003 to 2010, the first round of programme accreditation was completed: all study programmes for bachelor or master degrees had to undergo this process once.

The formal accreditation decision is taken by an independent agency, and the Dutch Accreditation Organisation (since 2003 known by its abbreviation NVAO) was established. The NVAO is operationally independent but was created by the higher education law and is mostly funded by the government, with the remainder of its income coming from accreditation fees. In addition, the universities' umbrella bodies had to turn their quality-management departments into independent agencies. These agencies could still organise external evaluation teams, but, instead of publishing the evaluation reports as they had done before, they had to be submitted to the NVAO. Moreover, the market for organising external quality assessment was opened to other agencies as well, though they had to be approved by the NVAO.

More precisely, the accreditation process orchestrated by NVAO contains three consecutive steps. A self-evaluation is followed by external assessment and lastly the decision of formal accreditation (Hillen, 2010). In order to be accredited the university must assess its programmes in terms of six themes and 21 standards. The six themes are: Aims and objectives of the programme; Contents of the curriculum; Faculty and staff; Facilities; Internal quality assurance; and Results and study outcomes. These six themes are found in most higher education accreditation schemes in EU member states (Schwartz & Westerheijden, 2007a).

Even if the accounting for the six themes is structured by the 21 standards, there is substantial room for manoeuvre. In the following I therefore use the example of medicine based on Hillen (2010). Here theme 1, *aims and objectives*, implies examining the extent which the programme meets the quality requirements set by the national and international professional community in the field of medical education. For Dutch medical programmes this implies compliance with the European Directives and with the Dutch Blueprint for undergraduate medical education. Theme 2 requires consistency between *curriculum* contents on the one hand and the aims and objectives of the programme on the other. An important issue is whether the curriculum enables students to achieve the intended competencies within the set timeframe. Another aspect of content is the use of a variety of modern learning methods. Also the curriculum should offer flexibility to enable students to make choices in the programme according to their own interests. With regard to theme 3, *faculty and staff*, the university must account for the number of teachers required to effectively run and deliver the programme. A benchmark for the student/teacher ratio is 16:1. In order to ensure good education, teaching should primarily be a task for active medical researchers and clinicians. There must also be a staff-development programme and regular assessment of the quality of teachers and the teaching programme. Theme 4, *facilities*, implies accounting for whether students have adequate access to an electronic learning environment, a library and a study landscape with digital study facilities, laboratories and a skills lab. Theme 5 examines the institution's system of *internal quality assurance*. There must be some kind of formalised evaluation process embedded in the institution's routines and a programme committee consisting of staff and students that is in charge of evaluating, maintaining and improving the quality of the programme. Moreover, institutions for higher education are bound by law to install an examination committee consisting of students and staff members, which is responsible for the quality and validity of the examinations. Finally, the *results and study outcomes* theme requires statistical demonstration of effective student progress through the programme. Final success rates of 80 per cent for bachelor and master programmes are considered the standard target in medical education.

The example from the field of medical studies displays a number of typical features of higher education accreditation. The six themes are common elements in most study-programme-oriented accreditations, though the specific articulations of these obviously vary. For example, on themes 3 and 4, most human and social sciences would have much more lax criteria for being seen to comply with curriculum and facilities standards. On the results and study outcomes theme, some accreditation organisations in other member states (e.g. Denmark) require the university to provide employment statistics for study-programme graduates. While these variations are obviously crucial for the individual study programmes, as they can decide whether they survive or not, they all point to a generalised technology for governing higher education. This technology entails that the accredited institution must turn back upon itself; it must reflect and take actions that it finds will improve its services within the framework of normative standards determined by the accreditation scheme. Finally, I have tried to show that accreditation in higher education was driven – both in the US and in Europe – mainly by concerns over the creation and functioning of a quasi-market for higher education services.

Accreditation of hospitals

If the creation and functioning of a quasi-market constituted the key political rationality informing accreditation in higher education, we will find a more diversified picture in the case of hospitals. The accreditation of hospitals has spread remarkably fast to most liberal democracies during the 1990s. Prior to 1990, only hospitals in the US, Canada (1953), Australia (late 1970s) and Spain (1981) were subjected to accreditation (Scrivens, 1995, pp. 21–4). This rapid spread is interesting for several reasons. Firstly, there is no evidence that hospital accreditation leads to better clinical outcomes (De Walque et al., 2008, pp. 15–21). Secondly, hospital accreditation is costly. Direct annual costs for the accreditation organisation alone range from €3.5 million in Ireland to €60 million in Britain (De Walque et al., 2008, 32). This does not include the costs imposed by the accreditation system on the hospitals, which no doubt are much larger. Thirdly, there is a general hostility from the medical community to accreditation, though when asked in more concrete terms about everyday work procedures many medical staff actually acknowledge that it has positive potential.

All hospital accreditation schemes are essentially based on a set of procedural standards and organisational structures that are supposedly conducive for securing the quality of hospital services (De Walque et al., 2008, 34). Notwithstanding this general similarity, the genealogy of accreditation is quite complex and varies importantly from one country to another. Important variations in accreditation schemes include the temporal experience with accreditation (long: only US, versus short: most other countries), mandatory versus voluntary status (in the EU around half are mandatory by law whereas the other half are voluntary (ibid., 2008, 27)), the degree of representation of the medical profession in the accreditation organisation (ibid., p. 28) etc.

I argue that hospital accreditation is not primarily about external, managerial control, though that is part of the story too. On the one hand, accreditation seeks to render the quality of medical services in ways that are amenable to public choice of health services and political interventions. On the other hand, accreditation works above all by the self-government of the medical staff, i.e. accreditation standards seek to make medical staff adhere to clinical guidelines developed by the medical profession itself. Thus, accreditation hinges on the governing of self-government, i.e. on making the self conduct or govern itself in particular ways. In the following, I first provide an overview of the history, spread and national diversity of hospital accreditation in the US and Western Europe. I then look in more depth into one case, the Danish Quality Model.

The invention and spread of hospital accreditation

Hospital accreditation first emerged in the US in 1917 when the Hospital Standardization Program was established by the American College of Surgeons in order to improve the quality of healthcare at the hospitals (Roberts et al., 1987). The background for this programme was the concern shown by surgeons, other medical groups and hospital managers over the appalling conditions in the US and Canadian hospitals in the early twentieth century. Firstly, there was no systematic assessment of a physician's competence to practise in a hospital. Secondly, patients were not examined upon admission and patients' histories and diagnoses were seldom recorded. Only a few hospitals had any procedures for conducting preoperative and postoperative evaluation of surgical patients. Furthermore, few efforts were made to determine the results of patient treatment and no one was held responsible for the quality of care provided to patients.

With the support of hospital surgeons, physicians and managers from all over the US and most of the Canadian provinces, the recently formed American College of Surgeons issued the Hospital Standardization Program in 1917. The standards evolved around ensuring the competence of medical staff, the availability of adequate laboratory facilities, the making and recording of precise patient diagnosis and a monthly audit of the medical work undertaken at the hospital (Roberts et al., 1987). Thus, the standards were above all informed by a concern over the medical quality of the hospital services and the absence of standards guaranteeing that the staff were actually trained physicians or surgeons (Scrivens, 1995, pp. 16–17). The standards then also implied a certain protection of the medical profession from outside competition. Over the next few decades, the standards would be refined and expanded. Also, the number of hospitals subjecting themselves and actually fulfilling the standards programme increased dramatically. This spread of the standards programme was driven by professional and managerial concerns over the esteem of their hospital, which in turn was influential for attracting paying patients, i.e. the programme was voluntary. As a consequence of the rapid spread of the standards programme its administration became too big a task for the College of Surgeons, and in 1953 it was taken over by the newly formed Joint Commission on the Accreditation of Healthcare Organizations (JCAHO).

It was only in 1965 that the voluntary standards programme was linked to federal legislation, when the US Congress passed the Social Security Amendments – containing provisions for the Medicare programme (Roberts et al., 1987). The Act stipulated that the standards programmes run by JCAHO were deemed as being in compliance with most of the Medicare Conditions of Participation for Hospitals and therefore met eligibility requirements for participation in the Medicare programme. A hospital certified for Medicare was also considered certified for Medicaid and thereby eligible for Medicaid participation. Consequently, hospitals that wished to receive patients under these two public health programmes had to participate in either a state accreditation or a JCAHO accreditation programme. In 1972, the type of medical audits conducted by the JCAHO became requirements of the Professional Standards Review Organization. Moreover, most states would subsequently require the hospitals working under their licensure systems to be approved by the JCAHO's accreditation programme. Finally, the major (health) insurance companies would allow their clients to be treated only at hospitals accredited by JCAHO (Scrivens, 1995, 101). In brief, in practice all hospitals have had a very strong economic incentive to subject themselves to accreditation.

Until the 1960s, the core of the accreditation programme revolved around a relatively limited set of minimum standards around the qualification of medical staff and patient processing and recording (Scrivens, 1995, p. 19).

With the JCHAHO's 1970 programme-standards manual, this would change towards a much more comprehensive set of standards encompassing a wide array of organisational procedures. Firstly, JCAHO's programme would increasingly focus on the use of systematic review procedures and the development of objective and valid criteria for measuring the actual quality of care being provided (Roberts et al., 1987). Secondly, this introduction of systematic review procedures entailed that the JCAHO would step up the regularity and scope of its external surveys of hospitals' compliance with the standards. This resulted in various medical practitioners complaining that the former procedurally oriented element received too much attention at the expanse of the latter substantive, clinically oriented element. Thus, in their eagerness to ensure JCAHO approval and thereby access to Medicare and Medicaid patients, hospital managements often seemed more concerned with ensuring compliance with formal audit procedures than with substantive clinical outcomes. Notwithstanding these criticisms, the JCAHO focused during the late 1970s on integrating all quality-assurance systems in the hospital primarily by boosting the number of organisational standards that hospitals needed to comply with.

Partially due to the critique of the JCAHO's accreditation programme focusing too narrowly on procedural standards at the expense of substantive, clinical outcomes, the JCAHO embarked in 1986 on a multi-year accreditation process designed to move away from its triennial inspection of whether the hospital complied with a very large set of procedural standards and to move towards an assessment of the processes and outcomes of care. The latter implied a more continuous process focusing on whether hospitals had adopted and adhered to substantive clinical guidelines and monitored clinical outcomes (Braun, Koss & Loeb, 1999). Moreover, the idea of determining a set of clinical indicators for each and every medical specialisation was abandoned in favour of letting the hospital itself settle the clinical measures suited best to its needs. In sum, the tendency over the last two decades has been to reduce the number of general process standards, increase the number of substantive clinical indicators and give hospitals more room to develop and select the latter ones.

Notwithstanding these changes, the hospital accreditation process has been taking place along the following general template at least since the 1980s. All member healthcare organisations are subject to a three-year accreditation cycle, while laboratories are surveyed every two years. The results of the hospital surveys are not publicised, but the JCAHO does provide the organisation's accreditation decision and any standards that were listed for improvement. Organisations deemed to be in compliance with all or most of the applicable standards receive a positive accreditation.

Even though the JCAHO has operated with unannounced surveys since 2006, about 99 per cent of inspected hospitals are accredited. Not surprisingly some critics have argued that serious problems in the delivery of care are sometimes overlooked or missed (Kowalczyk, 2007). The hospital must be familiar with the JCAHO's standards, examine current processes, policies and procedures relative to the standards and improve any areas that are not in compliance. The hospital should be in compliance with applicable standards during the entire period of accreditation, which means that surveyors will look for a full three years of implementation for several standards-related issues (Compliance 360, 2015).

Accreditation of hospitals first came to Europe in 1981 when it was introduced in the province of Catalonia in Spain (Roberts et al., 1987). During the 1990s accreditation started spreading to most European countries (Shaw et al., 2010; Fortes et al., 2011). By the end of the 2000s, at least 17 out of 27 EU member states had adopted some kind of hospital accreditation system (De Walque et al., 2008, 25). In contrast to the accredition of higher education, hospital accreditation has had little if anything to do with the EU common market for goods and services. While the European Court of Justice has issued several rulings seeking to strengthen the rigths of EU citizens to access public health services across member states, the latter have only reluctantly and selectively allowed for more patient mobility (Palm & Glinos, 2011). Today, member states have established mechanisms for reimbursement of patient treatment costs for patients admitted by agreement from the hospital of their home country. Even with the latest EU directive in this area, which came into force in the member states in 2013, it is still unclear if and how hospitals can be reimbursed in case of admitting patients from another member state without a specific referral from the hospital of that member state (EU, 2011).

The development of accreditation in Europe has thus less to do with marketisation, at least not at the EU level, and more to do with national concerns over the cost-effectiveness of health expenditures constantly growing and the ability to hold hospitals and the medical profession to account for the quality of their services. In all EU countries, public-health-service expenditures take up more than 10 per cent of GDP, and they are rising in most countries. For this reason alone, governments are eager to try to control the growth of health expenditures or, at the very least, ensure that they are spent as effectively as possible. A second related concern has to do with the frequent stories of medical malpractice. While these stories are often grossly exaggerated by the media, and their numbers mostly remain very limited compared to the number of patients being treated in hospitals (Baker, 2005), they often put strong pressure on responsible health authorites and hospital managers to take action, such as making hospitals adopt some kind of quality-assurance system (Scrivens, 1995; Kodate, 2010). Finally, there was a generalised hype about the potential of quality-management systems that wandered from the private into the public sector from the mid-1980s. The potential of these systems to ensure quality was also debated in the public health sectors in Europe (Lafell & Blumenthal, 1989). These interrelated political concerns driven by health authorities and hospital managers, rather than the medical profession's concern for clinical outcomes, seem to constitute some of the main forces behind drive towards hospital accreditation in Europe.

In most EU countries, hospital accreditation is funded by public money, either by the government or by international donor organisations. Accreditations usually involve a combination of self-assessments and scheduled external reviews (De Walque et al., 2008, p. 35). Unlike in the US, unannounced external surveys are very rare and used only in the UK and Luxembourg. It takes somewhere between seven and twelve months to prepare and conduct the self-assessment and the scheduled external review. The maximum number of days for a full on-site survey for a hospital is four days. The on-site external survey is conducted by multidisciplinary teams usually composed of managers, doctors and nurses. Documented evidence is required with regard to compliance with clinical practice indicators. Finally, the survey team and the hospital engage in dialogue both at the end of the visit concerning the main findings of the survey and in finalising the draft for accreditation submission.

The employment of hospital accreditation in Denmark

Since August 2009, all public Danish hospitals and clinics have been subjected to accreditation in shape of the Danish Quality Model (Den Danske Kvalitetsmodel, DDKM).[1] Most private hospitals and clinics are included too as this is a precondition for receiving patients financed by public money. The idea of introducing accreditation in Danish hospitals has been met with widespread critique from various parts of the medical community, including the nurses. As late as November 2011, around sixteen hundred doctors and other medical staff signed an open letter to the Director of Health in the Capital Region criticising excessive demands for documentation caused by poor ICT systems and in particular the two parallel accreditation systems operating in the Region, namely the DDKM and the US JCAHO model. The criticism was endorsed by nine hundred further medical staff outside the Capital Region, even if they 'only' had to deal with one accreditation system (DDKM).

At the most general level, the criticism of hospital accreditation launched by substantial, albeit far from all, parts of the medical profession revolves around two points. Firstly, it has been argued that there is no scientific evidence that accreditation leads to better clinical results, at least if evidence is understood as randomised controlled trials (EVIDENS, 2011). Secondly, accreditation was criticised for wasting quite substantial resources on documentation and standardisation, which could have been better spent on medical staff and equipment. On the one hand, no systematic analyses of the costs of running accreditation have been conducted, either in Denmark nor elsewhere (Greenfield & Braithwaite, 2008). On the other hand, certain non-validated estimates have circulated in the debate and served to fuel the critique against accreditation. Thus, during the height of the debate over accreditation in 1999, the head of research in the Danish Hospital Institute (DSI) claimed that the total running costs of operating accreditation at any particular hospital lie between one thousandth and one per cent of total hospital costs, probably closer to one per cent (So ein Ding müssen wir auch haben, 1999). This was rapidly taken up in the debate by some doctors to estimate that the costs of running accreditation in the hospitals of Copenhagen would amount to 80 million Kroner (in 1999 value). Notwithstanding this critique, the Minister of Health decided in 2001 that an accreditation system should be developed and that all Danish hospitals receiving public money must be subjected to it.

The decision to develop and apply a mandatory hospital accreditation model in Denmark was preceded by a number of historical developments involving a variety of different political rationalities, technological innovations and base political calculations that came to form a more or less coherent dispositive or assemblage of hospital quality management (Triantafillou, 2014). This *dispositive*, the making of which stretches back to 1980, consists of the following elements: methods of categorising disease treatments, computerisation of such treatments, concerns over cost-effectiveness, complaint registration, the availability of international hospital quality assessment systems, the mobilisation of organised medical interest groups, and a tradition of consultative policymaking procedures. The introduction of new methods of categorising disease treatment at hospitals and electronic computerisation of such treatments during the 1980s together enabled the articulation of concerns over cost-effectiveness. The combination of systematic registration of hospital patients' complaints and highly publicised incidents of medical malpractice around 1990 pushed health authorities to take action. After a number of minor and largely uncoordinated initiatives, the political interventions took inspiration from existing international hospital-quality assessment systems, notably the US JCAHO's system of accreditation and the British Health Quality Service model. They inspired two Danish counties to set up voluntary accreditation systems for all their hospitals around 2000. In order to ensure national coverage and at the same time appease the critical voices of the medical profession, the Ministry of Health embarked in 2001 on a protracted process of consultative policymaking involving most parts of the medical profession to develop a Danish accreditation system from scratch. The so-called Danish Quality Model was finalised in 2005, but implemented only in 2009. Surprisingly, the (now former) Minister of Health decided in April 2015 that the DDKM is no longer mandatory for hospitals, only for pharmacies and general practitioners. By the end of 2015, all Danish hospitals still used the DDKM, though discussions were taking place about whether it should be simplified.

The DDKM model focuses not really on how hospitals seek to abide by its standards but rather on whether hospitals adopt procedures that account for the ways in which they will deal with the standards and indicators (Triantafillou, 2016). While DDKM implies that all hospitals are subjected to a mandatory external assessment every three years, IKAS Institut for Kvalitet og Akkreditering i Sundhedsvæsenet – Institut for Quality and Accreditation in the Health Sector) emphasises that the purpose of this assessment 'is not that externals [assessors] assess the concrete quality of every form of treatment. DDKM must instead evaluate the hospital's preconditions to deliver good quality' (IKAS, 2012, p. 4). In spite of DDKM's overwhelming number of standards and indicators, they do allow the hospitals substantial discretion regarding the ways in which the standards are fulfilled. Even in vital areas such as patient security and risk management, hospitals must find their own way of implementing these (IKAS, 2012, pp. 2, 38). Even more importantly than allowing hospitals to implement standards differently, the DDKM urges – if not forces – them to do so in two ways. Firstly, many standards and their respective indicators are defined quite broadly, leaving a wide room for interpretation. For example, several of the organisational standards, such as the documentation of quality measures, allow for rather differential practices. Secondly, some standards explicitly demand that hospital staff develop and apply their own guidelines for everyday medical service work. All hospitals must develop local guidelines reflecting local hospital conditions and needs. This requirement is particularly clear in the patient process and sickness-specific standards, but it is also found to some extent within many of the organisational standards. It seems then that the local accountability practices propagated by DDKM are not primarily about ensuring compliance with particular standards or guidelines, though this does play a role, but more about making local hospital assess their use of such guidelines and develop these when needed.

In sum, most of the procedural standards in DDKM amount to a form of power that works by latching on to and facilitating a particular form of freedom of those over whom or, more precisely, through which that power is exercised (Triantafillou, 2016). Doctors and nurses are not told how to carry out their medical work but urged to act and take up the role of active and responsible civil servants constantly reflecting on how their work can be improved. Of course the freedom that doctors and nurses are encouraged to exercise is a rather specific one. On the one hand, it must be exercised within the space defined by the DDKM indicators and in line with the professional norms of medical conduct largely established by the medical profession itself. On the other hand, it is a freedom that must make itself visible to the outside world, notably to the public health authorities, through extensive and standardised documentation of the ways in which the guidelines developed and chosen by the hospital itself are adhered to.

Conclusion

In this chapter I have tried to show that accreditation may be regarded as a technology of government that seeks to render public sector institutions credible. It also renders public institutions amenable to government in partially new ways. Accreditation is in many ways similar to ex-post evaluation methods. Both seek to provide more or less systematic assessment of the value of a given public service and both seek to account for highly complex activities in ways that render these susceptible to governing, either by external policymakers or by the organisation itself. Yet two differences stand out. Firstly, accreditation involves the decision of whether or not the organisation meets accreditation standards and therefore whether it should be allowed to survive. Secondly, accreditation, at least in its current forms, systematically links self-assessment by way of national standards with state aspirations of securing the quality of health services. This latter dimension is a relatively recent development, emerging in the US from the 1960s and in Europe from the 1990s.

In a certain sense accreditation constitutes an extreme case of the wider quest to spur the public sector to govern itself. As a mode of governing, accreditation is above all characterised by its meta-character, a doubling of government by which government turns upon itself. On the one hand, to be accredited, the institutions must reflect upon itself along certain given standards, document how these reflections take place, what is decided to improve its services and how these decision are adhered to in daily procedures and routines. On the other hand, the institutions are usually by design given a very wide room on how to translate the given standards into concrete guidelines, procedures and routines. In fact, institutions are usually forced by the accreditation scheme to choose or even develop their own guidelines for good practice and then document that the institutions actually adhere to these. This is particularly clear in hospital accreditation, but it is also found in higher education programmes – under the themes of objectives and staff. In sum, accreditation is essentially an imperative imposed on the public sector to reflect upon, assess and govern itself in ways largely of its own choice, though the subject of accreditation is at the same time obliged to show how its choice of self-government resonates with the external political goals and socially desirable norms.

I have also tried to show that the introduction of accreditation in hospitals and universities cannot be reduced to a single, uniform neoliberal rationality. Rather the introduction of accreditation is informed by a historically unique blend of neoliberal rationalities and contingent political events some of which have little if anything to do with neoliberalism. In the case of higher education accreditation, the political rationality informing reforms is relatively uniform, though the technical and organisational underpinnings of accreditation are quite diversified. The overall rationale driving accreditation of colleges and universities is to ensure the functioning of a quasi-market of higher-education services in which students are supposed to make informed choice. In the US, this became relevant when electives were introduced and gradually replaced fixed courses and syllabuses at the end of the nineteenth century. The same political logic of market creation would drive the introduction of accreditation in European universities following the Bologna Process around 2000. The big difference of course was that in the US, with a large number of private universities, it was the universities driving this process. In (Continental) Europe it was the state driving the process. In order to be able to compete with other countries (and their universities) to attract students travelling around Europe to find the university best suited to their interests and needs, ministries of higher education found that they had to be able to show that the universities of their country had a high quality. While some European universities had already started their own accreditation schemes prior to the Bologna Process, notably in the areas of business and medicine, they were driven by the same political logic of competition.

In the case of hospital accreditation, the political rationalities are more diverse. It was above all concerns over the clinical quality of hospital services that drove North American doctors to push for accreditation in the early twentieth century. Thus, accreditation was driven by biomedical concerns over patients' health articulated mainly by the medical profession with support from hospital managers. By the same token, accreditation served to bolster the autonomy of physicians and surgeons by ensuring that non-educated staff were excluded from the clinical services at hospitals. However, this political rationale changed in the mid-1960s when it became mandatory for hospitals catering to Medicaid and Medicare patients to be accredited. From then on the process would be informed more by managerial and commercial concerns of hospital approval than by biomedical concerns about clinical quality. This change obviously reflects the fact that more than half US hospitals are private and that all hospitals had to comply with JCAHO accreditation standards to receive patients under the Medicare and Medicaid programmes (American Hospital Association, 2015). The introduction of accreditation in the mainly public hospital sectors of Europe from the 1990s was above all informed by concerns over cost-effectiveness or, more broadly, value-for-money produced by the public sector. With large and steadily growing public expenditures for public-health services, a generalised hype of quali-tyassurance systems from the mid-1980s and the availability of concrete hospital accreditation systems (in the US and Australia), most European health authorities found it desirable if not outright necessary to adopt or develop some form of hospital accreditation. Thus, in contrast to the US, neither clinical quality concerns nor strict commercial logics played any significant role in Europe, where we instead find a more straightforward constructivist neoliberal rationality, whereby the public administration must fold back upon itself in order to improve its way of governing.

Note

1 This section draws on my earlier studies of Danish hospital accreditation (Triantafillou, 2014, 2016).

7

Evidence-based policymaking: Towards epistemological infinitude?

Introduction

This chapter examines the evidence-based policy (EP) movement. It tries to map and understand how and why new experimental and statistical techniques for producing knowledge have spread from medicine to education, crime prevention, employment and other social areas.

EP is perhaps the clearest movement away from the neoliberal concern over epistemological finitude. While van Mises, Hayek and Popper were all concerned with excessive state intervention because of the cognitive limitations of the state and other actors, the EP movement seems to have a strong trust in the governing potentials of evidence. If only we can provide enough qualified knowledge about the effects of policy interventions and programmes, it is argued, we will be able to adopt the right policies to tackle given social problems. The advent and rapid diffusion of randomised controlled trials (RCT), various statistical regression techniques and systematic meta-reviews from medicine and public health into education, crime prevention, employment and social welfare policies seem to testify to a much more optimistic view of the abilities of scientific knowledge to inform 'good' policymaking.

The chapter first traces the critique of excessive planning and the propagation of minor experimental interventions through the works of Karl Popper (Popper, 1966) and Donald T. Campbell (Campbell, 1969) in the 1950s and 1960s. It shows that, while they both rejected centralised planning based on some grand omnipotent science of society, both insisted on the democratic and societal benefits of scientific knowledge. However, the latter was to be generated by minor experiments and to inform small-scale interventions intended to alleviate human misery, rather than promote happiness. RCTs were simply one among many techniques accepted to generate this kind of experimental knowledge.

The chapter then moves on to account for the spread of RCTs, statistical regression techniques and meta-reviews from medicine, health policies to education, crime prevention and employment policies. I will show how these ways of producing knowledge gradually became authoritative and crystallised into a so-called evidence hierarchy that systematically devalues other ways of producing knowledge. Examples are given of how this new regime of truth is used in the said policy areas to exclude and reject democratically supported policy measures.

The chapter finally discusses how the epistemological optimism of the contemporary evidence-based policy movement challenges our notion of neoliberal political rationality. It also discusses the political implications of this epistemological optimism, both its potential to break with received wisdom and conventions and its risk of favouring technocratic policymaking at the expense of democratic decision-making.

The emergence of the experimental society and its rapport with (critical) neoliberalism

EP is based on the apparently simple and innocuous assumption that politics should be founded on the best available knowledge (Triantafillou, 2015a). The notion that political governing will benefit from being based on truthful (scientific) knowledge is of course not very new. From Plato's philosopher kings (Plato, 1930, Book 5) and Machiavelli's advice to the prince to the Saint-Simonians and August Comte (Comte, 1877), there have always been some who believed that secular truths could work as the foundation for the making of political society. If we move from the world of lofty political ideals about the role of science and into the actual political use of knowledge, it has been shown that the making of modern territorial states has depended fundamentally on scientific knowledge in general and statistical knowledge in particular (Desrosières, 1998; Scott, 1998). More recently, the rapid increase of social-science research funded by the government and the military during the 1950s gave US social scientists a strong incentive not only to apply methods emulating the natural sciences but also to prove the relevance of these for policy interventions (Steinmetz, 2005, pp. 296–9). By resorting mainly to positivist methods of evaluating the effects of various political reforms, social scientists could simultaneously claim political relevance without being tied to specific political goals: they were supposedly simply delivering rational tools to promote the goals chosen by democratically elected governments (Mirowski, 2005, pp. 164–5).

At the end of the Second World War, Popper published his now famous *The open society and its enemies* (Popper, 1966). Here he argued against utopian planning and historicist metaphysics, on the one hand, and in favour of piecemeal social engineering based on limited interventions seeking to minimise societal evils, on the other (Popper, 1966, pp. 158–9). He concurred with Friedrich Hayek and Ludwig von Mises on the view that grand societal planning is bound to fail because no central planner can know the values and preferences of all the citizens in a given society. Accordingly, Popper argued against so-called utopian planning attuned to bring about societal happiness and harmony. Instead of grand state planning, Popper supported limited interventions targeting a particular institution, sector, or segment of the population with the goal of mitigating social evils rather than pursuing societal happiness. This limited and more humble character of government interventions would, Popper argued, make it easier to roll these back and try out new ones if they turned out to not bring about the desired results. More generally, limited or small-scale interventions would allow for 'piecemeal social experiments', such as insurance systems, taxation, or penal reforms, and generate useful policy learning without resorting to wholesale societal restructuring (Popper, 1966, p. 162).

The idea of a society open to the testing of received wisdom was taken a step further in the late 1960s by the American psychologist Donald T. Campbell and his insistence on experimentation as the basis for social policymaking (Campbell, 1969). Later, he would elevate this ethos into a societal vision: the experimenting society (Campbell, 1997). Campbell was a trained psychologist who earned a doctorate from the University of California, Berkeley, in 1947, was elected to the National Academy of Sciences in 1973 and served in 1975 as President of the American Psychological Association. Yet, Campbell's writings on the ethos and methods of experimentation, in which a society encouraged the ongoing formulation and testing of new ideas and policy measures, had a resonance not only in other social sciences than psychology but also in the ways in which US education and social policies began to be evaluated and tested from the 1970s onwards (Shadish & Epstein, 1987).

Like Popper, Campbell saw an ethos of experiment not only as important in developing science and as making for better policies but also as a way to challenge existing dogmas and authorities and, not least, to invigorate democracy. While Campbell was sceptical about Popper's principle of falsification, he did agree with the idea that society should conduct systematic policy experiments based on the principle of eliminative induction: the systematic testing of policy interventions, tried out in real life, and the elimination of those not bringing about the desired goals. More precisely, Campbell was propagating so-called quasi-experiments, which he found much more suited than RCTs to examine policy programmes and interventions in areas of in education and welfare (Campbell 1978; Cook & Campbell 1979)

The term 'quasi-experimentation', which was coined by Campbell and the statistician Julian C. Stanley in the early 1960s (Campbell & Stanley, 1963), broadly denotes the experimental interventions that in various ways deviate from the method of RCT and its requirement that an independent (treatment) variable is manipulated in order to determine its effect on a dependent (outcome) variable by way of a treatment and control group. Instead, quasi-experiments are designed for settings in which manifold contingencies are beyond the control of the experimenter. These contingencies are likely to give rise to many rival hypotheses that can threaten the validity of causal claims. Quasi-experimentation entails that plausible rival hypotheses are tested and, where possible, eliminated. It is thus a pragmatic, rather than a logical-analytical, induction that is key to Campbell's experimental method, which produces knowledge through processes of trial-and-error learning and selective retention. While Campbell regarded himself as a critical realist and rejected phenomenological reductionism of the real with the phenomenally given (Campbell, 1974), his ethos of experimental knowledge production is actually not that different from Dewey's pragmatist ideal of public interventions and experiments as a vehicle to promote policy learning and alleviate social problems (Dewey, 1957; see also Sanderson, 2009). By the same token, Campbell would increasingly accept the value of case studies and other qualitative methods in order to test the efficacy of public policies (Campbell, 1984).

In brief, from around the 1960s, experimentation in the area of public policymaking and service provision was articulated as an alternative to state planning. The latter was rejected because of its assumption that the state can gather the necessary intelligence of complex societies and the manifold needs of individual citizens. In contrast, experimentation was propagated as a way of endorsing public interventions not to promote general happiness and welfare but to alleviate misery on the basis of minor but systematic trial-and-error interventions. Scientific knowledge was accepted as a legitimate source of government intervention to the extent that it was constantly tested and susceptible to refutation if its assumptions were proved wrong. This relationship between state power and scientific knowledge was clearly in rapport with neoliberal rationalities of government and marked a break with both socialist and Keynesian-inspired welfare rationalities in which the state aspired to hold the truth about society and its need for interventions.

The spread of evidential techniques into welfare policies

Notwithstanding Campbell's emphasis on the need for a plurality of methods to be employed in the name of social experimentation, the next few decades would see the emergence of a so-called evidence hierarchy – a ranked list of knowledge-producing methods in which RCT would be regarded as superior. Thus, what started as a liberation movement or at least a serious alternative to state planning would soon establish its own hegemonic and exclusionary regime of truth. Starting in the fields of US psychology in the 1920s (Dehue, 2001) and in biomedical interventions during the late 1940s (Timmermans & Berg, 2003, pp. 89–90), RCT has more recently become the predominant ideal for (the Golden Standard) producing knowledge about the effect of not only medical but also a whole range of other policy interventions within education, crime prevention, employment and other welfare issues.

In the US, experiments are common for assessing the effectiveness of public interventions in the area of crime prevention and employment (Steiner, et al., 2009). Surprisingly, experimental techniques seem less frequently used in the field of education in the US (Cook & Gorard, 2007). The first boost of policy evaluation came with the employment creation and housing programmes of the 1930s. A further impetus came in the 1960s with the many social-welfare programmes (Rossi et al., 1999; Dehue, 2001). The demand for evaluation exceeded the capacity of the US GAO and created new employment possibilities for the increasing number of social science doctorates. Moreover, two new professional evaluation societies emerged in the 1970s (Evaluation Research Society and Evaluation Network) and were followed soon after by professional journals and standards. The notion that the selection of policy programmes and instruments should be determined by the evidence of their effects has for some time informed a number of employment programmes (Maynard et al., 1979; Bloom et al., 1997). As exemplified by the federal Workforce Investment Act of 1998, RCTs and other methods from the top of the evidence hierarchy were not the only accepted standards for producing evidence (Heinrich, 2007, p. 271). Yet the evidence hierarchy seems to be playing an increasing role in that attempt to prove effects, as it serves as a criterion for the screening of grant applications within education, employment, crime and drug-abuse control programmes (Birkeland et al., 2005; Weiss, Murphy-Graham, Petrosino & Gandhi, 2008; Petrosino, 2013). This regime of truth was reinforced by the Coalition for Evidence-Based Policy established in 2001 to promote the use of RCT to strengthen the effectiveness of social policies (Coalition for Evidence-Based Policy, 2011). In the following years, the coalition managed to convince congressional legislators to make evidence of effects an integral part of a number of federal social programmes.

In Europe, the use of experimental methods outside the area of medicine came much later and is still less prevalent than in the US (Petrosino, 2013).

Still, from not being used or even discussed at all, experimental methods and meta-reviews have in a relatively short term become the hegemonic, if far from realised, ideal for the making and assessment of education, crime prevention, employment and other welfare policies. The ideal of using evidence by way of experimental methods is clearly gaining political credence in Europe over the last decade or so partly due to the formation of the Campbell Collaboration in 2000. The founding of the Campbell Collaboration was directly inspired by the role played by the Cochrane Collaboration since 1993 in disseminating experiment-based knowledge within medicine and public health. During the annual meeting of the Royal Statistical Society in 1996, its president asked rhetorically:

> But what's so special about medicine? We are, through the media, as ordinary citizens, confronted daily with controversy and debate across a whole spectrum of public policy issues. But typically, we have no access to any form of systematic 'evidence base' – and therefore no means of participating in the debate in a mature and informed manner. Obvious topical examples include education – what does work in the classroom? – and penal policy – what is effective in preventing re-offending? (Smith 1996 cited in Petrosino, 2013)

The founding of the Campbell Collaboration in 2000 by British researchers and public managers to promote the use of evidence in social policymaking closely mirrored the Cochrane Collaboration. In fact, many of the same people who had established the Cochrane Collaboration were also key to the making of the Campbell Collaboration, notably the obstetrician Iain Chalmers and Michael Peckham, who ran the Research and Development Programme at the National Health Service and moved to become the Director of the School of Public Policy at the University College London (Petrosino, 2013).

Since its inception, the Campbell Collaboration has systematically identified and reviewed intervention studies in the areas of education, crime prevention, international development and a range of social programmes (Campbell Collaboration, 2014). It has gathered researchers and policymakers from a large number of countries through its annual colloquia where the developments in methods of gauging the efficacy of social policies are discussed (Campbell Collaboration, 2015). By 2015, the Campbell Collaboration seemed to be quite active in the areas of crime prevention and social welfare but less so in education and international development. In the area of crime prevention and social welfare the Campbell Collaboration is working closely with at least seven national organisations – four in the US, and one each in the UK, Canada and Denmark – to propagate the new methods of evidence in the crime prevention and social welfare policies and programmes in their home countries. In Britain, for example, the EPPI

Centre, which is located at University College London, has since 1993 been accumulating evidence of the efficacy of education, crime prevention and social-welfare programmes and tried to make this available to policymakers (Oakley et al., 2005; EPPI Centre, 2015). Of course, all of this does not say anything about the Campbell Collaboration's actual impact of experimental methods and meta-reviews in policymaking processes, and we should certainly be careful not to exaggerate this. My guess would be that, if asked about the Campbell Collaboration and its work, most policymakers in North America and Western Europe would probably not have a clue.

Apart from the area of medicine and public health, experimental methods have been particularly successful in establishing themselves as influential, if not hegemonic, in the areas of education and crime prevention. In the area of education, the Campbell Collaboration has probably contributed to spurring such methods, but the most influential force is with little doubt the OECD and its regular, international comparative surveys of schoolchildren's performance, the so-called PISA tests. Since 2000, the OECD's Programme for International Student Assessment (PISA) has every third year conducted standardised tests of 15-year-olds in key subjects, such as reading, writing, mathematics and problem-solving (OECD, 2015). The number of countries participating has gone up from 41 in 2000 to 65 in 2012. These tests have latched on to and probably contributed to reinforcing the general globalisation discourse that sees the development of human resources, such as intellectual skills and entrepreneurial drive, as fundamental to a nation's competitiveness vis-à-vis other states. At least, the tests are the subject of intense political and public focus, and every third year when its results are published teachers, school directors and ministers of education of laggard countries have to come up with all kinds of excuses and promises of improvement to ensure the country's future (Takayama, 2008; Pereyra et al., 2011; Baird et al., 2011). Of course, sober statisticians have been pointing out all along that, owing to differences in the application of the tests, inter-country comparisons should be made with extreme caution if not be outright avoided (Prais 2003; Wuttke 2008; Wiseman 2013). Even the OECD says that the tests are not intended to produce a ranking list but to provide policymakers with sources of inspiration for new teaching methods and systems and to assess whether they improve over time. Nevertheless, the standard reaction of the media and many policymakers in Western European countries that tend to perform relatively poorly in these tests is that their education systems need serious revisions and that the choice of teaching methods should be based not on the discretion of teachers but on evidence. Accordingly, many countries have seen the establishment of so-called educational clearing houses, i.e. institutions or networks developing, reviewing and disseminating information of the effects of various teaching methods. For example, as mentioned above, the EPPI-Centre located at University College London began examining the efficacy of education systems as early as 1993, though more systematic reviews took off only from 2000. In the US the What Works Clearinghouse was established in 2002 with support from the Department of Education (Institute of Education Sciences, 2015), and in Denmark the Danish Clearing House for Educational Research was established in 2006, a direct follower of an intense political debate about the quality of the Danish elementary school, sparked by the 2003 PISA test (Danish School of Education, 2015). Again, we should be careful not to exaggerate the influence of the new regime of truth in educational policies. At least, teachers and their unions in many European countries, particularly in the UK and France but not in Germany and Switzerland, have resisted the import of what they regard as quantitative and reductionist methods emanating from medicine, the general argument being that such methods tend to ignore important objectives of learning, such as creative and social skills, at the expense of easy-to-measure targets, such as proper writing and the resolution of maths assignments (Oakley et al., 2005; Dobbins, 2014).

Experimental methods actually have a fairly long tradition in crime prevention, though the real break came fairly recently. One of the first experimental studies undertaken in the area of crime prevention was the so-called Cambridge–Somerville study conducted in Massachusetts during the Second World War (Powers & Witmer, 1951). The study included a total of 650 delinquent boys, half of whom received specialised treatment and the other half the usual treatment, whose behaviour was followed for around five years after the ending of the programme. However, for a long time such studies remained few and far between. Even in the US, where the National Institute of Justice was established in 1968 to undertake research on the efficacy of criminal justice policies, development was slow (National Institute of Justice, 2014). In a review conducted in the mid-1970s of community programmes for the prevention and treatment of juvenile delinquency, Wright and Dixon (Wright & Dixon, 1977) could identify only 27 programmes using randomised or matched samples, and only nine of these combined randomisation with an outcome measure of delinquent behaviour. Again, in 1983, David Farrington, at that time a lecturer in psychological criminology at Cambridge University and later one of the leading figures in the quest for making crime prevention policies be based on experimental methods, would lament the very limited use of experimental methods in designing crime prevention interventions (Farrington, 1983, p. 257). In order to spur the use of experimental methods in this area, he argued, programme administrators had to relinquish control of assignment to experimenters and ethical problems of denial of treatment had to be overcome.

Such a change in the mind of managers of crime prevention programmes seems to have come about around 2000. By that time the number of research and government institutions engaged more or less intensely in the exploitation of experimental methods in crime prevention interventions had grown rapidly, particularly in the Anglophone countries. In the US, the Division and Academy of Experimental Criminology, a division of the American Society of Criminology, was founded in 1998 to promote the use and development of experimental evidence and methods in crime control policies. In 2001, the Jerry Lee Center of Criminology at the University of Pennsylvania was founded to research the causes and prevention of crime and spur public safety. The Center for Evidence-Based Crime Policy, George Mason University, was founded in 2008 and undertakes research on a wide range of criminal justice issues as well as evaluation of interventions for outcome effectiveness. Finally, the National Institute of Justice (mentioned above) is now firmly endorsing experimental methods as the key mode of assessing the efficacy of crime prevention programmes (National Institute of Justice, 2015b), and the results are being disseminated through the homepage CrimeSolutions.gov to help inform practitioners and policymakers about what works in criminal justice (National Institute of Justice, 2015a).

In Europe, the UK is clearly the leading country in terms of organisations engaged in evidence-based crime-prevention policies. These include the British Evidence for Policy and Practice Information and Co-ordinating Centre (EPPI-Centre), which has been dealing with crime prevention research at least since 2000: see above. Moreover, the Jerry Lee Centre for Experimental Criminology at Cambridge University, which was founded in 2007, runs one of the world's largest programmes of multi-site RCTs of crime prevention and supports the training of doctoral and post-doctoral students. The Jerry Lee Centre collaborates with UK police agencies, led by the Manchester Police, in conducting its so-called Tactical Experiments and Strategic Testing Programme (Cambridge University, 2015). Most other European countries have been quite slow in adopting experimental methods in crime prevention policies, though countries such as Germany, the Netherlands and Sweden have recently taken initiatives in that direction (Brottsforebyggande Rådet, 2004; Junger et al., 2007).

By the mid-2000s, then, experimentation had become a highly influential regulative ideal of crime prevention programmes. In an edited volume on the state of art of experimental methods in crime prevention (Farrington & Welsh, 2006), two influential scholars in the field of crime-prevention evaluation would rather modestly announce that 'support for evidence-based crime prevention is growing' (ibid., p. 2). Thus, from around 2000, there has been a substantial and increasing pressure in the Anglophone and several Western European countries not only to assess but also to design crime-prevention interventions on the basis of knowledge produced by RCT and quasi-experimental methods. While many, probably most, programmes in the area of crime prevention are – still – not evaluated and, if so, not by experimental methods, policymakers in the Anglophone countries and many Western European countries must now defend the non-use of experimental methods. Crime-prevention policies that are not based on evidence – by way of experimental methods – are easy prey for political contestation and closures.

The contemporary quest for evidence-based policymaking and its rapport with constructive neoliberalism

This section argues that, even if the contemporary quest for EP owes a lot to neoliberal problematisations of government, the two sit somewhat uneasily. This uneasiness has above all to do with the articulation of more or less strong convictions in the ability of science to show, once and for all, the best way to govern our societal problems.

In the preceding sections we have seen that the emergence and spread of experimental methods were strongly informed by a neoliberal critique of state planning. EP was, at least in its formulations by Popper and Campbell, taken to be a form of policy based on a tentative, piecemeal and refutable knowledge. Experimental methods were never intended to provide knowledge that once and for all would establish the most effective solutions to societal problems. Yet, this epistemological modesty and the limitations this put to the ambitions of government may be changing in favour of a more optimistic assessment of the capacity of science to provide policymakers with the – technically speaking – proper instruments to meet politically defined goals.

In much of the everyday lingo of politicians and public managers it is not difficult to discern an overtly optimistic faith in the ability of experimental knowledge to identify so-called best practice. In itself, the latter term suggests that it is possible to find once and for all the optimum solution to a given politically defined problem. Taken at face value, many of the official statements made by the incipient British New Labour government suggested an almost naive faith in the ability of science to override ideological concerns and, more importantly, provide the optimum solution for any given political problem. For example, then Home Secretary David Blunkett explained: 'This Government has given a clear commitment that we will be guided not by dogma but by an open-minded approach to understanding what works and why. This is central to our agenda for modernising government: using information and knowledge much more effectively and creatively at the heart of policymaking and policy delivery' (Blunkett, 2002).

Obviously, this and other statements by Blair formed part of communicating the Third Way strategy as a non-ideological way of governing society. In this strategy, 'evidence' came in handy as an apparently purely pragmatic and technical way of developing and implementing policy solutions. Thus the key message of New Labour's Modernising Government White Paper was that: 'policy decisions should be based on sound evidence. The raw ingredient of evidence is information. Good quality policy making depends on high quality information, derived from a variety of sources – expert knowledge; existing domestic and international research; existing statistics; stakeholder consultation; evaluation of previous policies' (Cabinet Office, 1999).

In this rendition, evidence seems to hold almost unlimited potential for construing the correct, non-ideological, policy (Davoudi, 2006). At least systematically produced knowledge should be employed to secure that public interventions are bringing about political goals in the most effective way. This quest shows a fundamental similarity with Max Weber's notion of the bureaucracy as a technical instrument for the realisation of political ends (Weber, 1978). For Weber, the very strength of the bureaucracy rested with its ability to develop the highest level of expertise within functional areas and impartially employ that expertise to determine the technically speaking most effective solution to given political goals. As is well known, Weber was acutely aware that the bureaucracy was an ideal-type that in many instances would not be able to uphold a tight division between technical expertise on the one hand and the articulation of political goals on the other. More importantly, he had serious qualms about the possible negative moral implications of the bureaucracy and its formal, instrumental rationality. Nevertheless, Weber found the bureaucracy not only technically superior but in many cases also morally more desirable than other forms of power, not least because the ideals of impartiality and *Sachlichkeit* which informed the bureaucratic ethos were replacing earlier forms of patronage and clientelism.

My point here is not to discuss the moral virtues or dangers of Weber's belief in the possibility of separating solutions identified by expert knowledge from the making of political goals but to argue that there is a certain similarity between this Weberian understanding of the role of expertise and some of the contemporary political renditions of the capacity of scientific evidence to produce the right political solutions. In fact, the former New Labour's take on this seems to go even further than Weber's ideal. Thus, in contrast to Weber, who was adamant on separating expertise driven by the quest for truth (Weber, 1948b) and politics driven by irrefutable values (Weber, 1948a), New Labour's thrill for evidence-based policy seemed at times to imply collapsing the two. Thus, the Third Way seemed to regard systematically accumulated experience and knowledge conducive not only to deciding on the best policy instruments but also to being able to identify the most suitable policy goals. At least, the very absence of this distinction and the opening this clears for large-scale interventions is inherently problematic and directly at odds with the critical mode of neoliberalism.

Yet, we should not exaggerate EPs conflict with neoliberal rationalities of government, neither the critical nor the constructivist ones. With regard to the critical mode of neoliberalism, it must be stressed that even the most optimistic formulations of the early New Labour government do not take evidence-based policy as a stepping stone for comprehensive state interventions. The liberal norm of respecting and even augmenting the self-governing capacities of civil society remain fundamental even in the areas of evidence-based policymaking. The recent obsession with nudging found in the UK and elsewhere testifies to the continued importance of citizen choice and empowerment. In 2010, the British coalition government led by Prime Minister David Cameron officially endorsed the deployment and testing of the efficacy of 'choice architectures' in areas of crime prevention, energy saving and healthy lifestyle (see also Cialdini, 2007; Ariely, 2008; Osborne & Thaler, 2010). Directly inspired by the book *Nudge* (Thaler & Sunstein, 2008), the Behavioural Insight Team was established in the British Cabinet Office to explore and employ more effective ways of governing: citizen conduct was explicitly seen as a technical mode of government overcoming the strong ideological connotation associated with both the statist interventions favoured by (Old) Labour and the market-oriented interventions favoured by Thatcherite-style Conservatism (Burgess, 2012). Tellingly, the Behavioural Insight Team, in popular terms the Nudge Unit, is led by David Halpern, a former adviser in Tony Blair's strategy unit. The implication of this particular utilisation of nudging and the insights of behavioural psychology is that an apparently non-ideological device ideally based only on scientific evidence is employed within a mode of political rule dominated by choice. It is not up to politicians or scientists to decide how citizens, companies and communities should act. Instead, informed by the work of scientists, politicians are supposed to implement architectures that enable citizens and others to exercise their freedom and choose a lifestyle that is in line with current norms of civility, health and industriousness.

With regard to the constructivist mode of neoliberalism, the contemporary quest for evidence-based policymaking is ambiguous too. On the face of it, the belief in best practice may entail that there is little or no room for professional discretion exercised by frontline workers. Doctors', teachers' and social workers' autonomy may be reduced to that of adopting the solutions that have proved their worth by experimental methods and systematic reviews of the results of such experiments. While this may be seen as highly negative by the professions, it may have a certain democratic potential in that the near-monopoly authority earlier found in fields such as medicine, education and research, and social work is now penetrated and broken up by the requirement for evidence (Timmermans & Berg, 2003, p. 21). Notwithstanding this democratic potential, the limiting of the room for the exercise of discretion and the non-use of the freedoms and self-steering capacities of civil servants would be at odds with constructivist neoliberalism.

Yet, is evidence-based policy really about limiting professional discretion and freedom in order to secure the pursuit of best practice? Hardly. While Popper's and Campbell's calls for experiments, a plurality of knowledge forms and tentative reforms may seem to be distant historical remnants, they are still part and parcel of contemporary evidence-based policy. Here is what the then Australian Prime Minister Rudd announced on 30 April 2008 when his government articulated the link between science and politics:

> A third element of the Government's agenda for the public service is to ensure a robust, evidence-based policy making process. Policy design and policy evaluation should be driven by analysis of all the available options, and not by ideology. When preparing policy advice for the Government, I expect departments to review relevant developments among State and Territory governments and comparable nations overseas. The Government will not adopt overseas models uncritically. We're interested in facts, not fads. But whether it's aged care, vocational education or disability services, Australian policy development should be informed by the best of overseas experience and analysis. In fostering a culture of policy innovation, we should trial new approaches and policy options through small scale pilot studies ... Policy innovation and evidence-based policy making is at the heart of being a reformist government. (Rudd, 2010).

On the one hand, the former Australian Prime Minister is clearly expressing a confidence in the role of scientific knowledge in informing policymaking to avoid fads and ineffective solutions. Such knowledge has potentially universal validity as suggested by his insistence that 'overseas' analyses be considered. On the other hand, he is also very clearly articulating an experimental ethos emphasising innovation and minor, tentative studies. He is aspiring not to universally (or eternally) valid solutions but rather to open-mindedness among politicians and public administrators alike to constantly interrogate existing ways of doing things. In Denmark, shifting governments – of both Liberal and Social Democratic bents – have since the early 2000s all officially endorsed the blessings of evidence-based policymaking, though so far experimentally produced knowledge is mainly used in the areas of public health and education (Bhatti et al., 2006). However, following a recent debate on whether the desire for evidence in the area of social policies had gone too far, the former Danish minister of social welfare argued that 'Evidence is sound reason. And we need more of that, not less, in the social area.' But he went on to add:

> This does not mean that all social interventions from tomorrow should be based on randomised experiments at the highest step of the evidence ladder. Nor that social pedagogues in the future should wear a white coat and carry a laminated manual under their arm, and ignore both professional insights and the unique social DNA of the individual citizens ... Because even in the most hard-core evidence-based interventions a precondition for success is that the professional employees – social pedagogues, psychologists, social counsellors – contribute to the project insight, professionalism and reflection. The manuals are in other words a support tool, not a blueprint. Finally, it is a fundamental premise for the evidence-based interventions that they should be adapted to the individual participants in order to work. (Sareen, 2014, my translation from Danish)

Of course, these few examples above do not in any was encompass the entire range of political receptions of evidence-based policy. Yet, they do indicate that at least some contemporary key policymakers in the liberal democracies find that public administration should be guided less by the Weberian-inspired optimism of identifying the (one and only) most effective solution to a given political problem but more by an active, experimental ethos constantly looking for new and better ways of doing things. In doing so, civil servants should actively use and be willing to modify their professional knowledge and standards, but they should not abandon their professional discretion in their everyday work with citizens.

Regardless of the uneasy and not entirely straightforward relationship between neoliberalism and EP, the latter comes with a number of political dangers. Interestingly, much of the critical writing in this area revolves above all around EP not being sufficiently scientific (House of Commons, 2006). According to this understanding, the problem with EP is neither that it purports to be neutral nor that it may limit professional autonomy and discretion but that politics still prevail in the selection, use and application of evidence in policymaking. So, instead of evidence-based policy we get 'policy-based evidence' (Boden & Epstein, 2006). In a slightly different vein, an academic authority in the field like Ray Pawson argues that we need to focus more on programme theory in order to understand better the causalities of shifting social problems (Pawson, 2006). While there can be absolutely no doubt that politicians ignore, skew and abuse evidence, there may be more problematic sides of EP than its lack of scientificity or its choice of a wrong style of science. Both these criticisms imply that, if only we get EP to adopt more (of the right form of) science, then there really is no problem.

First, such criticisms overlook EP's systematic inclusions and exclusions of research objects and the forms of power it enables. With regard to the inclusions and exclusions of EP, we find a very clear pattern of attention. Because the methods are attuned to study behavioural changes of selected groups targeted by one more or less clearly defined intervention, a wide range of policy areas are by default excluded from the scrutiny of systematic knowledge. Take an area such as taxation, perhaps the most crucial area for the survival of any state. The same could go for defence policies. Why has no one ever considered systematically assessing the efficacy of such systems? We could of course come up with all kinds of speculative answers evoking the political sensitivity and strong conflicting interests in these areas. Yet, I think the answer is much more mundane and straightforward: the methods of truth production topping the list of the evidence hierarchy are simply not technically suited to analysing complex policy processes with a variety of political goals and interests and an even greater array of political instruments at play. Thus, experimental methods are fine for examining programmes targeting the underage, the sick, the criminal, the drug abuser and the unemployed but not the company engaged in tax fraud or the lobbyist peddling contracts for new military equipment.

Secondly, if we turn to those policies and programmes that actually are subjected to the truth tests of experimentation, we face the now familiar dangers of modifying these programmes in ways that render them assessable in terms of a few simple quantifiable indicators. By now there is a whole literature dealing with the unintended or perverse effects of performance measurement in the public sector in general (Smith, 1995; Pidd, 2005), and in areas of health (Freeman, 2002; Bevan & Hood, 2006), education (Baker et al., 2010), crime prevention (Leggett, 2003; Grizzle, 2002) and employment services (Sanger, 2003; Bruttel, 2004) in particular. These effects include such things as data manipulation, cherry picking (focusing on the easy, but measurable tasks only), parking (paying limited or no attention to the weakest citizens), abstaining from collaboration and disregarding long-term goals. Methods of knowledge production suited to appreciate collaboration, targeting the ones most in need and focusing on long-term objectives, such as case studies and informal experience-sharing among peers, are usually at the lower end of the hierarchy. Therefore, they are often discarded as anecdotal knowledge of little value.

Finally, the most important danger of EP is its claim to neutrality in which it is assumed that technical means can be neatly separated from political goals (Triantafillou, 2015b). Put differently, while evidence-based policy may owe its origins to an attitude of experimentation and the valuing of different forms of knowledge, there is today also a certain faith in the possibility of finding out once and for all what constitutes so-called best practice to achieve a given goal. Yet, one probably does not have to be a Foucauldian analyst to acknowledge that procedures, schemes, tools and technologies of intervention are structuring the possible field of action and producing effects in ways that go well beyond any articulation of political goals. In other words, the choice of policy instruments and tools that may be endorsed as the result of systematic experimental studies may not only have effects that go well beyond political intentions; they may shape those very intentions. As I have tried to show in the case of the Australian and Danish unemployment services, the narrow focus on measuring and assessing how many fast people get into jobs will systematically favour a work-first approach at the expense of an employment policy more focused on a human-development – not to mention social-security – approach (Triantafillou, 2011). More generally, if we accept that political power entails governing other people's conduct, then the production of evidence and the recommendations emanating from this production are explicitly attuned to shape and to legitimise the exercise of power with a particular focus on those who owing to their age or conduct are seen as failing to meet contemporary, liberal norms of citizenship, namely the child, the sick, the criminal and the unemployed. For these groups that are deemed unable or unwilling to exercise their freedom in line with liberal norms of responsibility, healthiness, civility and employability, the state or, more broadly, public administration has a series of illiberal instrumentations at its disposal that may lend their legitimacy from knowledge produced according to the evidence hierarchy.

Conclusion

I have argued in this chapter that EP sits somewhat uneasily with neoliberal rationalities of government but it would be wrong to regard them as antithetical. At minimum, this kind of knowledge can be used by the public to hold professionals accountable to their decisions and actions within the said policy fields. EP may penetrate spheres of professional enclosures and modify relationships of authority between the public administration and the citizens it supposedly serves. However, it may also narrow down the discretion of professional choice exercised in the provision of public services to the point where the room for the exercise of freedom is so limited that we are dealing with sovereign power rather than liberal government. While only a few politicians today genuinely seem to believe in the existence of a best practice in the sense of universally valid policy instruments to achieve given policy goals, we do find several instances of political strategies, such as the Third Way, flirting dangerously with the idea that science can somehow provide non-ideological policy solutions that are limited not only to the instrumentation of politics, as Weber would have it, but potentially also to policy goals and visions.

Notwithstanding such political articulations that are clearly at odds with critical neoliberalism, the main trend has been and still seems to be that EP is essentially about experimentation, piecemeal reforms and the constant possibility of refuting the knowledge upon which reforms are based. By the same token, EP in its present forms does not seem attuned to comprehensive state planning at the expense of civil-society-based activities and solutions. Also, the fear posed by many public-sector professionals, such as doctors, teachers and social counsellors, that EP will eliminate professional discretion and freedom, seems overstated. My argument here is not the much referred-to one that EP is all rhetoric and little or no action, which of course is true. So far, EP is mainly a regulative ideal and not something that effectively pervades policymaking, at least not outside medicine and certain public-health interventions. My argument is rather that, to the extent that EP has gained political credence as a regulative ideal, it entails that the public administration must constantly question itself, test its policy-delivery solutions and see to that its interactions with citizens in order to better their situation are based on available evidence. EP then will encourage if not force public administration and its employees to use and continually develop their use of professional knowledge and standards. Conversely, they are unlikely to be allowed not to exercise their professionally regulated freedom.

8

A new civil-servant persona?

Introduction

The reforms explored in the preceding chapters call in various ways for a reorientation of the orientation of the civil service. Civil servants must attune their routines and ways of providing public service in ways that are amenable to performance-accounting and accreditation and in line with available evidence on the efficacy of policy instruments. However, these are not the only demands that civil servants face. Over the last few decades, they have also been expected to be more responsive to the visions of policymakers and to the needs of citizens and civil-society groups. Moreover, they must be more flexible in order to allow for innovation. Above all they must be able to engage with citizens in ways that help the latter mobilise their own resources and empower them. While many scholars are keen to make a firm distinction between New Public Management, Public Value Management and New Public Governance, just to mention the most prominent labels of recent public-management reforms and schemes, they all insist on the need for civil servants to change their conduct in order to become more responsive, flexible and (citizen-) empowering.

By the notion of the civil-servant persona I am referring to the kind of self-comportment that civil servants are expected to exercise in order to be able to function properly in the public administration. Michel Foucault used the term 'ethics' or ethical work to account for the self's work on itself, i.e. the reflections and practical ways by which an individual (or a group) constitutes itself as a subject in rapport with existing codes of conduct and prevailing forces of power (Foucault, 1987, pp. 25–32). It is the substance of this ethical work, i.e. the reflections and techniques of self-subjectification, which makes up the bureaucratic persona. This understanding of ethics has informed a limited set of studies of modern civil servants in Western and colonial societies (Osborne, 1994; du Gay, 1996; Minson, 1998; Triantafillou, 2004b). Unlike some other writings, which tend to see modern Weberian-style bureaucracy as machine-like and bereft of ethics (e.g. Bauman, 1989; Schumacher, 1995), this Foucauldian-inspired understanding of bureaucratic conduct creates a conceptual space for analysing the fundamental importance and historical variation of the styles of ethical work undertaken by civil servants. In particular, it allows us to explore the link between the bureaucratic personae on the one hand, and the wider public management reforms and political rationalities informing these on the other.

This chapter first explores shifting patterns in the educational requirements for civil servants. It then moves on to examine how norms and techniques of entrepreneurship are increasingly saturating public administration. Thirdly, I analyse discourses and techniques seeking to form a new empowering civil-servant persona. Finally, I discuss the link between the bureaucratic persona and the wider public-management reforms and political rationalities informing these.

Education for the new civil-servant persona

Civil servants are part and parcel of any territorial state. In Western Europe, civil servants were the essentially subject of the monarch and employed to ensure the latter's will during the seventeenth and eighteenth centuries. With the advent of liberal democracy during the nineteenth and early twentieth centuries, civil servants were required to shift their allegiance to the elected government. Notwithstanding the dramatic changes taking place in public administration during these centuries, entrance to the civil service – at least the middle and top tiers – has required a professional education. However, the kind of professional education required has changed quite radically in most liberal democracies over the last two or three decades.

At the most general level we see a shift from law (Continental Western Europe) and liberal arts (United Kingdom) as the dominant education of civil servants to more technical and managerial degrees. In Continental Western Europe, legal studies have until recently played the predominant role in educating civil servants. This is particularly clear in Germany, where lawyers – people with a university degree in law – have taken up the bulk of senior administration positions both before and after the Second World War (Kickert, 2005; Goetz, 2011). Administrative lawyers have also played a very dominant role in France, Italy and the Netherlands (Kickert, 2005). In the Nordic countries, lawyers replaced the nobility in the central administration during the eighteenth century to strengthen the monarch's control of the state apparatus and enhance the latter's effectiveness (Feldbæk, 2000, pp. 322–5). The law degree has gradually lost its dominant role in favour of specialised, technical degrees on the one hand, and more general degrees in economics, political science and public administration on the other (van der Meer, 2011). In France and the Netherlands, for example, degrees in public administration importantly supplemented law for entrance to the central administration from the middle of the twentieth century (Bezes & Jeannot, 2011, p. 193; van der Meer & Dijkstra, 2011, p. 174). Even in Germany, where lawyers for a very long time have enjoyed something close to a *Juristenmonopol* in the top tier of the civil service, there is a slow but clear tendency of recruiting civil servants with other degrees (Goetz, 2011, p. 54). The education and recruitment of civil servants underwent important innovations in many Western European countries from around the 1960s, when public administration emerged as a university major (Tony Verheijen & Connaughton, 2003) – either in its own right (the Netherlands) or as a sub-discipline of political science (Denmark, see Hansen, 2011, p. 105). While the syllabus of these new studies also included public law, they focused more broadly on public and welfare economics, public budgeting, organisation theory, performance management and evaluation. Similar studies have emerged in many Eastern European countries following the end of the Cold War (Verheijen, 1999). While the extent to which civil servants with a degree in public administration have replaced administrative lawyers remains unclear, it seems fair to say that the former play an increasingly important role in public administration vis-à-vis administrative lawyers.

In the UK, an Oxbridge education in the liberal arts was regarded as instrumental to meet the ambition of creating a civil-service vocation in the British civil service (Drewry & Butcher, 1988; Osborne, 1994, p. 305). Of course, lawyers played an important role in many parts of the civil service but much less so compared to Continental Europe. Exams were held at regular intervals not to match the suitability of a civil-servant candidate to a particular position but to test his or her general vocation to office. A broad education in the liberal arts was seen as the best way to ensure this. Paradoxically, mastering classical Greek was seen as particularly useful. Because Greek was regarded as the language of civilisation and reason, its mastery was seen as a sign of generalised expertise. More importantly, its mastery was linked to the creation of an ethic of distance that would allow civil servants to access the general public interest and distance themselves from narrow particularistic interests (Jenkyns, 1980, pp. 65–6). Following the expanse of specialised welfare services from the 1960s, the liberal arts have lost importance vis-à-vis more specialised professional degrees. This decline of the relative importance of liberal-arts-trained generalists took further pace from the 1980s, after which the British civil service has seen a substantial boost in the recruitment of specialised professionals and a significant reliance on external experts in management, finance and contracting (Greer & Jarman, 2011, pp. 20–7).

Finally, the US makes up a very different case. Owing to its size and the separation of powers between the federal level and the 50 very different states, it is highly problematic to make any general characterisation of the US civil-service system and its recruitment of civil servants. Notwithstanding this qualification, the US civil-service system has since 1850 been widely characterised as a dual system. This reflects the coexistence of civil servants hired for purposes of political patronage and policy advice on the one hand and administrators hired by way of merit-based exams on the other (Ingraham, 1995, pp. 23, 53). The recruitment between the two types of civil servants varies substantially between the various branches of the civil service and over time, though with a clear tendency of a dropping rate of merit-based or competitive recruitment (Ingraham & Moynihan, 2003). It is also clear that neither law studies nor classical studies have played the dominant roles they did in Continental Europe and the UK respectively. Recruitment has generally been much more specialised than in most European systems. Statistics are hard to find, but, according to one of the leading scholars in the field, the general pattern at the federal level is that civil servants are either specific experts, such as people with a degree in the agricultural sciences at the Department of Agriculture, or general-policy advisers with a degree in economics or (public or business) administration (Peters, 2015). State civil-service systems tend to be pretty much the same but with more people trained in public administration.

The substantial changes in the educational background of civil servants during the latter half of the twentieth century have manifold and quite diverse causes that differ from one country to another. At the most general level, the expansion of the welfare state during the twentieth century has – even in the US – led to a significant growth of technical staff with a professional expertise in health, education, engineering and social work. Yet, we have also seen an increase in the number of civil servants with more general-type degrees in economics, political science, public administration, management and finance. Their role in the public administration has less to do with providing welfare services and more with governing the public sector itself. Whereas administrative lawyers are attuned by their cultural background to rule by law and ensure that policies comply with existing laws, the new civil service must attend to tasks such as policy advice, budget control, performance management, contractual management and human-resource management. They would also be the ones in charge of performance-accounting, implementing accreditation schemes and making sure that public policymaking is evidence-based.

Apart from the governing of the public administration itself, the new civil servants must also contribute to the effective governing of society. However, unlike the welfare profession groups that grew during the twentieth century, such as doctors, teachers, social workers and engineers, the new groups of civil servants are concerned less with the direct provision of public services and more with how the public administration can better utilise its resources and, not least, the unused immobilised resources of civil society. While the former task seems to correlate with an entrepreneurial ethos, the latter mobilisation of civil-society resources has led to calls for an empowering or facilitating civil servant. While these two personae are not the same, they do display a number of similarities. Negatively defined, they both differ substantially from the kind of persona instilled through legal training or the classical arts. Positively, defined thus, the entrepreneurial and empowering ethos both correlate with a civil-service persona preoccupied less with governing the public administration itself and enhancing its capacity to empower civil society and communities to solve their problems by themselves.

The making of entrepreneurship in the civil service

From the end of the nineteenth century up until the 1980s, the public administrations of most liberal democracies were run in more or less proximity to Max Weber's bureaucratic ideal type (Weber, 1978, pp. 956–1005). Thus, legality, *Sachlichkeit* and (party political) neutrality were key codes of conduct. Moreover, those public administrations that did not adhere to these norms or were fairly far from realising these were criticised accordingly by local opposition or other governments. Thus, Max Weber's analytical ideals served to a large extent as regulative ideals, i.e. as codes or norms of conduct. This regulative dimension seems to be increasingly challenged by other norms. Perhaps, this is clearest in the case of civil servants and the ethos sustaining their work. The civil-servant persona seems to move from those primarily hired because of their expertise in a societal field to those hired because of their subjective qualities (Minson, 1998). By the same token, the civil servant must now negotiate ideals of matter-of-factness and impartiality with norms of customer orientation and citizen dialogue (du Gay, 2000). Of course expertise within professional fields such as health, learning or social work is still relevant for those working in the front line providing services to citizens. Yet, public-service professionals and in particular their managers must now be willing to develop and realise themselves in and through their work. Public managers must be experts not in the service their agency is in charge of delivering but in performance and personnel management, budgets, shifting political strategies, customer dialogue and the development of organisational mission and values.

The instilling of an entrepreneurial ethos in civil servants hinges on a wide range of mundane techniques of government that have invaded the public administration of OECD countries since the 1980s. These include legal regulations, non-legal contracts (individual and organisational), citizen charters, informal codes of conduct and performance-related pay, just to mention the most influential ones. Some of these are new and some are old techniques used for the partially new purpose of creating an entrepreneurial ethos. In the following sections, I explore legal regulations, citizen charters and economic instruments and discuss their particularity vis-à-vis Weberian norms of bureaucratic conduct.

Transforming the legal codification of bureaucratic conduct

In most liberal democracies, civil servants' conduct has been codified in labour or administrative law in order to ensure a merit-based and impartial civil service (Wise, 1996). This has often entailed tightly regulated career-advancement and payment structures that have provided little room for local managerial discretion. The rise of NPM and new HRM practices has put the *legal* position of civil servants under pressure in a number of European countries over the last two decades or so. Accordingly, many countries have seen the elimination of special civil-service rights and responsibilities. In Europe, these include Denmark, Italy, the Netherlands, Sweden and Switzerland (van der Meer et al., 2013).[1] Outside Europe, we find similar developments in civil-servant labour law in Australia and Canada, though Australia recently partially reversed this trend following several cases of civil-service scandals (Caron & Giauque, 2006; J. Halligan, 2013). In the US, the Clinton administration abolished the Federal Personnel Manual and its many rules and guidelines in order to promote flexibility and responsiveness of civil servants (Ingraham & Moynihan, 2003). In sum, most of the leading OECD countries have eroded regulations and legal rights protecting civil servants from direct government influence and narrow party-political strategies. Consequently, the differences between the labour laws regulating private and public sector employees have been diminished. In sum, in a number of countries, we see changes in the civil-servant labour regulations that erode the special status of civil servants in order to make way for more customer-oriented, flexible and innovative civil servants.

Yet, in several Central and Eastern European countries and, more recently, in the UK, the development has been quite the opposite. They have adopted legal regulations codifying the special character of the civil-servant employment and secure principles of neutrality, impartiality and *Sachlichkeit* (Bryane, 2012; van der Meer et al., 2013). The main explanation for this alternative trend in Central and Eastern European countries seems to be their attempt to divest themselves of the Communist state apparatus and build an administrative organisation that allows expertise and (political) neutrality to become more prominent. These reforms were encouraged by the accession process to the European Union (Verheijen, 1999). The UK saw the adoption of the Constitutional Reform and Governance Act 2010, which provides the British civil service with a legal basis formally establishing the core values of the civil service – i.e. impartiality, integrity, honesty and neutrality – and the principle of merit-based appointment of the position of civil servants. The impetus for the British push towards legal codification of Weberian norms of bureaucratic conduct seems to reflect two things. On the one hand, Britain has a longstanding tradition of common law with an inbuilt reluctance to legal codification of civil-service responsibilities and rights. While the Northcote–Trevelyan report of 1853 contributed to establishing a merits-based and impartial British civil service, it was tellingly never put into law (Pilkington, 1999) . On the other hand, the increasingly unclear roles and responsibilities of civil servants resulting from the NPM reforms rolled out since the 1980s had resulted in a strong pressure on these Weberian-style bureaucratic norms (van der Meer et al., 2013, p. 103). In brief, whereas in many Central and Eastern European countries Weberian-style bureaucracy had to be invented from scratch, the British case was one of trying to defend the erosion of these longstanding norms from an overzealous government committed to bend the civil service according to its party-political strategies in general and to norms of flexibility and responsiveness in particular.

The pursuit of flexibility by legal means constitutes a significant break from Max Weber's ideal of rule-based administration. Weber regarded rule-based administration as the epitome of the formal rationalisation of political authority and as absolutely superior to all previous forms of rule in terms of both its technical efficacy and its democratic potential. It is superior in terms of technical efficacy, Weber argued, because it enables a strict horizontal and vertical division of labour which enabled the optimum use of the skills of each and every employee in the bureaucratic organisation – be that public or private (Weber, 1978, pp. 973–80). It has a superior democratic potential in that it enabled a more or less clear division between goal-setting by elected political representatives of the people on the one hand, and the implementation of these goals by rule-following expert civil servants on the other (Weber, 1948a). It is well known that the strict rule-following during the last several decades has been regarded as the root of many if not all public sector maladies, notably the lack of incentives, sound judgement, individual responsibility and not least the lack of flexibility.

Most academics take a sober approach to bureaucratic rules by trying to distinguish between rules necessary to uphold democratic accountability and transparency (often labelled green tape) on the one hand and rules leading to inefficient work practices (often labelled red tape) (Bozeman, 2000; Sanjay & Scott, 2002). For such scholars and the OECD, the problem is essentially how to hold on to the green tape and at the same time cut the counterproductive red tape, i.e. rules reducing flexibility and innovation in public administration (OECD, 2003).[2] Of course, it is no easy task to distinguish between the rules favouring legal, political and perhaps even learning accountability on the one hand and the rules resulting in lack of flexibility and innovation on the other. Often the very same rule may be essential to ensuring accountability but also a source of inflexibility. For example, legal requirements of public transparency in public administration's policy advice to politicians may render political decision-making cumbersome because of the potential critical voices raised by the media or the government opposition. Another example may be the increasing procedural requirement in the public-health and other sectors to adhere to particular guidelines and to document that such guidelines are actually followed, i.e. accreditation. As shown in Chapter 6, such rule-based systems seek to promote learning (accountability) by forcing public agencies to systematically accumulating their experiences and results. Yet this may reduce flexibility and result in administrative overload (Lewis & Triantafillou, 2012). Thus, civil servants are today expected to be flexible in the sense of bending though not transgressing the rules in order to adopt smarter and more effective solutions to societal problems. In order to promote efficiency, flexibility and responsiveness, the new laws regulating bureaucratic conduct in most of (Continental) Western Europe have eroded legal rights to protect civil servants from direct government influence attuned to favour narrow party-political strategies. Accordingly, civil servants must perform a fine balancing act in their everyday work of adhering to existing rules, on the one hand and, on the other, constantly testing these rules, reinterpreting them in order to come up with new ways of meeting political demands and goals that seem to change with increasing pace.

Citizen charters

Citizen charters constitute one of the key instruments in many OECD countries seeking to make civil servants more responsive to citizens' needs. While this instrument has been used in various forms, the general idea is to make civil servants treat citizens as customers whose individual needs must be catered to. This idea has without doubt been articulated most strongly in the Anglophone countries.

The British Citizen Charter was established in 1991 and its purpose was explained by then Prime Minister John Major in the following way: 'to make public services answer better to the wishes of their users, and to raise the quality overall' (British Government, 1991). It was subsequently updated and continued by New Labour. However, two fundamental elements have persisted. Firstly, each and every department had to formulate a citizen charter stipulating the standards of service that citizens could expect to receive. Standards included verifiable quantitative measures (such as waiting times) and qualitative ones (relationship between providers and users). Secondly, standard marks were awarded to all departments by their users, thereby making public both those departments that did well and those that did not. The Citizen's Charter Unit regularly published progress reports, monitoring of the overall results and the new goals. Moreover, independent bodies, such as Offer, Ofsted, Audit Commission, NHS Executive and so on, have been involved in measuring and evaluating the results mostly to instigate a learning process and to improve services, rather than just to sanction poor service (Schiavo, 2000). Thus, public managers were directly and civil servants indirectly pressured to attune their activities in ways that would secure a high level of user satisfaction (Duggett, 1998). In line with the British tradition of common law, the Citizen's Charter was launched as a non-legal instrument. In 1994, Diane Goldsworthy, Deputy Director of the Citizen's Charter Unit, explained:

> As you know, there have been suggestions that the Citizen's Charter needs 'legislative teeth' in order to achieve results and to protect accountability. I do not share this view. Legislation to empower citizens to obtain their entitlements from public services could in practice become a constraint on developing more flexible, responsive public services that reflect what people want today. (Goldsworthy, 1994)

The OECD's PUMA group seems to have played an important role in informing and not least propagating the British Citizen Charter to other countries. At least, several other countries were quick to adopt similar measures. In the Anglophone countries, the customer service plans were introduced in the US in 1993 by the Clinton administration, and the Australian Government Service Charters were introduced by the Howard government in 1998. Not surprisingly, the specific design and implementation of these schemes differed from the British one (McGuire, 2001). Despite these differences these schemes have all been the object of substantial political attention and put strong pressures on civil servants to pay more attention to the needs of individual citizens than to administrative procedures and regulations.

In Continental Europe, citizen service charters have evolved in Belgium, Finland, France, Italy, the Netherlands, Norway, Portugal and Spain (Nikos, 2001; Torres, 2004). The developments in these countries were mainly driven by national governments, even if Eurobarometer surveys from the late 1990s onwards of customer satisfaction with public services in the member states may have reinforced this movement (European Commission, 2000, 2002, 2003, 2004). While introduced to modernise the public sector and remind civil servants of their duty to cater to citizens, the use of citizen charters has played a rather different and generally less important role outside the Anglophone countries. In France, for example, the introduction of the public service charter in 1992 appears not to have done much to enhance responsiveness to the citizen-consumer. Here, the service charter has been less about empowering citizen-consumers and more about reasserting republican principles of equal citizenship (Clark, 2000). In Italy, a strong public-law tradition has blocked the effective implementation of the non-legal mechanism of the *Carta dei servizi* introduced in 1993 under direct inspiration from the British initiative (Schiavo, 2000). Only quantitative standards were introduced and in a way that did not allow inter-organisational comparison and therefore left little room for external assessment.

The distinctiveness of the kind of responsiveness that the citizen charters seek to evoke from civil servants may be clarified by contrasting it to the kind of impartiality implied by Weber's notion of the ethos of office (Weber, 1978, p. 1404). The latter essentially implies that civil servants are able to engage in a form of self-comportment by which they loyally obey a political superordinate regardless of their own personal convictions. The ethos of responsiveness differs in two fundamental ways from the kind of obedience expected by the Weberian-style civil servant. First of all, responsiveness is not about obedience but about paying attention to and reflecting on how to meet needs and interests. To be responsive implies that the civil servant must be cognisant of such needs and interests, must be able to reflect on the extent to which these are reasonable and then try to accommodate the ones that are deemed to be so. In contrast, the only kind of reflection required by the Weberian bureaucrat when receiving an order from a superior is whether this order is in accordance with existing laws and regulations. Secondly, whereas the Weberian civil servant's obedience is targeted towards one person only, their superior, the responsiveness ideal should include all so-called stakeholders, i.e. all those with a direct interest in a given case or policy. Stakeholders will often include individuals and groups both within public administration, such as politicians, top managers within and between various public agencies, and outside public administration, such as organised interest groups, for-profit companies, NGOs and not least citizens targeted for public services. In brief, instead of following rules and regulations, civil servants must now provide services by being cognisant of the needs of relevant stakeholders, assessing which of these claims seem to hold the strongest problem-solving potential, and be willing to change their ways of service provision at the whims of shifting customer ratings.

Performance pay

Under the broad heading of performance (related) pay, several liberal democracies have seen the introduction of economic instruments seeking to promote entrepreneurial conduct by way of economic incentives. Well into the 1980s, the bulk of public-sector employees in the OECD countries were paid according to fixed incremental salary scales. Civil servants were usually paid according to an incremental system directly linked to a fixed pattern of career steps.[3] By the early 2000s, almost all OECD countries had introduced some kind of performance-related payment system in parts of their public administration (OECD, 2005, p. 10). Not surprisingly, we find substantial variations in the degree to which performance is actually applied throughout the public sector. Only a few countries seem to have a systematic and extensive performance-pay policy, namely Denmark, Finland, Korea, New Zealand, Switzerland and the UK (OECD, 2005, p. 12). Moreover, in many cases only managerial staff or specific departments or agencies are required to operate on a performance-pay basis (OECD, 2005, p. 11). While some systems favour individualised systems, other are more collective in focusing on working groups or even whole agencies. Finally, performance-pay systems have generally been linked to the decentralisation of the management of budgets and human resources, though again we find substantial variation between countries (OECD, 2005, pp. 36–7).

Notwithstanding important variations in the prevalence and the homogeneity of performance-pay systems in the public sectors of liberal democracies, they do seem to share the assumption that the civil servant is equipped with an innate entrepreneurial drive that may be harnessed for the purpose of improving public services. This assumption has above all been informed by public choice and rational-choice institutional theory. Performance-pay systems are driven by the assumption that the behaviour of civil servants is essentially structured by their pursuit of self-interest whether in terms of material benefits (money) or social benefits (prestige). Based on this assumption, performance-pay systems, if properly designed, may steer the behaviour resulting from the pursuit of self-interest in a direction that is more or less closely aligned with central political goals.

Over the last decade or so, much literature has criticised the understanding of the civil servant as being driven narrowly by self-interest for being, if not outright wrong, then at least far too simplistic and overlooking other strong motivating forces, such as altruism and the intrinsic value of the job (Perry, 2000). While I tend to agree with this critique launched by theories of public-service motivation and stewardship theory (Schillemans, 2013), these theories may unwittingly reproduce the image of an entrepreneurial civil-servant persona. True, public-service motivation theory may provide a much more nuanced image, but this theory too is driven by the governmental problematisation: how – by what sources and means – are the entrepreneurial drives of the civil servant best developed and maintained? On the face of it, public-service motivation and stewardship theory are akin to Weber's conception of the civil servant as driven by a *Beruf* (Max Weber, 1948a, 1948b). In particular, the notion of intrinsic value found in public-service motivation theory may seem close to Weber's notion of *Beruf*, or calling, which he linked to the pursuit of a particular profession characterised both by a specific expertise or savoir-faire and a particular set of moral values. However, whereas Weber was preoccupied with understanding the value-rationalities informing individual conduct, he never articulated this as the governmental question: how can the motivational drives of civil servants be harnessed in ways that make them continuously reflect on improving the efficiency and or quality of the public services? In sum, while public service motivation theory and likeminded theories may provide a much-needed critique and nuancing of the understanding of the civil servant, they are likely to contribute to the consolidation of the entrepreneurial civil-servant persona.

The making of the empowerment persona

So far, I have addressed a few of the many reflections and reforms seeking to promote an entrepreneurial civil-servant persona continuously concerned with improving the efficiency and quality of the public services. Yet entrepreneurship is not the only important new ethos that civil servants must subject themselves to. Another important ethos is that of empowerment. Today, civil servants are supposed no longer (only) to determine the technically speaking most effective solution but (also) to empower and thereby enable citizens to find their own solutions. As I will suggest below, this call comes from a surprising variety of academic and political sources.

Academic discourses on the need for the facilitating civil servant

Depending on political preference, we may loathe or laugh at former US President Ronald Reagan's one-liner: 'The nine most terrifying words in the English language are, "I'm from the government and I'm here to help"' (Reagan, 1986). However, from the far right to the far left, politicians, think tanks (OECD, 2011b), political philosophers (Barber, 1984; Daly, 1994), public-administration scholars (Denhardt & Denhardt, 2000; Callahan, 2007) and NGOs have for the last three decades or so lamented the paternalism and dependency created by public administrators seeking to provide services to those deemed in need. Also, despite their differences, they have coalesced around the virtues of empowerment and called for more enabling forms of public administration (Cruikshank, 1999). The call for an empowering or enabling public administration implies a kind of bureaucratic persona that differs fundamentally from Weber's ideal of matter-of-factness. Thus, at the most general level, the empowerment is not about ensuring the objective factuality of a societal problem to be analysed and handled by the civil servant, but about governing the subjective capacities of citizens and other so-called stakeholders to address the societal problem affecting them.

A brief exposure of a few prolific public-administration or management scholars over the last couple of decades may shed some light on the new kind of civil-servant persona deemed necessary for the early twenty-first century. The book *Reinventing government* has – no doubt correctly – been taken as the blueprint of New Public Management and the legitimation of market principles in public-service delivery. However, Osborne and Gaebler put a good deal of labour into expressing the importance of empowering local communities:

> It stands to reason that when communities are empowered to solve their own problems, they function better than communities that depend on services provided by outsiders. (Osborne & Gaebler, 1992, p. 51)

Osborne and Gaebler are adamant that community empowerment does not amount to a rolling back of government interventions. Rather, it entails a reformation of government and public-service delivery to become catalysts or facilitators of communities with a view to increase the capacity and responsibility of the latter to handle societal problems. Accordingly, Osborne and Gaebler refer to the example of the closure of the large mental institutions in the US and elsewhere in the 1970s as a failure, because government did not prepare and enable communities to deal with the mentally ill (Osborne & Gaebler, 1992, p. 73). In brief, the generalised solution to the kind of dependency resulting from public-service delivery is to empower citizens and communities by latching on to the norms and governing techniques of participatory democracy. This is a very far cry from the critical neoliberalism proposed by Hayek and Mises. Instead, Osborne and Gaebler are propagating a decidedly US communitarian version of constructivist liberalism.

Let us now compare Osborne and Gaebler's call for an empowering civil service with the *Public Value Management* approach suggested by Mark Moore, professor at the John F. Kennedy School of Government. The public sector is put into the world to create public value (Moore, 1995, p. 28). Refreshingly simple, but then the problem begins. If public value is defined by its ability to meet the needs of individual citizens, which is what Moore assumes, then how can public managers know what public value is and how to produce it? In the words of Moore, 'Public managers create public value. The problem is that they cannot know for sure what that is. Even if they could be sure today, they would have to doubt tomorrow, for by then political aspirations and public needs that give point to their efforts might well have changed' (Moore, 1995, p. 57).

Moore is here rearticulating the core neoliberal critique of government, namely its inability to ever get to know the diverse interests and preferences of individual citizens. However, instead of inferring from the epistemological finitude of government that the latter should be limited to a set of constitutional rules securing individual freedoms, Moore draws a quite different conclusion: government must show that it is actually creating something akin to public value by being more active and outward-reaching. True, Moore suggests that public managers use cost-benefit and ex-post evaluations to assess the value of policies and programmes, but he also emphasises the potential of civil servants engaging extensively with a wide range of private citizens and organisations. The latter suggestion of extensive engagement with a wide array of stakeholder is further developed in the follow-up publication *Public value. theory & practice* (Bennington & Moore, 2011). Several other academics have endorsed Public-Value Management and explained that it entails extensive interactions between the public administration and a variety of so-called stakeholders, such as neighbourhood leaders, those with knowledge about services as professionals or users, and those in a position of oversight as auditors or regulators (Goss, 2001). Public-value management thus hinges on an activist form of government in which civil servants engage in close dialogue with private stakeholders in order to ensure the legitimacy of the public administration and empower relevant stakeholders (Stoker, 2006).

In Chapter 3, I explored the bourgeoning research field of captured by the broad heading *new public governance*. This field too articulates the need for a more participatory form of public administration in the twenty-first century. Much of this work is based on the societal diagnosis by which the state is regarded as being under increasing fiscal pressures and pressure on its sovereignty from both global regimes and local governments. Above all, citizens, private companies, NGOs and other third-sector organisations are increasingly demanding influence on policies directly affecting them.

Accordingly, the key challenges facing civil servants are essentially navigating this complex strategic situation of diminishing state sovereignty and needing to latch on to the knowledge and resources of other public agencies and above all private actors (Koppenjan & Klijn, 2004). While most NPG scholars are remarkably sober about the many problems facing civil servants, and refuse to elevate NPG to a normative template of policy solutions (e.g. Pierre & Peters, 2005), the ontological diagnosis they make informs a very specific problematisation of government, namely: how can the civil servant facilitate and mobilise the resources of civil society? Thus, the obvious normative implication of the NPG literature is that civil servants must instil in themselves an ethos of empowerment in order to tap into the unused resources of citizens in tackling societal problems.

Techniques of empowerment

Apart from public administration discourses on the new civil-servant persona, a whole range of techniques have emerged over the last decade or two with a view to assisting civil servants in their role as facilitator. These includes public conversations, interactive ICT systems, participatory budgeting, citizen juries, study circles, collaborative policymaking and alternative dispute resolution (Salamon, 2002; Bingham et al., 2005). Other techniques or instruments include appreciative inquiry summits, consensus conferences, focus-group sessions and various types of workshops (Creighton, 2005, pp. 102–38). Several of these techniques have been employed in policy areas including urban renewal (Bingham, 2006), crime prevention (Steinheider & Wuestewald, 2008), transport (Koppenjan, Charles & Ryan, 2008), environmental protection and public health (Laverack, 2006). In sum, a number of techniques are available to civil servants seeking with more or – often – less success in trying to tackle societal problems by facilitating and unearthing the resources and self-steering capacities of relevant stakeholders.

Despite the emergence of a number of more or less novel techniques of deliberation and participation, techniques are not sufficient to transform public administration into an enabling or empowering organisation. Civil servants need to inculcate certain personal skills or, more broadly, a certain ethos or persona. Whether this person is called the collaborative manager (O'Leary & Bingham, 2009) or the boundary spanner (Williams, 2012), the civil servant must cultivate a mode of self-comportment that favours facilitation and collaboration with a view to empowering the users of public services. Lester Salamon has argued that the civil servant needs to be able to master negotiation and persuasion, collaboration and enablement (Salamon, 2002, pp. 15–17). He takes the latter to make relevant stakeholders participate in networks, persuading the stakeholders to collaborate, and provides these with enough incentive to elicit co-operative behaviour. Accordingly, the civil servant must turn themselves into objects of reflection and government in order to think about how they – as civil servants of the early twenty-first century – can use their skills to enhance the capacities of others. In short, in order to govern others, such as citizens deemed in need or network stakeholders, civil servants must govern hemselves in accordance with norms of activism and empowerment (Triantafillou & Nielsen, 2001).

Perhaps the best way to grasp the distinctiveness of a bureaucratic persona driven by an ethos of empowerment is to counterpose it to the Weberian notion of *Sachlichkeit*. *Sachlichkeit*, or matter-of-factness, constitutes a cornerstone in Weberian-style bureaucracy and the key condition for the technical superiority of bureaucracy. It is one thing to have civil servants impartially pursuing the goals stipulated by elected politicians within the existing framework of rules and regulations; it is another to have this pursuit undertaken by the systematic use of relevant expertise. Weber envisaged that civil servants in the modern bureaucracy would be educated and trained at the highest level to ensure that they would identify and develop the most effective instruments to implement given political goals. By implication, their choice of such instruments would be determined not by individual or political proclivities but by what was regarded by expert knowledge to constitute the most effective solution. To the extent that the Weberian-style expert bureaucrats needed to work on their own subjectivity, it entailed disciplining themselves in order to remain impartial from illegitimate influences. In contrast, the ideal civil servants of the early twenty-first century must constantly work on themselves in order become facilitators. As civil servants are no longer to deliver the solution to the problems of civil society, they must constantly reflect upon the ways in which can engage as a person with the lifeworld and interests of the relevant stakeholders and thereby stimulate their self-governing and problem-solving capacities.

Conclusion

This chapter has tried to show that the regulative ideals informing the making of the bureaucratic persona in many liberal democracies have seen a shift over the last few decades from ones emphasising the importance of upholding a strict separation between public and private spheres to ones stressing the need for civil servants to engage in extensive interactions with public and private stakeholders. This shift may be linked to a wider change in the political rationalities of government informing the working of the public sectors from classical liberalism to constructivist neoliberalism.

Whereas classical liberalism and critical neoliberalism both favour a limited and constitutional-oriented modality of government, constructivist liberalism emphasises the importance of an activist and enabling form of government. Of course, we should be careful not to exaggerate the strategic correlation between general political rationalities and specific codes of bureaucratic conduct. Yet the Weberian ethos of bureaucratic persona, emphasising rule-following, impartiality and *Sachlichkeit*, does seem to fit well into a classical liberal mode of government in which the separation between the public and private spheres or, more precisely, between state and civil society is absolutely fundamental. If the defining problem of classical liberalism (and partly critical neoliberalism) is how to exercise state power without undermining the self-governing powers of civil society, then it is absolutely fundamental for civil servants to internalise a distinction between public and private in their everyday work. Moreover, as representatives of state power, civil servants must make sure that their interventions in other people's lives in the name of the public interest adhere strictly to the constitutional rules that at once allow and limit the state's intrusion into civil society. Finally, while classical liberalism and critical neoliberalism both remain highly sceptical of the ability of experts to get to know the needs of civil society, the ideal of *Sachlichkeit* does seem compatible with these forms of liberalism to the extent that this ideal is employed not to identify some abstract notion of the public good but to undertake discrete and limited interventions to alleviate concrete social problems and market imperfections.

In contrast, the new bureaucratic norms of responsiveness, entrepreneurship and empowerment seem squarely at odds with both classical liberalism and critical neoliberalism. Today, a key critique of civil servants is that they adhere too closely to the many rules regulating their work and that they are unwilling to engage more directly with civil-society actors. To constructivist neoliberalism the problem is not how to limit the state's interventions in civil society but how to reform the state and the modus operandi of its employees in ways that mobilise the capacities and resources of individuals and groups in civil society. Above, I explored a few of the many techniques employed to steer the conduct of civil servants in to become more responsive to citizens' demands, to think constantly about how to improve the public services and to engage private stakeholders in the tackling of societal problems. If the defining problem for constructivist neoliberalism is how to spur the self-governing capacities of the individuals and groups of civil society, then the appropriate bureaucratic ethos is not those of impartiality, rule-following and *Sachlichkeit* but rather those of responsiveness, entrepreneurship and empowerment. Accordingly, the key recruitment criteria are neither a degree in law (to ensure a constitutional and rule-based mode of administration), competitive exams (to ensure merit and *Sachlichkeit*) or classical languages and culture. Rather, the suitable education for many civil servants is some kind of management study attuned to the governing of various performance systems on the one hand and the mobilisation of human resources both inside and outside the public sector on the other. If the recruitment to the middle and top echelons of many public administrations today seems to show no clearly discernible pattern apart from some kind of management education, it may very well be because what is required is less a definite expertise in a substantive policy area, though such skills are still widely found among frontline civil servants, but a generalised capacity to pay attention to political signals and, above all, steer organisational processes and their human relations.

The calls for performance-accountability and accreditation seem to fit quite well with the wider changes in the recruitment patterns emphasising general management skills and the norms of entrepreneurship in the public sector. However, as noted in the preceding chapter, the call for evidence-based policy seems to fit less well with these trends. In fact, it seems tempting to see the call for EP as a rejuvenation of Weber's ideal of *Sachlichkeit*. At least, the call for evidence-based policy entails that the public administration must constantly question itself, test its policy-delivery solutions and see to it that its interactions with citizens in order to better their situation are based on available evidence. EP then will encourage if not force the public administration and its employees to use and continually develop their use of professional knowledge and standards.

The persistence of some kind of *Sachlichkeit*, now in the form of EP, is but one indication that we are not seeing some kind of epochal change by which the bureaucratic norms of rule-following, impartiality and *Sachlichkeit*, are being wholly replaced by norms of responsiveness, entrepreneurship and empowerment. Rather, it seems that all the older, Weberian-type norms are still very much part and parcel of public administration in liberal democracies. In fact, many of the conflicts and contestations evolving around contemporary civil servants seem to reflect the clash between the old and the more recent norms of bureaucratic conduct (Minson, 1998; du Gay, 2000). The developments in the UK, which saw the adoption of the Constitutional Reform and Governance Act 2010, not only reflect the ongoing conflicts between older and more recent codes of conduct but also suggest that classical liberalism and its attention to control the exercise of sovereign power is still a highly influential political rationality. Even if most other liberal democracies have relaxed the regulations aimed at upholding the integrity of the civil service in the name of responsiveness and flexibility, Weberian-style codes of conduct continue to play an influential and legitimising force for the civil service.

This mix of distinct and partly contradictory codes of bureaucratic conduct puts many civil servants in a very difficult position. No matter what they do, their conduct may be criticised by one or more of the many norms that they are expected to conform to. If judged in terms of some of our leading sociological scholars, such unclear and unstable normative requirements are essentially bad as they are likely to lead to ontological insecurity (Giddens, 1991) or the corrosion of character (Sennett, 1998). However, if we hinge our critical analysis not on some more or less historically invariant anthropological normativity but rather on the civil servants' possibility for exercising freedom, i.e. the room for their ethical work, then the verdict may be a bit more complex. Yes, the normative terrain framed by the calls for responsiveness, entrepreneurship and empowerment is a highly power-laden one. And true, it is a sophisticated kind of power – liberal government – working through the freedom or subjectivity of the civil servant (Rose, 1999). Yet, the co-existence of quite distinct liberal rationalities of government creates a certain openness and strategic reversibility of the kinds of sovereign, disciplinary and governmental power exercised over civil servants. The space for bureaucratic ethics or self-work may even be enhanced to the extent that civil servants strategically exploit the co-existence of at least two distinct liberal rationalities of government and their distinct regulative bureaucratic ideals. Finally, we may speculate that some civil servants actually enjoy and take a professional pride in navigating in a normative terrain that favours responsiveness to citizens' needs, the continuous attempt to improve public-service provision and interactions with citizens in ways that may empower the latter.

Notes

1 Some countries, such as Belgium, France, Germany and Spain, have not made any substantial changes to the labour laws or statutes regulating civil-servant employment (Torres & Pina, 2004; van der Meer et al., 2013).

2 Here it matters less that some research indicates that Weberian-style public bureaucracies are no hindrance to innovation in the sense of coming up with new methods and solutions to policy problems (Jakobsen & Thrane, 2016).

3 The introduction of privatised tax collection in parts of the US at the end of the nineteenth century in order to incentive tax collectors constitutes an important exception to this pattern (Thorndike, 2001, p. 734).

9

Conclusion

This chapter first sums up the findings made in the previous chapters on the relationship between neoliberal power and contemporary public administration and management reforms. It then moves on to discuss the academic and normative implications of the findings.

The findings

I started this book by asking the question whether the kind of power exercised through contemporary public-administration and management reforms suggests that we are still in the age of neoliberalism. The short answer is yes, though with some important caveats. Above all, I have examined a very limited and by no means representative set of scholarly public-management discourses and administrative mechanisms. In particular, the mechanisms of accountability, performance-auditing, accreditation and EP constitute a very limited set of the universe of contemporary public-management schemes and techniques in liberal democracies. Moreover, performance-auditing and accreditation were deliberately chosen as extreme examples of the governmentalisation of government and, thereby, of the constructivist modality of neoliberalism.

Notwithstanding these qualifications, I think it is defensible to claim that constructivist neoliberalism does indeed constitute a crucial rationality of government underpinning public-administration and management reforms in the early twenty-first century. Even the quest for more traditional forms of accountability and EP are importantly informed by constructivist neoliberalism, though other rationalities of government are clearly at play here as well.

More precisely, Chapter 2 examined six distinct approaches critically analysing power in public administration and management. I argued that, while they hold a strong critical potential, the Foucauldian-inspired approach seems to be the one that most adequately interrogates the link between this kind of power and the various bodies of knowledge purporting to tell the truth about the best way to govern. Accordingly, Michel Foucault's analytics of power–knowledge relations in general, and his notion of government in particular, informed my examination of contemporary forms of public-management reforms. Yet, I also paid attention to how government and other forms of indirect power may work in tandem with coercive techniques of power, such as legal regulations and various economic and penal sanctions.

In Chapter 3, it was argued that neoliberalism may be understood as particular ways of problematising the art of governing, rather than seeing it as an ideology veiling and legitimising more substantial, material interests or as a discourse providing a more or less coherent blueprint for political and administrative reforms. On the basis of this understanding of neoliberalism, two general types of neoliberalism were identified: a critical and a constructivist problematisation of the art of governing. The former is akin to classical liberalism in that it is generally sceptical about the possibility and the benefits of state intervention because of the state's limited ability to be cognisant of the processes and needs of individual citizens and groups. Critical neoliberalism takes the market as a mechanism of information exchange. This market not only needs to be protected from the state, it also needs to be constructed by a proper constitutional framework. It is the recognition that the market is a thoroughly human artefact, a technical device of information distribution, rather than a more or less given sphere of freedom, that makes some, but not all, critical neoliberalists argue in favour of some level of state interventions in order to secure the functioning of the market. For constructivist neoliberalism, the key problematisation is not how the state can govern in a situation of ignorance and at the same time protect individual liberties but rather how the state can augment freedoms in ways that are instrumental to wider political and societal goals. Accordingly, instead of a critical ethos seeking to find the appropriate limits to state intervention, constructivist liberalism adopts an enabling ethos that interrogates not the need for state intervention but the efficacy with which state intervention may best facilitate and mobilise the resources of civil society and public administration itself. Finally, I argued that the mutual relation between critical and constructivist neoliberalism is agonistic rather than antagonistic. That is, they are clearly in conflict but they share certain basic premises that circumscribe the nature of their conflict.

The book then moved on to explore the emergence and employment of accountability systems in liberal democracies over the last few decades. Chapter 4 pointed out that these systems enabled the exercise of new forms of power. In particular, they enable governing at a distance by way of governmentalising those authorities, NGOs and even individual citizens engaged in providing public services to improve the well-being of society. I argued that the quest for accountability seems to be self-perpetuating in the sense that the technological possibilities created with the ICT revolution of the late twentieth century combined with neoliberal rationalities of government have given an impetus to constantly develop, improve and disseminate new and more sophisticated ways of accounting for activities linked to the making of public services. Thus, the interlocking of a system seeking to convert complex activities into more or less simple quantifiable accounts and a political rationality bent on unleashing and controlling the self-steering capacities and resources of public administrations and civil-society actors seems to amount to a self-perpetuating quest for new and better forms of accountability.

In Chapter 5 I argued that in the decades following the Second World War and with particular force from the 1980s, SAIs were increasingly supplementing their technical and legal control of executive government with performance auditing. Thus, SAIs seem to become part of the wider neoliberal concern of whether government governs itself efficiently. My analysis of performance auditing of public-health interventions showed that performance audits more or less systematically pay relatively limited attention to substantial outcomes in favour of an almost manic preoccupation with auditee procedures attuned to promote a solid knowledge base, clear division of labour and co-ordination between relevant partners, evaluation measures and guidelines for disseminating results.

Taking its point of departure in the complex sectors of public health and academia, Chapter 6 examined accreditation, a governing technique that may represent the most extreme case of the wider movement of making the public sector accountable for its actions. As a mode of governing, accreditation is above all characterised by its meta-character, a doubling of government by which government turns upon itself. On the one hand, to be accredited, the public agency subjected to accreditation must reflect upon itself along certain given standards, document how these reflections take place, what is decided to improve its services, and how these decision are adhered to in daily procedures and routines. On the other hand, the agency is usually by design given very wide room on how to translate the given standards into concrete guidelines, procedures and routines. In fact, institutions are usually forced by the accreditation scheme to choose or even develop their own guidelines for good practice and then document that they actually adhere to these. The introduction of accreditation in hospitals and universities cannot be reduced to a single, uniform neoliberal rationality. Rather the introduction of accreditation is informed by a historically unique blend of neoliberal rationalities and contingent political events some of which have little if anything to do with neoliberalism.

Chapter 7 examined the EP movement with a view to mapping and understanding how and why new experimental and statistical techniques for producing knowledge have spread from medicine to education, crime prevention, employment and other social areas. I argued that that EP sits somewhat uneasily with neoliberal rationalities of government, but it would be wrong to regard them as antithetical. At minimum, this kind of knowledge can be used by the public to hold the professions accountable to their decisions and actions within the said policy fields. EP may penetrate spheres of professional enclosures and modify relationships of authority between the public administration and the citizens it supposedly serves. Yet, it may also narrow down the discretion of professional choice exercised in the provision of public services to the point where the room for the exercise of freedom is so limited that we are dealing with sovereign power rather than liberal government. I argue that, to the extent that EP has gained political credence as a regulative ideal, it entails that the public administration must constantly question itself, test its policy-delivery solutions and see to it that its interactions with citizens in order to better their situation are based on available evidence. EP then will encourage if not force public administration and its employees to use and continually develop their use of professional knowledge and standards.

Finally, I argued in Chapter 8 that the regulative ideals informing the making of the bureaucratic persona in many liberal democracies have seen a complex and partly contradictory shift over the last few decades. On the one hand, we have seen the proliferation of regulative ideals stressing the need for civil servants to engage in extensive interactions with public and private stakeholders. This seems to have occurred at the expense of emphasising the importance of upholding a strict separation between public and private spheres. This shift may be linked to a wider change in the political rationalities of government informing the working of the public sectors from classical liberalism to constructivist neoliberalism. On the other hand, the persistence of some kind of *Sachlichkeit*, now in the form of EP, indicates that we are not seeing some kind of epochal change by which the bureaucratic norms of rule-following, impartiality and *Sachlichkeit* are being wholly replaced by norms of responsiveness, entrepreneurship and empowerment. This co-existence of quite distinct liberal rationalities of government creates a certain openness and strategic reversibility of the kinds of sovereign, disciplinary and governmental power exercised over civil servants.

In sum, the administrative reforms and mechanisms employed over the last few decades in the quest for accountability, credibility and evidence display a significant diversity in terms of their historical antecedents and their political rationality. Yet, these diverse forms of public-administration and management reforms do have something in common in that they all – albeit in quite distinct ways – seek to provide an answer to the constructivist neoliberal problematisations of government: how best to make public administrations govern themselves more effectively? To some extent, they are all part and parcel of the movement whereby neoliberal power exercised through the public administration turns back upon itself in order to become more efficient and provide better quality. It does so by constructing new ways of making the performance of the public administration visible and amenable to government.

Academic and political implications

If it is correct that the contemporary quest for accountability, credibility and evidence in the public administrations in liberal democracies is informed by neoliberal political rationalities, then where does that leave our understanding of neoliberalism? I have argued that in order to render intelligible the said kinds of power exercised through contemporary public-administration and management reforms we have to distinguish between two forms of neoliberalism: a critical one and a constructivist one. As argued in Chapters 2 and 3, most academic understandings of neoliberalism link it with a generalised faith in market-based solutions in which the role of the state is reduced to ensuring the functioning of the market and the competiveness or employability of its population. This understanding is in line with critical neoliberalism, a strand that can be identified not only in the writings of Ludwig van Mises and Friedrich Hayek but also in a range of libertarian thinkers. I also agree that a number of contemporary political reform ideas, in particular in the US but also to some extent in Western Europe, can be understood in these terms. However, the administrative reforms and mechanisms examined in this book have little if anything to do with market solutions. In fact, the proponents of these reforms do not even try to justify them as such. The reforms and mechanisms seeking to provide or, more precisely, produce accountability, credibility and evidence in public administration are not even seeking to limit state interventions. Rather they are expanding power in the sense that government is subjected to itself, i.e. government. What we are seeing is not the limitation of state interventions – and more space for civil society – but the governmentalisation of government.

In the attempt to grasp this expansion and folding back of power upon itself, modernity critiques, realist critiques, Gramscian-inspired discourse analysis and political economy approaches all seem to fall short, though in different ways. As I explained in more detail in Chapter 2, these approaches are either not questioning neoliberal rationalities at all (the realist critique and partially modernist critique) or are addressing neoliberalism in a rather narrow way with the effect of overstating the repressive aspects of neoliberalism and overlooking its immanent critique of power exercised through the public administration. One may object, in my view correctly, that (critical) neoliberalism's critique of state power is a very limited one. Even critical neoliberalism will mainly be concerned over the power exercised by the state and tend to ignore the forms of power exercised by corporations, organised employers and wealthy individuals. Nevertheless, when both the political left and the political right can agree to criticise NPM reforms, such as performance auditing, accreditation and the incessant quest for evidence, for being too resource-demanding, inefficient and encroaching on professional autonomy, then it is because much of these reforms goes against the grain of critical neoliberalism. Most political reforms of a critical neoliberal bent criticise NPM reforms and mechanisms not because they want to completely dismantle state power, which they regard as essential to protect individual liberties and market transactions, but because they see these public-management mechanisms as an excessive and wasteful form of government intervention. Thus, in order to understand the kinds of power analysed in this book, we must either nuance our understanding of neoliberalism, which I have tried to do here by developing the notion of constructivist neoliberalism, or allow for one or more political rationalities that are not liberal, or both.

In the cases of accountability, performance-auditing, accreditation and evidence-based policymaking, we do indeed find at play other political rationalities than constructivist neoliberalism. For example, in the case of accountability we find classical liberal ideals informing the control of the exercise of sovereign power by the elected executive. In the early stages of US accreditation, we found both concerns over professional autonomy and critical neoliberal ideas of ensuring a market for educational services. Finally, the quest for evidence in policymaking builds to a certain extent on classic Enlightenment ideals and the belief that expert knowledge can successfully be employed to improve policymaking, an assumption that critical neoliberals deplore. Notwithstanding the importance of these other political rationalities, I have a hard time seeing these as much more than strategic supplements to the constructivist neoliberal rationality that seems to pervade said reforms through and through. As mentioned in Chapter 3, other terms have been coined to distinguish between a more market-oriented and a more welfare-oriented liberalism, such as 'liberal new-welfarism' (Ferrera, 2013). I am quite sympathetic to this conception as it allows for a rationality both committed to welfare – in the sense of striving to provide equal life chances – and to liberty – in the sense of allowing for self-development and ensuring non-discrimination. However, this conception does not really help us grasp the movement whereby power or, more broadly, government turns upon itself. The kind of power encapsulated by the governmentalisation of government is not really about making concerns over welfare and liberalism meet. Rather, it is about constructing new ways in which government can be held accountable for its efficiency and effectiveness by itself. It is also about constructing new forms of regulated administrative freedom in the sense of urging, if not forcing, public agencies and civil servants to be active, constantly reflecting on how they can improve their services, and taking steps to do so.

Some Foucauldian scholars may object that the distinction between critical and constructivist neoliberalism does not make much sense. They may point out that according to Foucault one of the defining features of neoliberalism is exactly its constructivist element. As explained in Chapter 3, Foucault and Burchell characterised neoliberalism not by its immanent critique of state intervention but by its constructivist element (Burchell, 1996, pp. 27–9; Foucault, 2008, pp. 120–1, 259–61). In his lectures on neoliberal governmentalities evolving during the middle of the twentieth century, Foucault distinguished between an American modality emphasising the role of the free market (the Chicago School) and a West German modality emphasising the role of the state in securing the functioning of the market mechanisms (the Ordoliberalen) (Foucault, 2008). Both involved an element of constructivism, though this was much more extensive and intellectually argued in the making of the West German Social Market Economy approach. Unlike the US case, the task for the Ordoliberalen was not to make already existing markets function better but to build both a market and a state that could legitimately contribute to the making and managing of the former.

My point is not whether or not Foucault's account is historically correct but to stress that, if we want to understand contemporary reforms and mechanisms of power, we have to go beyond Foucault's analysis of the Chicago School and the Ordoliberalen, if for no other reason than that the two latter strands of thought showed little concern for improving the efficiency and quality of public administration. Put differently, it would be rather puzzling if we could simply assume that the kinds of neoliberal rationalities articulated during the middle of the twentieth century around the making and management of the economy would be the same as the one articulated more than half a century later around regulating the performance of government. While I do believe that we are still in an age in which neoliberalism is a predominant rationality of government, the kind of neoliberalisms articulated through contemporary public-administration and management reforms are best understood as evolving around two poles, critical and constructivist. Moreover, the latter constructivist one is clearly predominant, at least when gauged by the reforms examined in this book. In sum, in order to better understand contemporary forms of public administration and management reforms, there is a need for Foucauldian-inspired scholars to further discuss and develop the notions of neoliberalism on the one hand, and inquire into its strategic relationship with other political rationalities and instruments of power on the other.

Apart from conceptual elaboration of the notion of neoliberalism, I also think there is a need for more in-depth empirical studies of the public sector and public-management reforms in order to show just how power in public administration and management is actually working. In itself it is not very interesting to assert that contemporary power is informed by constructivist neoliberalism. What we need to know is how this rationality – potentially together with other political rationalities – is played out in concrete mechanisms, procedures and techniques of administration. What are the unexpected twist and turns? What new forms of domination are the more indirect and freedom-based forms of management linking up to? And, what new forms of freedom are encouraged and how are they used by local interests and struggles? Thus, we need more studies to expose how neoliberalism at once enables the exercise of new forms of power through public administration and management, on the one hand, and articulates various critiques of state power and encourages new forms of (regulated) freedom, on the other. In particular, we need to pay attention to the interplay and carefully assess the prospects and costs of the construction of new forms of regulated freedoms in the public administration rather than simply dismissing them out of hand as being just that: neoliberal.

This brings us to the political implications of my analysis. There are several features of the quest for accountability, credibility and evidence that deserve critique or to be problematised. In Chapter 1 and, in particular, Chapter 2, I accounted for some of the most important critical analyses of NPM reforms and their link to neoliberalism. While these critiques are very important, they uniformly overlook the absence of political limits to state intervention in the rationales of constructivist liberalism. In contrast to both classical liberalism and Hayek's critical neoliberalism, which essentially rested on an immanent critique of the epistemological impossibility of comprehensive state planning, and thereby a constant reminder of the dangers of governing too much, the constructive neoliberal thought has no such immanent concerns. This is not to say that constructivist neoliberalism is propagating state planning. Rather, it is concerned with constructing the practices of freedom or the capacities necessary for citizens and organisations to steer themselves properly, i.e. in line with contemporary norms of legality, civility, industriousness and entrepreneurship. I have striven to show that it is the same kind of constructivist ambition that is at stake in many public sector reforms, i.e. the attempt to make public organisations and civil servants take responsibility for meeting political goals and exercise their freedom properly by steering them at a distance. Constructivist neoliberalism then seems to offer few if any breaks on the ambitions of power exercised through contemporary public-administration and management reforms. At least, when it comes to governing government itself (public administration), current forms of rule seem very optimistic about the role of knowledge. Thus, the production of more and better knowledge seems to be taken as a necessary but also realistic precondition for making the public administration be governed – by others and by itself – in a more democratic and effective way.

How are we to assess this lack of immanent critique of the exercise of power found in many contemporary public-administration and management reforms? In principle, I find highly problematic any form of power that does not systematically ask itself whether it is really desirable or necessary to be exercised. In its pure form, constructivist neoliberalism has no such inbuilt brakes. Fortunately, contemporary administrative power is not informed by constructivist neoliberalism only. It is also informed by classical liberalism, critical neoliberalism and welfarist rationalities. Thus, the constructivist and, therefore, interventionist ambitions of constructivist neoliberalism is negotiated and restrained in the everyday exercise of power by other rationalities and forces.

But apart from the lack of immanent self-restraint, is neoliberal power really so problematic? I have tried to show that freedom is a fundamental feature of the mechanisms enabling the quest for accountability, accreditation and evidence-based policymaking. Here I am thinking of the new powers and responsibilities implied by the delegation of administrative discretion and de facto policymaking to public administration and its many types of civil servants. The clearest example of this is probably accreditation that often entails, at least in the public-health sector, that the professionals and employees act to define the standards and guidelines according to which they want to govern themselves and be assessed by others. These freedoms are important and should not be easily discarded as they may be seen as morally desirable to those enjoying them and may also be important for understanding why this kind of power seems to be so hard to fight and resist.

Yet, I have also indicated that these new forms of freedom also come with important limitations. While some kinds of activism, freedom and autonomy are seen as desirable, legitimate and even necessary, others are regarded as illegitimate and punished more or less severely. Thus, civil servants are under constant pressure to make their activities accountable, credible and based on evidence. They are expected to ensure that they constantly develop themselves and their work in ways that contribute to improve organisational performance, regardless of whether the standards for assessing this have been chosen by external superiors or by local civil servants themselves. In doing so, civil servants are supposed to exercise their freedom to choose or develop the methods that will improve their performance in the best possible way. They will often also be expected to contribute to the definition of what constitutes best practice in their area by developing and compiling evidence. In brief, such conduct cannot be reduced to rule-based obedience. In fact, public administrators and employees are told over and over again that they must be more innovative and take more initiatives and unleash their entrepreneurial drives and ideas to create an efficient public sector. For those civil servants who are unable or unwilling to play this more or less structured game of freedom, various illiberal forms of power may be employed, ranging from lowering of salaries to arresting of careers and firing people. I think it is our task as critical analysts to interrogate constantly the new management reforms and mechanisms both by way of refining our conceptualisation and by way of conducting empirical studies of concrete instances of the evolving forms of neoliberal power.

References

Aberbach, J. D. (1990). *Keeping a watchful eye: the politics of congressional oversight*. Washington, DC: Brookings Institution.

Aberbach, J. D., & Christensen, T. (2005). Citizens and consumers. *Public Management Review*, 7(2), 225–46. http://doi.org/10.1080/14719030500091319.

Agrawal, A. (2001). Common property institutions and sustainable governance of resources. *World Development*, 29(10), 1649–72. http://doi.org/http://dx.doi.org/10.1016/S0305-750X(01)00063-8.

Akkas, S. A. (2004). Appointment of judges: a key issue of judicial independence. *Bond Law Review*, 16(2), Art. 8.

Algemene Rekenkamer (2013). *Quality indicators in the care sector*. The Hague.

Algemene Rekenkamer (2015). *2014 Annual report of Netherlands Court of Audit*. The Hague.

American Hospital Association (2015). Fast Facts on US Hospitals. Chicago: AHA. www.aha.org/research/rc/stat-studies/fast-facts2015.shtml.

ANAO (2014). *Implementation of recommendations. The Auditor-General ANAO report no.8 2014–15 performance audit*. Canberra.

Ariely, D. (2008). *Predictably irrational: the hidden forces that shape our decisions*. New York: HarperCollins.

Arrow, K. J. (1951). *Social choice and individual values*. New York: Wiley & Sons.

Arrow, K. J. (1985). The economics of agency. In J. W. Pratt & R. J. Zeckhauser (eds), *Principals and agents: the structure of business* (pp. 37–51). Boston: Harvard Business School.

Australian National Audit Office (2015). *External review*. Canberra. Retrieved from www.anao.gov.au/About-Us/External-Audit.

Bäckström, H. (1999). *Den krattade manegen: Svensk arbetsorganisatorisk utveckling under tre decennier*. Uppsala University.

Baird, J.-A., Isaacs, T., Johnson, S., Stobart, G., Yu, G., Sprague, T. & Daugherty, R. (2011). *Policy effects of PISA*. Oxford: Oxford University Centre for Educational Assessment.

Baker, E. L., Barton, P. E., Darling-Hammond, L., Haertel, E., Ladd, H. F., Linn,

R. L., ... Shepard, L. A. (2010). Problems with the use of student test scores to evaluate teachers, *EPI Briefing paper, no. 278*. Washington, DC.

Baker, T. (2005). *The medical malpractice myth*. Chicago: University of Chicago Press.

Barber, B. (1984). *Strong democracy: participatory politics for a new age*. Berkeley: University of California Press.

Barber, B. (1998). *A place for us: how to make society civil and democracy strong*. New York: Hill and Wang.

Barry, A. (2001). *Political machines: governing a technological society*. London: Athlone Press.

Barry, A. (2012). Political situations: knowledge controversies in transnational governance. *Critical Policy Studies*, 6(3), 324–36. http://doi.org/10.1080/19460171.2012.699234.

Bauman, Z. (1989). *Modernity and the Holocaust*. Cambridge: Polity Press.

Becker, G. (1964). *Human capital*. New York: National Bureau of Economic Research.

Behn, R. D. (2001). *Rethinking democratic accountability*. Washington, DC: Brookings Institution Press.

Behn, R. D. (2014). PerformanceStat. In M. Bovens, R. E. Goodin & T. Schillemans (eds), *The Oxford handbook of public accountability*. Oxford: Oxford University Press.

Beller, A., & Has, R. (2014). New challenges for the cooperation between civil society and the public sector: the national voluntary service in Germany. In T. Brandsen, W. Trommel & B. Verschuere (eds), *Manufacturing civil society. principles, practices and effects* (pp. 116–35). Basingstoke: Palgrave Macmillan.

Bennington, J., & Moore, M. H. (2011). Public value in complex and changing times. In J. Bennington & M. H. Moore (eds), *Public value. theory & practice* (pp. 1–30). Basingstoke: Palgrave Macmillan.

Bevan, G., & Hood, C. (2006). What's measured is what matters: targets and gaming in the English public health care system. *Public Administration*, 84(3), 517–38.

Bezes, P., & Jeannot, G. (2011). The development and current features of the French civil service system. In F. M. van der Meer (ed.), *Civil service systems in Western Europe* (pp. 185–215). Cheltenham: Edward Elgar.

Bhatti, Y., Hansen, H. F. & Rieper, O. (2006). *Evidensbevægelsens udvikling, organisering og arbejdsform. En kortlægningsrapport*. Copenhagen: AKF Forlaget.

Bingham, L. B. (2006). The new urban governance: processes for engaging citizens and stakeholders. *Review of Policy Research*, 23(4), 815–26. http://doi.org/10.1111/j.1541-1338.2006.00234.x.

Bingham, L. B., Nabatchi, T., & O'Leary, R. (2005). The new governance: practices and processes for stakeholder and citizen participation in the work of government. *Public Administration Review*, 65(5), 547–58. http://doi.org/10.1111/j.1540-6210.2005.00482.x.

Birkeland, S., Murphy-Graham, E. & Weiss, C. (2005). Good reasons for ignoring good evaluation: The case of the drug abuse resistance education (D.A.R.E.)

program. *Evaluation and Program Planning*, 28(3), 247–56. http://doi.org/10.1016/j.evalprogplan.2005.04.001.
Bloom, H., Orr, L., Bell, S., Cave, G., Doolittle, F., Lin, W. & Bos, J. (1997). The benefits and costs of JTPA Title II-A programs: key findings from the National Job Training Partnership Act Study. *The Journal of Human Resources*, 32(3), 549–76.
Blunkett, D. (2002). Speech to the ESRC 2 February. London: Economic and Social Research Council. Cited from: Wells, P. (2007), New Labour and evidence based policy making 1997–2007, *People, Place & Policy Online* (2007), 1(1), 22–9.
Boden, R., & Epstein, D. (2006). Managing the research imagination? Globalisation and research in higher education. *Globalisation, Societies and Education*, 4(2), 223–36. http://doi.org/10.1080/14767720600752619.
Boltanski, L., & Chiapello, E. (2005). *The new spirit of capitalism*. London and New York: Verso.
Boström, M., & Garsten, C. (2008). The treadmill of accountability. In M. Boström & C. Garsten (eds), *Organizing transnational accountability* (pp. 231–49). Cheltenham: Edward Elgar.
Bouckaert, G., & Walle, S. van de (2003). Comparing measures of citizen trust and user satisfaction as indicators of 'good governance': difficulties in linking trust and satisfaction indicators. *International Review of Administrative Sciences*, 69, 329–43.
Bovens, M. (1998). *The quest for responsibility*. Cambridge: Cambridge University Press.
Bovens, M., Schillemans, T. & Goodin, R. E. (2014). Public accountability. In M. Bovens, T. Schillemans & R. E. Goodin (eds), *The Oxford handbook of public accountability* (pp. 1–20). Oxford: Oxford University Press.
Box, R., Marshall, G. S., Reed, B. J. & Reed, C. M. (2001). New public management and substantive democracy. *Public Administration Review*, 61(5), 608–19.
Bozeman, B. (2000). *Bureaucracy and red tape*. Upper Saddle River, NJ: Prentice Hall.
Braun, B. I., Koss, R. G. & Loeb, J. M. (1999). Performance measure data into the joint commission accreditation process. *Evaluation & The Health Professions*, 22(3), 283–97.
Brenner, N., & Theodore, N. (2010). Cities and the geographies of 'actually existing neoliberalism'. In G. Bridge & S. Watson (eds), *The Blackwell city reader* (pp. 411–18). Chichester: John Wiley & Sons.
Brewer, B. (2007). Citizen or customer? Complaints handling in the public sector. *International Review of Administrative Sciences*, 73(4), 549–56. http://doi.org/10.1177/0020852307083457.
British Government (1991). *The citizen's charter raising the standard*. London.
Brottsforebyggande Rådet (2004). *Effektiva polisiära åtgärder mot brott – En sammanställning av forskning och beprövad erfarenhet*. Stockholm.
Brown, D. M. (1999). Information systems for improved performance management; development approaches in US public agencies. In R. Heeks (ed.), *Reinventing government in the information age* (pp. 113–34). London: Routledge.

Brown, R. (2004). *Quality assurance in higher education: the UK experience since 1992*. London: Routledge.

Brown, W. (2006). American nightmare: neo-liberalism, neo-conservatism, and de-democratization. *Political Theory*, 34(6), 690–714.

Brubacher, J. S., & Rudy, W. (1968). *Higher education in transition: a history of American colleges and universities*. New York: Harper & Row.

Brubaker, R. (1991). *The limits of rationality: an essay on the social and moral thought of Max Weber*. London: Routledge.

Bruno, I. (2009). The 'indefinite discipline' of competitiveness: benchmarking as a neoliberal technology of government. *Minerva*, 47(3), 261–80.

Bruttel, O. (2004). Contracting-out and governance mechanisms in the public employment service. In *TLM.NET conference 'Quality in labour market transitions: a European challenge'*. Amsterdam: Royal Netherlands Academy of Arts and Sciences.

Bryane, M. (2012). Issues in anti-corruption law: how can code of conduct laws be drafted in order to reduce corruption in a public sector like Romania's. *European Law Journal*, 18(2), 289–322.

Buchanan, J. M. (1975). *The limits of liberty*. Chicago: Chicago University Press.

Buchanan, J. M., & Brennan, G. (1985). *The reason of rules*. Cambridge: Cambridge University Press.

Buchanan, J. M., & Tullock, G. (1962). *The calculus of consent: logical foundations of constitutional democracy*. Ann Arbor: University of Michigan Press.

Bundesrechnungshof (2015). History. Berlin. Retrieved from www.bundesrechnungshof.de/en/bundesrechnungshof/geschichte.

Burchell, G. (1996). Liberal government and techniques of the self. In A. Barry, T. Osborne and N. Rose. (eds), *Foucault and political reason* (pp. 19–36). London: UCL Press.

Burgess, A. (2012). 'Nudging' healthy lifestyles: the UK experiments with the behavioural alternative to regulation and the market. *European Journal of Risk Regulation*, 3(1), 3–30.

Cabinet Office. (1999). *Modernising government White Paper, CM4310*. London.

Callahan, K. (2007). Citizen participation: models and methods. *International Journal of Public Administration*, 30(11), 1179–96.

Cambridge University. (2015). Jerry Lee Centre of Experimental Criminology. www.crim.cam.ac.uk/research/experiments/.

Campbell Collaboration (2014). The monograph series Campbell systematic reviews. Retrieved 15 October 2015, from www.campbellcollaboration.org/lib/?go=monograph.

Campbell Collaboration (2015). What helps? What harms? Based on what evidence? Retrieved 10 October 2015, from www.campbellcollaboration.org/artman2/uploads/1/C2_GeneralBrochure_low_May09.pdf.

Campbell, D. T. (1969). Reforms as experiments. *American Psychologist*, 24(4), 409–29.

Campbell, D. T. (1974). Evolutionary epistemology. In P. A. Schilpp (ed.), *The Philosophy of Karl Popper* (pp. 413–63). La Salle: Open Court.

Campbell, D. T. (1978). Qualitative knowing in action research. In M. Brenner, P. Marsh & M. Brenner (eds), *The social context of methods* (pp. 184–209). London: Croom Helm.

Campbell, D. T. (1984). Can we be scientific in applied social science? In R. Connor, D. G. Altman & C. Jackson (eds), *Evaluation studies review annual* (9th ed., pp. 26–48). London: Sage Publications.

Campbell, D. T. (1997). *The experimenting society: essays in honour of Donald T. Campbell*. (W. N. Dunn, ed.). New Brunswick: Transaction.

Campbell, D. T., & Stanley, J. C. (1963). Experimental and quasi-experimental designs for research on teaching. In N. L. Gage (ed.), *Handbook of research on teaching*. Chicago: Rand McNally.

Caron, D. J., & Giauque, D. (2006). Civil servant identity at the crossroads: new challenges for public administrations. *International Journal of Public Sector Management*, 19(6), 543–55.

Catlaw, T., & Sandberg, B. (2012). 'Dangerous government': info-liberalism, active citizenship, and the open government directive. *Administration & Society, DOI: 10.11*. http://doi.org/DOI: 10.1177/0095399712461912.

Christensen, T., & Lægreid, P. (2002). A transformative perspective on administrative reforms. In T. Christensen and P. Lægreid, P. (eds), *New public management. the transformation of ideas and practice* (pp. 13–39). Aldershot: Ashgate.

Christensen, T., & Lægreid, P. (2006). Agencification and regulatory reforms. In T. Christensen & P. Lægreid (eds), *Autonomy and regulation: coping with agencies in the modern state*. Cheltenham: Edward Elgar.

Cialdini, R. (2007). *Influence: the psychology of persuasion*. New York: Harper Business.

Clark, D. (2000). Public service reform: a comparative West European perspective. *West European Politics*, 23(3), 25–44.

Clarke, J., & Newman, J. (1997). *The managerial state*. London: Sage.

Coalition for Evidence-Based Policy (2011). *Coalition mission & activities*. Washington, DC. Retrieved from http://coalition4evidence.org/wordpress/wp-content/uploads/Coalition-purpose-agenda-Sept-2011.pdf.

Compliance360 (2015). Healthcare: requirements addressed. Retrieved 22 October 2015, from www.compliance360.com/healthcare/requirements.asp.

Comte, A. (1877). *The system of positive polity*. London: Longmans, Green & Co.

Connell, R., Fawcett, B. & Meagher, G. (2009). Neoliberalism, new public management and the human service professions: introduction to the special issue. *Journal of Sociology*, 45(4), 331–8.

Cook, T. D., & Campbell, D. T. (1979). *Quasi-experimentation: design & analysis issues for field settings*. Boston: Houghton Mifflin.

Cook, T. D., & Gorard, S. (2007). Where does good evidence come from? *International Journal of Research and Method in Education*, 30(3), 307–23.

Council of the European Union (2000). Presidency conclusions (Vol. Lisbon). Brussels.

Cour des comptes (2015). History. Cour des comptes. Paris. Retrieved from www.ccomptes.fr/en/Our-organisations/History.

Creighton, J. L. (2005). *The public participation handbook*. San Francisco: Jossey-Bass.

Cruikshank, B. (1999). *The will to empower: democratic citizens and other subjects*. Ithaca: Cornell University Press.

Dahler-Larsen, P. (2014). Constitutive effects of performance indicators: getting beyond uninteded consequences. *Public Management Review*, 16(7), 969–86.

Daly, M. (1994). *Communitarianism: a new public ethics*. Belmont: Wadsworth Pub. Co, ITP.

Damgaard, B., & Lewis, J. (2014). Accountability and citizen participation. In M. Bovens, T. Schillemans & R. E. Goodin (eds), *The Oxford handbook of public accountability* (pp. 258–72). Oxford: Oxford University Press.

Danish School of Education (2015). The Danish Clearinghouse for Educational Research. http://edu.au.dk/en/research/research-areas/danish-clearinghouse-for-educational-research/.

Davies, J. S. (2011a). *Challenging governance theory: from networks to hegemony*. Bristol: Policy Press.

Davies, J. S. (2011b). The limits of post-traditional public administration: towards a Gramscian perspective. *Critical Policy Studies*, 5(1), 47–62. http://doi.org/10.1080/19460171.2011.555682.

Davoudi, S. (2006). Evidence-based planning – rhetoric and reality. *disP – The Planning Review*, 42(165), 14–24. http://doi.org/10.1080/02513625.2006.10556951.

De Bruijn, H. (2002). Performance measurement in the public sector: strategies to cope with the risk of performance measurement. *International Journal of Public Sector Management*, 15, 578–94.

De Walque, C., Seuntjens, B. & Vermeyen, K. (2008). *Comparative study of hospital accreditation programs in Europe*. Brussels: The Belgian Health Care Knowledge Centre.

Dean, M. (1999). *Governmentality: power and rule in modern society*. London: Sage Publications.

Dehue, T. (2001). Establishing the experimenting society: the historical origin of social experimentation according to the randomized controlled design. *The American Journal of Psychology*, 114(2), 283–302.

Denhardt, R. B., & Denhardt, J. V. (2000). The new public service: serving rather than steering. *Public Administration Review*, 60(6), 549–59.

Dent, M. (2006). Patient choice and medicine in health care – responsibilisation, governance and proto-professionalization. *Public Management Review*, 8(3), 449–62.

Desrosières, A. (1998). *The politics of large numbers: a history of statistical reasoning*. Cambridge, MA: Harvard University Press.

Dewey, J. (1957). *Reconstruction in philosophy*. Boston: Beacon Press.

Dibben, P., Wood, G. & Roper, I. (2004). *Contesting public sector reforms: critical perspectives, international debates*. Basingstoke: Palgrave Macmillan.

Dilulio, J. J. (2014). *Bring back the bureaucrats*. West Conshohocken, PA: Templeton Press.

Dobbins, M. (2014). French education politics after PISA and Bologna – rupture or continuite? In K. Martens, P. Knodel & M. Wintzio (eds), *Internationalization of education policy. a new contellation of statehood in education?* (pp. 115–40). London: Palgrave Macmillan.

Drewry, G., & Butcher, T. (1988). *The civil service today*. Oxford: Blackwell.

du Gay, P. (1993). Entrepreneurial management in the public sector. *Work, Employment and Society*, 7(4), 643–8.

du Gay, P. (1996). Making up managers: enterprise and the ethos of bureaucracy. In S. Clegg & G. Palmer (eds), *The politics of management knowledge* (pp. 19–35). London: Sage.

du Gay, P. (2000). *In praise of bureaucracy: Weber, organization and ethics*. London: Sage.

Duggett, M. (1998). New developments in public administration: country report Citizen's Charter: people's charter in the UK. *International Review of Administrative Sciences*, 64(2), 327–30.

Dunleavy, P. (1985). Bureaucrats, budgets and the growth of the state: reconstructing an instrumental model. *British Journal of Political Science*, 15(3), 299–328.

Dunleavy, P. (1991). *Democracy, bureaucracy and public choice*. New York: Harvester Wheatsheaf.

Eagleton-Pierce, M. (2014). The concept of governance in the spirit of capitalism. *Critical Policy Studies*, 8(1), 5–21. http://doi.org/10.1080/19460171.2014.883854.

Eardley, T. (1997). *New relations of welfare in the contracting state: the marketisation of services for the unemployed in Australia. Social Policy Research Centre discussion papers, no. 79* Sydney: University of New South Wales.

Editorial (2011). Special section on peer review. *International Journal of Government Auditing*, 38(4), 5.

Enders, J., & Westerheijden, D. F. (2014). The Dutch way of new public management: a critical perspective on quality assurance in higher education. *Policy and Society*, 33(3), 189–98.

EPPI Centre. (2015). About the EPPI-Centre. Retrieved 20 October 2015, from http://eppi.ioe.ac.uk/cms/Aboutus/AbouttheEPPI-Centre/tabid/63/Default.aspx.

Esping-Andersen, G. (1990). *The three worlds of welfare capitalism*. Cambridge: Polity.

Esping-Andersen, G. (2000). *A welfare state for the 21st century? Ageing societies, knowledge-based economies, and the sustainability of European welfare states. Report to the Portuguese presidency of the European Union, prepared for the Lisbon Summit*. Retrieved from http://lege.net/nnn.se/seminar/pdf/report.pdf.

Etzioni, A. (1993). *The spirit of community*. New York: Crown.

Etzioni, A. (1997). *The new golden rule: community and morality in a democratic society*. London: Profile.

EU (1999). Joint declaration of the European Ministers of Education Convened in Bologna on the 19th of June 1999. Brussels.

EU (2011). Directive 2011/24/EU of the European Parliament and of the Council of

9 March 2011 on the application of patients' rights in cross-border healthcare. Brussels.
European Commission (2000). *Eurobarometer 53: les Européens et les services d'interet generaux*. Brussels: CEC.
European Commission (2002). *Eurobarometer 58: Consumers' opinions about services of general interest*. Brussels: CEC.
European Commission (2003). *CCEB Eurobarometer European consumers and services of general interest*. Brussels: CEC.
European Commission (2004). *White Paper on services of general interest*. Brussels: CEC.
European Court of Auditors (2010). *Fagfellevurdering av Riksrevisjonen i Norge*. Oslo.
EVIDENS (2011). Cochrane: ingen evidens for akkreditering. *Ugeskrift for Læger*, 173(50), 3232–3.
Farrington, D. P. (1983). Randomized experiments on crime and justice. *Crime and Justice*, 4, 257–308.
Farrington, D. P., & Welsh, B. C. (2006). *Preventing crime: what works for children, offenders, victims, and places*. Philadelphia: Springer.
Feldbæk, O. (2000). Vækst og reformer – Dansk forvaltning 1720–1814. In D. Tamm (ed.), *Dansk Forvaltningshistorie, vol. I* (pp. 227–339). Copenhagen: Jurist- og Økonomforbundets Forlag.
Ferrera, M. (2013). Welfare state transformations: from neo-liberalism to neo-welfarism? In V. A. Schmidt & M. Thatcher (eds), *Resilient liberalism in Europe's political economy* (pp. 77–111). Cambridge: Cambridge University Press.
Flew, T. (2012). Six theories of neoliberalism. In *Emerging and enduring inequalities: the annual conference of the Australian Sociological Association 2012, 26–29 November 2012*. Brisbane: University of Queensland.
Folkers, A. (2016). Daring the truth: Foucault, parrhesia and the genealogy of critique. *Theory, Culture & Society*, 33(1), 3–28.
Fortes, M. T., de Mattos, R. A. & Baptista, T. W. D. F. (2011). Accreditation or sccreditations? A comparative study of accreditation in France, United Kingdom and Cataluña. *Revista Da Associacão Médica Brasileira*, 57(2), 1–8.
Foucault, M. (1977). *Discipline and punish: the birth of the prison*. London: Penguin.
Foucault, M. (1978). *The history of sexuality, vol. 1, An introduction*. London: Penguin.
Foucault, M. (1980a). The confession of the flesh. In C. Gordon (ed.), *Michel Foucault: power/knowledge* (pp. 194–228). New York: Harvester Wheatsheaf.
Foucault, M. (1980b). Truth and power. In C. Gordon (ed.), *Michel Foucault: power/knowledge* (pp. 109–33). New York: Harvester Wheatsheaf.
Foucault, M. (1982). The subject and power. In H. L. Dreyfus & P. Rabinow (eds), *Michel Foucault: beyond structuralism and hermeneutics* (pp. 208–26). London: The Harvester Press.
Foucault, M. (1987). *The use of pleasure: the history of sexuality, vol. 2*. London: Penguin.

Foucault, M. (1989). Problematics. In S. Lotringer (ed.), *Foucault live* (pp. 416–22). New York: Semiotext(e).

Foucault, M. (2008). *The birth of biopolitics: lectures at Collège de France 1978–79*. (M. Senellart, ed.). Basingstoke: Palgrave Macmillan.

Fountain, J. E. (2001). Paradoxes of public sector customer service. *Governance*, 14(1), 55–73. http://doi.org/10.1111/0952-1895.00151.

Freeman, T. (2002). Using performance indicators to improve health care quality in the public sector: a review of the literature. *Health Services Management Research* , 15 (2), 126–37. http://doi.org/10.1258/0951484021912897.

Friedman, M. (1962). *Capitalism and freedom*. Chicago: Chicago University Press.

Fung, A. (2004). *Empowered participation: reinventing urban democracy*. Princeton: Princeton University Press.

Funnell, W. (1998). Executive coercion and state audit: a processual analysis of the responses of the Australian Audit Office to the dilemmas of efficiency auditing, 1978–84. *Accounting, Auditing and Accountability Journal*, 11(4), 436–59.

Gendron, Y., Cooper, D. J. & Townley, B. (2001). In the name of accountability – state auditing, independence and new public management. *Accounting, Auditing & Accountability Journal*, 14(3), 278–10.

General Accountability Office (2005). *Transfer students: postsecondary institutions could promote more consistent consideration of coursework by not basing determinations on accreditation*. Washington, DC.

General Accountabilty Office (2012a). *Actions needed to evaluate the impact of efforts to estimate costs of reports and studies*. Washington, DC. Retrieved from www.gao.gov/products/GAO-12-480R.

General Accountability Office (2012b). *Government auditing standards. GAO-12-331G*. Washington, DC.

General Accountabilty Office (2015). *Hospital value-based purchasing*. Washington, DC.

General Accounting Office (1972). *Standards for audit of governmental organizations, programs, activities & functions*. Washington, DC.

Giddens, A. (1991). *Modernity and self-identity: self and society in the late modern age*. Cambridge: Polity.

Goetz, K. H. (2011). The development and current features of the German civil service system. In F. M. van der Meer (ed.), *Civil service systems in Western Europe* (pp. 37–65). Cheltenham: Edward Elgar.

Goldsworthy, D. (1994). The citizen's charter. *Public Policy Administration*, 19, 59–65.

Goss, S. (2001). *Making local governance work*. London: Macmillan Press.

Greenfield, D., & Braithwaite, J. (2008). Health sector accreditation research: a systematic review. *International Journal for Quality in Health Care*, 20(3), 172–83.

Greer, S. L., & Jarman, H. (2011). The British civil service system. In F. M. van der Meer (ed.), *Civil service systems in Western Europe* (2nd ed., pp. 13–35). Cheltenham: Edward Elgar.

Grizzle, G. A. (2002). Performance measurement and dysfunction: the dark side of quantifying work. *Public Performance & Management Review*, 25(4), 363–9.

Guthrie, J. E., & Parker, L. (1999). A quarter of a century of performance auditing in the Australian federal public sector: a malleable masque. *ABACUS*, 35(3), 302–32.

Habermas, J. (1989). *The structural transformation of the public sphere*. Cambridge: Polity Press.

Halachmi, A. (2014). Accountability overloads. In M. Bovens, T. Schillemans & R. E. Goodin (eds), *The Oxford handbook of public accountability* (pp. 560–73). Oxford: Oxford University Press.

Hall, P. A. (1993). Policy paradigms, social learning, and the state: the case of economic policymaking in Britain. *Comparative Politics*, 25(3), 275–96.

Halligan, J. (2013). The evolution of public service bargains of Australian senior public servants. *International Review of Administrative Sciences*, 79(1), 111–29.

Hansen, M. B. (2011). The development and current features of the Danish civil service system. In F. M. van der Meer (ed.), *Civil service systems in Western Europe* (pp. 99–114). Cheltenham: Edward Elgar.

Hansen, M., & Triantafillou, P. (2011). The Lisbon Strategy and the alignment of economic and social concerns. *Journal of European Social Policy*, 21(3), 197–209.

Hardt, M., & Negri, A. (2000). *Empire*. Cambridge, MA and London: Harvard University Press.

Harvey, D. (2005). *A brief history of neoliberalism*. Oxford: Oxford University Press.

Hasselbladh, H., Bejerot, E. & Gustafsson, R. (2008). *Bortom new public management. Insitutionell transformation i svensk sjukvård*. Lund: Academica Adacta.

Hayek, F. (1944). *The road to serfdom*. London: Routledge & Kegan Paul.

Hayek, F. (1960). *The constitution of liberty*. London: Routledge and Kegan Paul.

Hayek, F. (1976). *Law, legislation and liberty, Vol. 2: The mirage of social justice*. London: Routledge and Kegan Paul.

Hayek, F. (1979). *Law, legislation and liberty. Vol. III*. London: Routledge and Kegan Paul.

Hayne, C., & Salterio, S. E. (2014). Accounting and Auditing. In T. Bovens, M. Goodin and R. E. Schillemans (eds), *The Oxford handbook of public accountability*. Oxford: Oxford University Press.

Heinrich, C. J. (2007). Evidence-based policy and performance management: challenges and prospects in two parallel movements. *The American Review of Public Administration*, 37(3), 255–77.

Henning, N., & Rasmussen, H. B. (2013). Personal interview, conducted 3 September, Copenhagen, Rigsrevisionen.

Hillen, H. F. (2010). Quality assurance of medical education in the Netherlands: programme or systems accreditation? *Tijdschrift Voor Medisch Onderwijs*, 29(1), 73–9.

Hoecht, A. (2006). Quality assurance in UK higher education: issues of trust, control, professional autonomy and accountability. *Higher Education*, 51, 541–63.

Holmstrom, B., & Milgrom, P. (1991). Multitask principal-agent analyses: incentive contracts, asset ownership, and job design. *Journal of Law, Economics, & Organization*, 7, 24–52.

Homburg, V., & Bekkers, V. (2005). E-government and NPM: a perfect marriage? In V. Bekkers & V. Homburg (eds), *The information ecology of e-government* (pp. 155–70). Amsterdam: IOS Press.

Hood, C. (1991). A public management for all seasons? *Public Administration*, 69(1), 3–19.

Hood, C. (2006a). Gaming in the target world: the targets approach to managing British public services. *Public Administration Review*, 66(4), 515–21.

Hood, C. (2006b). The tools of government in the information age. In M. Moran, M. Rein & R. E. Goodin (eds), *The Oxford handbook of public policy* (pp. 469–81). Oxford: Oxford University Press.

Hood, C., & Dixon, R. (2015). *A government that worked better and cost less? Evaluating three decades of reform and change in UK central government*. Oxford: Oxford University Press.

Horkheimer, M., & Adorno, T. W. (1972). *Dialectic of enlightenment*. New York: Continuum.

Hoskin, K. (1996). 'The awful ideal of accountability': inscribing people into the measurement of objects. In R. Munro & J. Mouritsen (eds), *Accountability: power, ethos & the technologies of managing* (pp. 265–82). London: International Thompson Business Press.

Hoskin, K., & Macve, R. (1994). Writing, examining, disciplining: the genesis of accounting's modern power. In A. Hopwood & P. Miller (eds), *Accounting as a social and institutional practice* (pp. 67–97). Cambridge: Cambridge University Press.

House of Commons (2006). *Scientific advice, risk and evidence based policy making, HC 900-II*. London.

Humphrey, D., & Owen, C. (2003). Struggling for Supremacy: the case of UK public institutions. *Critical Perspectives on Accounting*, 41, 1–22.

Hunter, I. (2001). *Rival enlightenments: civil and metaphysical philosophy in early modern Germany*. Cambridge: Cambridge University Press.

IKAS (2012). *Indledning til den danske kvalitetsmodel for sygehuse, version 1* (Vol. 2012). Aarhus: IKAS.

Improbable Research (2012). Improbable Research. Retrieved from www.improbable.com/ig/winners/#ig2012.

Ingraham, P. W. (1995). *The foundation of merit: public service in American democracy*. Baltimore: Johns Hopkins Press.

Ingraham, P. W., & Moynihan, D. P. (2003). Civil service and administrative reform in the US. In J. Halligan (ed.), *Civil service systems in Anglo-American countries* (pp. 174–94). Cheltenham: Edward Elgar.

Institute of Education Sciences (2015). About the WWC. Retrieved 22 October 2015, from http://ies.ed.gov/ncee/wwc/aboutus.aspx.

INTOSAI (2004). *INTOSAI 50 years. 1953–2003*. Vienna.

INTOSAI Professional Standards Committee (2014). *Fundamental principles of performance auditing. ISSAI 300*. Vienna.

Jackson, S., & Bohrer, J. (2010). Quality assurance in higher education: recent developments in the United Kingdom. *Research in Comparative and International Education*, 5(1), 77–87.

Jakobsen, M. L. F., & Thrane, C. (2016). Public innovation and organizational structure: searching (in vain) for the optimal design. In J. Torfing & P. Triantafillou (eds), *Enhancing public innovatgoin by transforming public goverance?* Cambridge: Cambridge University Press.

Jay, M. (1996). *The dialectical imagination: a history of the Frankfurt School and the Institute of Social Research, 1923–1950*. Berkeley: University of California Press.

Jenkyns, R. (1980). *The Victorians and ancient Greece*. London: Blackwell.

Jensen, M. C., & Meckling, W. H. (1976). Theory of the firm: managerial behavior, agency costs and ownership structure. *Journal of Financial Economics*, 3(4), 305–60.

Joaquin, M. E., & Greitens, T. J. (2011). The accountability-performance link. *Public Performance & Management Review*, 34(3), 323–49. http://doi.org/10.2753/PMR1530-9576340301.

Jobert, B., & Muller, P. (1987). *L'ètat en action: politiques publiques et corporatismes*. Paris: Presses Universitaires.

Junger, M., Feder, L., Clay, J., Côté, S. M., Farrington, D. P., Freiberg, K., … Tremblay, R. E. (2007). Preventing violence in seven countries: global convergence in policies. *European Journal on Criminal Policy and Research*, 13(3–4), 327–356. http://doi.org/10.1007/s10610-007-9053-4.

Justitieombudsmännen (2015). Riksdagens Ombudsmän. Retrieved 3 August 2015, from www.jo.se/sv/Om-JO/Historik/.

Kickert, W. J. M. (2005). Distinctiveness in the study of public management in Europe. *Public Management Review*, 7(4), 537–63.

Kimmell, S. L., Marquette, R. P. & Olsen, D. H. (1998). Outcomes assessment programs: Historical perspective and state of the art. *Accounting Education*, 13, 851–68.

Kodate, N. (2010). Events, public discourses and responsive government: quality assurance in health care in England, Sweden and Japan. *Journal of Public Policy*, 30(3), 263–89.

Kooiman, J. (1993). Governance and governability. In J. Kooiman (ed.), *Modern governance: new government-society interactions* (pp. 35–48). London: Sage.

Koppenjan, J. F. M., Charles, M. B. & Ryan, N. F. (2008). Managing competing public values in public infrastructure projects. *Public Money & Management*, 28(3), 131–4.

Koppenjan, J., & Klijn, E.-H. (2004). *Managing uncertainties in networks*. New York: Routledge.

Kostadinova, P. (2015). Improving the transparency and accountability of EU Institutions: the impact of the Office of the European Ombudsman. *JCMS: Journal of Common Market Studies*, http://doi.org/10.1111/jcms.12245.

Kouzmin, A., Löffler, E., Klages, H. & Korac-Kakabadse, N. (1999). Benchmarking and performance measurement in public sectors. Towards learning for agency effectiveness. *The International Journal of Public Sector Management*, 12(2), 121–44.

Kowalczyk, L. (2007). Surprise check faults MGH quality of care. *The Boston*

Globe, 17 March, http://archive.boston.com/yourlife/health/diseases/articles/2007/03/17/surprise_check_faults_mgh_quality_of_care/?page=full.

Lafell, G., & Blumenthal, D. (1989). The case for using industrial quality management science in healthcare organisations. *Journal of the American Medical Association*, 262, 2869–873.

Larner, W., & Craig, D. (2005). After neoliberalism? Community activism and local partnerships in Aotearoa New Zealand. *Antipode*, 37(3), 402–24.

Larner, W., & Walters, W. (2000). Privatisation, governance and identity: the United Kingdom and New Zealand compared. *Policy and Politics*, 28(3), 361–77.

Lascoumes, P., & Le Gales, P. (2007). Introduction: understanding public policy through its instruments? From the nature of instruments to the sociology of public policy instrumentation. *Governance*, 20(1), 1–21. http://doi.org/10.1111/j.1468-0491.2007.00342.x.

Latour, B. (1987). *Science in action: how to follow engineers and scientists through society*. Buckingham: Open University Press.

Latour, B. (2004). Why critique has run out of steam? From matters of fact to matters of concern. *Critical Inquiry*, 30(2), 225–48.

Latour, B. (2005). *Reassembling the social: an introduction to actor-network theory*. Oxford: Oxford University Press.

Latour, B. (2010). An attempt at a 'compositionist manifesto'. *New Literary History*, 41(3), 471–90.

Laverack, G. (2006). Improving health outcomes through community empowerment: a review of the literature. *Journal of Health, Population and Nutrition*, 24(1), 113–20.

Leggett, T. (2003). What do the police do? Performance measurement and the SAPS. *Institute for Security Studies Papers*, 66, 1–15.

Lembruch, G., & Schmitter C. P. (1982). *Patterns of corporatist policy-making*. London: Sage.

Lemke, T. (2002). Foucault, governmentality, and critique. *Rethinking Marxism*, 14(3), 49–64.

Lester, M. S., Anheier, H. K., List, R., Toepler, S. & Sokolowski, S. W. (1999). *Global civil society: dimensions of the nonprofit sector*. Baltimore: Johns Hopkins Center for Civil Society Studies.

Lewis, J., & Triantafillou, P. (2012). From performance measurement to learning: a new source of government overload? *International Review of Administrative Sciences*, 78(4), 597–614.

Lindblom, C. E. (1959). The science of 'muddling through'. *Public Administration Review*, 19(2), 79–88.

Lindblom, C. E. (1977). *Politics and markets: the world's political-economic systems*. New York: Basic Books.

Lonsdale, J. (2015). Personal email communication, 6 October.

Lorentzen, H., & Henriksen, L. S. (2014). The invention and institutionalization of volunteer centers: a comparative analysis of Norway and Denmark. *Nonprofit and Voluntary Sector Quarterly* , 43(3), 589–608. http://doi.org/10.1177/0899764013476765.

Lowe, T. (2013). New development: the paradox of outcomes – the more we measure, the less we understand. *Public Money & Management*, 33(3), 213–16.

Lowndes, V., & Pratchett, L. (2012). Local governance under the coalition government: austerity, localism and the 'big society'. *Local Government Studies*, 38(1), 21–40. http://doi.org/10.1080/03003930.2011.642949.

MacKenzie, D., Muniesa, F. & Siu, L. (2007). *Do economists make markets? On the performativity of economics*. Princeton: Princeton University Press.

Majone, G. (1994). The rise of the regulatory state in Europe. *West European Politics*, 17, 77–101.

Majone, G., & Wildavsky, A. (1978). Implementation as evolution. In H. Freeman (ed.), *Policy studies review annual*. Beverly Hills: Sage.

Marx, K. (1994). Preface to A contribution to the critique of political economy. In L. H. Simon (ed.), *Karl Marx: selected writings* (pp. 209–13). Indianapolis: Hackett.

Mattson, I., & Strøm, K. (1995). Parliamentary committees. In H. Döring (ed.), *Parliaments and majority rule in Western Europe* (pp. 249–307). Mannheim: Mannheim Centre for European Social Research (MZES).

Maynard, R., Brown, R. & Schore, J. (1979). *The supported work demonstration: effects during the first 18 months after enrollment*. New York: Manpower Demonstration Research Corp. Retrieved from www.eric.ed.gov/PDFS/ED197223.pdf.

McGuire, L. (2001). Service charters – global convergence or national divergence? A comparison of initiatives in Australia, the United Kingdom and the United States. *Public Management Review*, 3(4), 493–524.

Meijer, A. J. (2007). Publishing public performance results on the internet: do stakeholders use the internet to hold Dutch public service organizations to account? *Government Information Quarterly*, 24(1), 165–85. http://doi.org/http://dx.doi.org/10.1016/j.giq.2006.01.014.

Mill, J. S. (1974). On liberty. In J. S. Mill (ed.), *Utilitarianism, on liberty, essay on Bentham*. New York: Meridan.

Miller, H. T., & Fox, C. J. (2007). *Postmodern public administration. Revised edition*. Armonk, NY: M. E. Sharpe.

Miller, J. W. (1972). *Organizational structure of nongovernmental post secondary accreditation*. Washington, DC: Catholic University of America.

Mincer, J. (1974). *Schooling, experience and earnings*. New York: National Bureau of Economic Research.

Minson, J. (1998). Ethics in the service of the state. In M. Dean & B. Hindess (eds), *Governing Australia*. Sydney: Cambridge University Press.

Mirowski, P. (2005). Economics/philosophy of science. In G. Steinmetz (ed.), *The politics of method in the human sciences: positivism and its epistemological others* (pp. 142–72). Durham, NC: Duke University Press.

Mirowski, P. & Plehwe D. (eds) (2009), *The road from Mont Pelerin: the making of the neoliberal thought collective*. Cambridge, MA: Harvard University Press.

Mitchell, T. (1998). Fixing the economy. *Cultural Studies*, 12(1), 82–101.

Moini, G. (2011). How participation has become a hegemonic discursive resource:

towards an interpretivist research agenda. *Critical Policy Studies*, 5(2), 149–68. http://doi.org/10.1080/19460171.2011.576524.

Mommsen, W. (1974). *The age of bureaucracy*. Oxford: Blackwell.

Moore, M. (1995). *Creating public value*. Cambridge, MA: Harvard University Press.

Morel, N., Palier, B., & Palme, J. (2012a). Beyond the Welfare State as we knew it? In N. Morel, B. Palier & J. Palme (eds), *Towards a social investment Welfare State? Ideas, policies and challenges* (pp. 1–31). Bristol: Policy Press.

Morel, N., Palier, B., & Palme, J. (2012b). *Towards a social investment Welfare State? Ideas, policies and challenges*. Bristol: Policy Press.

Morse, E. (1981). Auditing efficiency and economy. In B. Geist (ed.), *State audit: developments in public accountability* (pp. 199–216). Basingstoke: Macmillan.

Mosse, D. (1997). The symbolic making of a common property resource: history, ecology and locality in a tank-irrigated landscape in South India. *Development and Change*, 28, 467–504.

Mulgan, R. (2000). 'Accountability': an ever expanding concept? *Public Administration*, 78(3), 555–73.

Mulgan, R. (2003). *Holding power to account: accountability in modern democracies*. Basingstoke: Palgrave Macmillan.

Muller, P. (1995). Les politiques publiques comme construction d'un rapport au monde [Public policies as the framing of a perception of reality]. In A. Faure, G. Pollet & P. Warin (eds), *La construction du sens dans les politiques publiques: débats autour de la notion de référentiel* [*The construction of meaning in public policies. Debates on the notion of referential*] (pp. 153–81). Paris: L'Harmattan.

Muniesa, F., & Linhardt, D. (2011). Trials of explicitness in the implementation of public management reform. *Critical Perspectives on Accounting*, 22(6), 550–66. http://doi.org/http://dx.doi.org/10.1016/j.cpa.2011.06.003.

National Audit Office (2004). *International peer review of the value for money practice of the Office of the Auditor General of Canada – peer review report*. London.

National Audit Office (2014a). *Adult social care in England: overview*. London.

National Audit Office (2014b). *Out-of-hours GP services in England*. London.

National Audit Office (2015a). History of the NAO. Retrieved 10 October 2015, from www.nao.org.uk/about-us/our-work/history-of-the-nao/.

National Audit Office (2015b). *Progress in improving cancer services and outcomes in England*. London.

National Committee of Inquiry into Higher Education (1997). *Higher education in the learning society*. London: HMSO.

National Institute of Justice (2014). *25 years of criminal justice research*. Washington, DC.

National Institute of Justice (2015a). About crimesolutions.org. Retrieved 22 October 2015, from www.crimesolutions.gov/.

National Institute of Justice (2015b). NIJ tests and evaluates programs. Retrieved 23 October 2015, from www.nij.gov/topics/technology/standards-testing/pages/welcome.aspx.

Newman, J. (2000). Beyond the new public management? Modernizing public services. In J. Clarke, S. Gewirtz & E. McLauglin (eds), *New managerialism – new welfare?* (pp. 45–61). London: Sage.

Nikos, M. (2001). Trends of Administrative reform in Europe: towards administrative convergence? *International Public Management Review*, 2(2), 39–53.

Niskanen, W. (1971). *Bureaucracy and representative government*. Chicago: Aldine, Atherton.

North Central Association of Colleges and Schools (1993). *A Handbook of accreditation*. Tempe, AZ.

Nozick, R. (1974). *Anarchy, state and utopia*. Oxford: Blackwell.

O'Leary, R., & Bingham, L. B. (2009). *The collaborative public manager: new ideas for the twenty-first century*. Washington, DC: Georgetown University Press.

Oakley, A., Gough, D., Oliver, S. & Thomas, J. (2005). The politics of evidence and methodology: lessons from the EPPI-Centre. *Evidence & Policy*, 1(1), 5–31.

Öberg, S. A. (2003). Förvaltning og revision. In I. Mattson & O. Petterson (eds), *Svensk Författningspolitik* (pp. 148–62). Stockholm: SNS Förlag.

OECD (1995). *Governance in transition: public management reforms in OECD countries*. Paris: OECD/PUMA.

OECD (2003). *From red tape to smart tape: administrative simplification in OECD countries*. Paris.

OECD (2005). *Performance-related pay policies for government employees*. Paris. Retrieved from www.oecd-ilibrary.org/governance/performance-related-pay-policies-for-government-employees_9789264007550-en.

OECD (2009a). *Community capacity building creating a better future together*. Paris.

OECD (2009b). *Focus on citizens: public engagement for better policy and services*. Paris.

OECD (2009c). *Privatisation in the 21st century: recent experiences of OECD countries*. Paris.

OECD (2011a). *Demand-side innovation policies*. Paris.

OECD (2011b). *Partnership for democratic governance: concluding report 2007–2011*. Paris.

OECD (2011c). *Together for better public services: partnering with citizens and civil society*. Paris.

OECD (2015). PISA: background and basics. Retrieved 24 October 2015, from www.oecd.org/pisa/aboutpisa/pisafaq.htm.

Office of the Auditor General Canada (2005). *International peer review of the performance audit practice of the United States Government Accountability Office*. Ottawa: Office of the Auditor General Canada.

Office of the Auditor General Canada (2011). *Key information for policymakers to assess efforts to improve quality while reducing costs GAO*. Ottawa.

Office of the Auditor General Canada (2013). *Spring report of the Auditor General of Canada, chapter* 5. Ottawa.

Office of the Auditor General Canada (2015a). *BEHAVIORAL HEALTH. Options for low-income adults to receive treatment in selected states*. Ottawa.

Office of the Auditor General Canada (2015b). *MEDICAID: key issues facing the program*. Ottawa.

Office of the Auditor General of Norway (2014). *International peer review of the performance and financial audit practices of the United States Government Accountability Office*. Oslo. Retrieved from www.gao.gov/about/international peerreviewrpt2014.pdf.

Olson, M. (1965). *The logic of collective action: public goods and the theory of groups*. Cambridge, MA: Harvard University Press.

Osborne, D., & Gaebler, T. (1992). *Reinventing government*. Reading, MA: Addison-Wesley.

Osborne, G., & Thaler, R. (2010). We can make you behave. Opinion, *The Guardian*, 28 January.

Osborne, S. P. (2010). Introduction: the (new) public governance: a suitable case for treatment? In S. P. Osborne (ed.), *The new public governance?* (pp. 1–16). London: Routledge.

Osborne, T. (1994). Bureaucracy as a vocation: governmentality and administration in nineteenth-century Britain. *Journal of Historical Sociology*, 7(3), 289–313.

Ostrom, E. (1990). *Governing the commons: the evolution of institutions for collective action*. Cambridge: Cambridge University Press.

Outcomes Assessment Committee (1993). *Report of the 1992–93 Outcomes Assessment Committee*. Sarasota, FL.

Overbeek, H. (1993). *Restructuring hegemony in the global political economy: rise of transnational neo-liberalism in the 1980s*. London: Routledge.

Overbeek, H., & Van Appeldoorn, B. (2012). *Neoliberalism in crisis*. Basingstoke: Palgrave.

Palier, B. (2007). Tracking the evolution of a single instrument can reveal profound changes: the case of funded pensions in France. *Governance*, 20(1), 85–107. http://doi.org/10.1111/j.1468-0491.2007.00345.x.

Palm, W., & Glinos, I. A. (2011). Enabling patient mobility in the EU: between free movement and coordination. In E. Mossialos, G. Permanand, R. Baeten & T. K. Hervey (eds), *Health systems governance in Europe: the role of EU law and policy* (pp. 509–60). Cambridge: Cambridge University Press.

PAT-Net (2015). Public Administration Theory Network. PAT-Net. Retrieved from www.patheory.net/.

Paul, E. F. (2004). Hayek on Monopoly and antitrust in the crucible of United States vs. Microsoft. *NYU Journal of Law and Liberty*, 1, 167–204.

Pawson, R. (2006). *Evidence-based policy: a realist perspective*. London: Sage.

Pech, J. (1997). *Voice, choice and contract: customer focus in programs for unemployed people. Policy discussion paper, no. 9*. Canberra: Department of Social Security.

Peck, J. (2010). *Constructions of neoliberal reason*. Oxford: Oxford University Press.

Pereyra, M. A., Kotthoff, H. Y. & Cowen, R. (2011). *PISA under examination: changing knowledge, changing tests, and changing schools*. Rotterdam: SensePublishers. http://doi.org/http://dx.doi.org/10.1007/978-94-6091-740-0.

Perry, J. L. (2000). Bringing society in: toward a theory of public service motivation. *Journal of Public Administration, Research and Theory*, 10(2), 471–88.

Peters, G. B. (2015). E-mail correspondence, 7 December.

Petrakaki, D., Hayes, N. & Introna, L. (2009). Narrowing down accountability

through performance monitoring technology. *Qualitative Research in Accounting & Management*, 6(3), 160–79. http://doi.org/10.1108/11766090910973911.
Petrosino, A. (2013). Reflections on the genesis of the Campbell Collaboration. *The Experimental Criminologist*, 8 (July), 9–12.
Pidd, M. (2005). Perversity in public service performance measurement. *International Journal of Productivity and Performance Management*, 54(5/6), 482–93. http://doi.org/10.1108/17410400510604601.
Pierre, J., & Peters, B. G. (2005). *Governing complex societies: trajectories and scenarios*. Basingstoke: Palgrave Macmillan.
Pilkington, C. (1999). *The civil service in Britain today*. Manchester: Manchester University Press.
Plant, R. (2009). *The neo-liberal state*. Oxford: Oxford University Press.
Plato (1930). *The Republic* (P. Shorey, Ed.). London: William Heinemann.
Pollitt, C. (2003). Performance audit in Western Europe: trends and choices. *Critical Perspectives on Accounting*, 14(1–2), 157–70.
Pollitt, C., & Bouckaert, G. (2011). *Public management reform: a comparative analysis* (3rd edition). Oxford: Oxford University Press.
Pollitt, C., & Summa, H. (1997). Reflexive watchdogs? How supreme audit institutions account for themselves. *Public Administration*, 75(2), 313–36. Retrieved from http://dx.doi.org/10.1111/1467-9299.00063.
Popper, K. R. (1966). *The open society and its enemies* (5th revised edition). London: Routledge & Kegan Paul.
Posner, P. L., & Shahan, A. (2014). Audit institutions. In M. Bovens, R. E. Goodin and T. Schillemans (eds), *Oxford handbook of public accountability*. Oxford: Oxford University Press.
Power, M. (1996). Making things auditable. *Accounting, Organizations and Society*, 21(2–3), 289–315.
Power, M. (1997). *The audit society: rituals of verification*. Oxford: Oxford University Press.
Power, M. (2003). Evaluating the audit explosion. *Law & Policy*, 25(3), 185–202.
Powers, E., & Witmer, H. (1951). *An experiment in the prevention of delinquency*. New York: Columbia University Press.
Prais, S. J. (2003). Cautions on OECD'S recent educational survey (PISA). *Oxford Review of Education*, 29(2), 139–63. http://doi.org/10.1080/0305498032000080657.
Pressman, J., & Wildavsky, A. (1973). *Implementation: how great expectations in Washington are dashed in Oakland; or, Why it's amazing that federal programs work at all: this being a saga of the Economic Development Administration as told by two sympathetic observers who seek to build morals* (3rd edition). Berkeley: University of California Press.
Putnam, R. (1995a). Bowling alone: America's declining social capital. *Journal of Democracy*, 6(1), 65–78.
Putnam, R. (1995b). Tuning in, tuning out: the strange disappearance of social capital in America. *PS: Political Science and Politics*, 28(4), 664–83.

Radcliffe, V. S. (1998). Efficiency audit: an assembly of rationalities and programmes. *Accounting, Organizations and Society*, 23(4), 377–410.

Rawls, J. (1972). *A theory of justice*. Oxford: Oxford University Press.

Reagan, R. (1986). News conference, 12 August. Chicago, IL. www.presidency.ucsb.edu/ws/?pid=37733.

Rees, R. (1985). The theory of principal and agent – Part I. *Bulletin of Economic Research*, 37(1), 3–26.

Reeves, R. (2004). *Accountability for learning: how teachers and school leaders can take charge*. Alexandria, VA: Association for Supervision and Curriculum Development.

Resnick, D. P. (1987). Assessment, curriculum, and expansion: a historical perspective. *New Directions for Higher Education*, 59, 77–88.

Rhodes, R. A. W. (1994). The hollowing out of the state. *Political Quarterly*, 65, 138–51.

Richards, D., & Smith, M. (2006). The tensions of political control and administrative autonomy: from NPM to a reconstituted Westminster model. In T. Christensen & P. Lægreid (eds), *Autonomy and regulation: coping with agencies in the modern state* (pp. 181–202). Cheltenham: Edward Elgar.

Rigsrevisionen (2013). *Rigsrevisionens virksomhed i 2012*. Copenhagen.

Rigsrevisionen (2015a). *Evaluering af beretninger*. Copenhagen.

Rigsrevisionen (2015b). *Rigsrevisionens aktiviteter til evaluering af effekt og kvalitet*. Copenhagen.

Riksrevisjonen. (2015). *Riksrevisjonens undersøkelse av offentlig folkehelsearbeid Dokument 3:11*. Oslo.

Roberts, J. S., Coale, J. G. Redman, R. R. (1987). A history of the Joint Commission on Accreditation of Hospitals. *Journal of the American Medical Association*, 258(7), 936–40.

Rose, N. (1996). Governing 'advanced' liberal democracies. In A. Barry, T. Osborne & N. Rose (eds), *Foucault and Political Reason* (pp. 37–64). London: UCL Press.

Rose, N. (1999). *Powers of freedom*. Cambridge: Cambridge University Press.

Ross, G. (1995). *Jacques Delors and European integration*. Cambridge: Polity Press.

Rossi, P. H., Freeman, H. E. & Lipsey, M. W. (1999). *Evaluation: a systematic approach*. Thousand Oaks, CA: Sage Publications.

Rudd, K. (2010). Prime Minister: Address to heads of agencies and members of senior executive service, 30 April 2008. In Australian Government Productivity Commission, *Strengthening evidence-based policy in the Australian Federation. Roundtable proceedings. Canberra, 17–18 August 2009*. Melbourne: Commonwealth of Australia.

Sahlin-Andersson, K. (2002). National, international and transnational constructions of new public management. In T. Christensen & P. Lægreid (eds), *New public management: the transformation of ideas and practice* (pp. 43–72). Aldershot: Ashgate.

Sahlin-Andersson, K., & Engwall, L. (2002). *The expansion of management knowledge. carriers, flows, and sources*. Stanford: Stanford University Press.

Salamon, L. M. (2002). *The tools of government*. Oxford: Oxford University Press.

Sanderson, I. (2009). Intelligent policy making for a complex world: pragmatism, evidence and learning. *Political Studies*, 57(4), 699–719.

Sanger, M. B. (2003). *The welfare marketplace: privatization and welfare reform*. Washington, DC: Brookings Institution.

Sanjay, P. K., & Scott, P. G. (2002). Red tape: a review and assessment of concepts and measures. *J-PART*, 12(4), 553–80.

Sareen, M. (2014). Evidens er bare sund fornuft. Altinget.dk. www.altinget.dk/artikel/sareen-evidens-er-bare-sund-fornuft.

Schiavo, L. L. (2000). Quality standards in the public sector: differences between Italy and the UK in the Citizen's Charter initiative. *Public Administration*, 78(3), 679–98.

Schillemans, T. (2008). Accountability in the shadow of hierarchy: the horizontal accountability of agencies. *Public Organization Review*, 8, 175–94.

Schillemans, T. (2013). Moving beyond the clash of interests: on stewardship theory and the relationships between central government departments and public agencies. *Public Management Review*, 15(4), 541–62.

Schmidt, V. A., & Radaelli, C. M. (2004). Policy change and discourse in Europe: conceptual and methodological issues. *West European Politics*, 27(2), 183–210.

Schmidt, V. A., & Thatcher, M. (2013). Theorizing ideational continuity: the resilience of neo-liberal ideas in Europe. In *Resilient liberalism in Europe's political economy* (pp. 1–50). Cambridge: Cambridge University Press.

Schmitter C., P. (1974). Still the century of corporatism? *The Review of Politics*, 36(1), 85–131.

Schultz, T. W. (1961). Investment in human capital. *American Economic Review*, 51(1), 1–17.

Schumacher, E. F. (1995). *A guide for the perplexed*. London: Vintage Books.

Schwartz, S., & Westerheijden, D. F. (2004). *Accreditation and evaluation in the European higher education area*. Dordrecht: Springer.

Schwartz, S., & Westerheijden, D. F. (2007a). *Accreditation and Evaluation in the European Higher Education Area*. Dordrecht: Springer.

Schwartz, S., & Westerheijden, D. F. (2007b). Accreditation in the framework of evaluation activities: a comparative study in the European higher education area. In D. F. Westerheijden & S. Schwartz (eds), *Accreditation and evaluation in the European higher education area* (pp. 1–41). Dordrecht: Springer.

Scott, J. E. (1998). *Seeing like a state: how certain schemes to improve the human condition have failed*. New Haven: Yale University Press.

Scrivens, E. (1995). *Accreditation: protecting the professional or the consumer?* Buckingham: Open University Press.

Sebkova, H. (2002). Accreditation and quality assurance in Europe. *Higher Education in Europe*, 27(3), 239–47.

Selden, W. K. (1960). Why accreditation? *The Journal of Higher Education*, 31(6), 296–301.

Selznick, P. (1994). *The moral commonwealth: social theory and the promise of community*. Berkeley: University of California Press.

Sennett, R. (1998). *The corrosion of character: the personal consequences of work in the new capitalism*. New York: Norton.

Sevillia, M., & Ruffner, J. (2004). Public sector modernisation: modernising accountability and control. *OECD Journal on Budgeting*, 4(2), 123–41.

Shadish, W. R., & Epstein, R. (1987). Patterns of program evaluation practice among members of Evaluation Research Society and Evaluation Network. *Evaluation Review*, 11, 555–90.

Sharma, N. (2007). Interactions and interrogations: negotiating and performing value for money reports. *Financial Accountability & Management*, 23(3), 289–311.

Shaw, C. D. (2006). Accreditation in European healthcare. *Joint Commission Journal on Quality and Patient Safety*, 32(5), 266–75.

Shaw, C. D., Kutryba, B., Braitwaite, J., Bedlicki, M. & Warunek, A. (2010). Sustainable health care accreditation: messages from Europe in 2009. *International Journal for Quality in Health Care*, 22(5), 341–50.

Simon, H. (1946). The proverbs of administration. *Public Administration Review*, 6(1), 53–67.

Skolnik, M. L. (2010). Quality assurance in higher education as a political process. *Higher Education, Management and Policy*, 22(1), 1–20.

Smith, A. (1996). Mad cows and ecstasy: chance and choice in an evidence-based society. *Journal of the Royal Statistical Society. Series A (Statistics in Society)*, 159(3), 367–83. http://doi.org/citeulike-article-id:7205425\rdoi:10.2307/2983324.

Smith, G. (2009). Citizen oversight of independent police services: bifurcated accountability, regulation creep, and lesson learning. *Regulation & Governance*, 3(4), 421–41. http://doi.org/10.1111/j.1748-5991.2009.01061.x.

Smith, M. J. (2010). From big government to big society: changing the state–society balance. *Parliamentary Affairs*, 63(4), 818–33.

Smith, P. (1995). On the unintended consequences of publishing performance data in the public sector. *International Journal of Public Administration*, 18(2&3), 277–310.

So ein Ding müssen wir auch haben. (1999). *Ugeskrift for Læger*, 161(47), 6512–15.

Sørensen, E., & Triantafillou, P. (2009). The politics of self-governance: an introduction. In E. Sørensen & P. Triantafillou (eds), *The politics of self-governance* (pp. 1–22). Farnham: Ashgate.

Springer, S. (2012). Neoliberalism as discourse: between Foucauldian political economy and Marxian poststructuralism. *Critical Discourse Studies*, 9(2), 133–47. http://doi.org/10.1080/17405904.2012.656375.

Steiner, P. M., Wroblewski, A. & Cook, T. D. (2009). Randomized experiments and quasi-experimental designs in educational research. In K. E. Ryan & J. B. Cousins (eds), *The SAGE international handbook of educational evaluation* (pp. 75–97). London: Sage Publications.

Steinheider, B., & Wuestewald, T. (2008). From the bottom-up: sharing leadership in a police agency. *Police Practice and Research*, 9(2), 145–63. http://doi.org/10.1080/15614260802081303.

Steinmetz, G. (2005). Sociology. In G. Steinmetz (ed.), *The Politics of Method in the Human Sciences: Positivism and Its Epistemological Others* (pp. 275–323). Durham, NC: Duke University Press.

Stoker, G. (2006). Public value management: A new narrative for networked governance? *The American Review of Public Administration*, 36(1), 41–57.

Stoleru, L. (1974). *Vaincre la pauvreté dans les pays riches*. Paris: Flammarion.

Takayama, K. (2008). The politics of international league tables: PISA in Japan's achievement crisis debate. *Comparative Education*, 44(4), 387–407. http://doi.org/10.1080/03050060802481413.

Taylor, I., & Kelly, J. (2006). Professionals, discretion and public sector reform in the UK: re-visiting Lipsky. *International Journal of Public Sector Management*, 19(7), 629–42.

Thaler, R. H., & Sunstein, C. (2008). *Nudge: improving decisions about health, wealth and happiness*. New Haven: Yale University Press.

Thomas, R., & Davies, A. (2005). Theorizing the micro-politics of resistance: new public management and managerial identities in the UK public services. *Organization Studies*, 26(5), 683–706.

Thompson, B. (2000). Tragically difficult: the obstacles to governing the commons. *Environmental Law*, 30, 241–78.

Thorndike, J. J. (2001). Reforming the internal revenue service: a comparative history. *Administrative Law Review*, 53, 717–80.

Timmermans, S., & Berg, M. (2003). *The gold standard: the challenge of evidence-based medicine and standardization in health care*. Philadelphia: Temple University Press.

Torfing, J., & Triantafillou, P. (2013). What's in a name? Grasping new public governance as a political-administrative system. *International Review of Public Administration*, 18(2), 9–25.

Torres, L. (2004). Trajectories in public administration reforms in European Continental countries. *Australian Journal of Public Administration*, 63(3), 99–112.

Torres, L., & Pina, V. (2004). Reshaping public administration: the Spanish experience compared to the UK. *Public Administration*, 82(2), 445–64.

Trask, R. R. (1991). *GAO history, 1921–1991*. Washington. DC: GAO.

Traunmuller, R., & Lenk, K. (1996). New public management and enabling technologies. In N. Terashima & E. Altman (eds), *Advanced IT tools*. London: Chapman and Hall.

Triantafillou, P. (2004a). Addressing network governance through the concepts of governmentality and normalization. *Administrative Theory & Praxis*, 26(4), 489–508.

Triantafillou, P. (2004b). From blood to public office: constituting bureaucratic rulers in colonial Malaya. *Journal of Southeast Asian Studies*, 35(1), 25–40.

Triantafillou, P. (2007). Benchmarking in the public sector: a critical conceptual framework. *Public Administration*, 85(3), 829–46.

Triantafillou, P. (2011). Metagovernance by numbers: technological lock-in of Australian and Danish employment policies? In J. Torfing & P. Triantafillou (eds), *Interactive policymaking, metagovernance and democracy*. Colchester: ECPR Press.

Triantafillou, P. (2012). *New forms of governing: a Foucauldian inspired analysis*. Basingstoke: Palgrave Macmillan.
Triantafillou, P. (2014). Against all odds? Understanding the emergence of accreditation of the Danish hospitals. *Social Science & Medicine*, 101, 75–85.
Triantafillou, P. (2015a). The political implications of performance management and evidence-based policymaking. *American Review of Public Administration*, 45(2), 167–81.
Triantafillou, P. (2015b). The politics of neutrality and the changing role of expertise in public administration. *Administrative Theory & Praxis*, 37(3), 174–87.
Triantafillou, P. (2016). Government by standards: the making and managing of accountability in Danish hospitals. *Social Theory & Health*, 14, 239–55.
Triantafillou, P., & Nielsen, M. R. (2001). Policing empowerment: the making of capable subjects. *History of the Human Sciences*, 14(2), 63–86.
Van Berkel, H., & Wijnen, W. (2010). Accreditation in the Netherlands: does accountability improve educational quality? *Research in Comparative and International Education*, 5(1), 88–97.
van der Knaap, P. (2015). Policy analysis and performance audit at the 'highest level': looking for evidence and responsiveness. In F. van Nispen and P. Scholten (eds), *Policy analysis in the Netherlands* (pp. 121–36). Bristol: Policy Press.
van der Meer, F. M. (ed.) (2011). *Civil service systems in Western Europe*. Cheltenham: Edward Elgar.
van der Meer, F. M., & Dijkstra, G. S. A. (2011). The civil service system of the Netherlands. In F. M. van der Meer (ed.), *Civil service systems in Western Europe* (pp. 149–83). Cheltenham: Edward Elgar.
van der Meer, F. M., van den Berg, C. F. & Dijkstra, G. (2013). Rethinking the 'public service bargain': the changing (legal) position of civil servants in Europe. *International Review of Administrative Sciences*, 79(1), 91–109.
Vandenbroucke, F. (2001). Foreword. In G. Esping-Andersen, D. Gallie, A. Hemerijck & J. Myles (eds), *Why we need a new welfare state* (pp. viii–xxiv). Oxford: Oxford University Press.
Venugopal, R. (2015). Neoliberalism as concept. *Economy and Society*, April, 1–23. http://doi.org/10.1080/03085147.2015.1013356.
Verheijen, T. (1999). *Civil service systems in Central and Eastern Europe*. Cheltenham: Edward Elgar.
Verheijen, T., & Connaughton, B. (2003). Public administration education and Europeanization: prospects for the emancipation of a discipline? *Public Administration*, 81(4), 833–51. http://doi.org/10.1111/j.0033-3298.2003.00373.x.
Verhoest, K., Peters, B. G., Bouckaert, G. & Verschuere, B. (2004). The study of organisational autonomy: a conceptual review. *Public Administration and Development*, 24(2), 101–18. http://doi.org/10.1002/pad.316.
von Mises, L. (1944). *Bureaucracy*. New Haven: Yale University Press.
von Mises, L. (1990). *Epistemological problems in economics*. Indianapolis: The Liberty Fund.
von Mises, L. (1996). *Human action*. New York: Foundation for Economic Education.

Vrangbæk, K. (1999). New public management i sygehusfeltet – udformning og konsekvenser. In E. Z. Bentsen, F. Borum, G. Erlingsdottir & K. Sahlin-Andersson (ads), *Når styringsambitioner møder praksis – den svære omstilling af sygehus- og sundhedsvæsenet i Danmark og Sverige* (pp. 33–56). Copenhagen: Handelshøjskolens Forlag.

Wacquant, L. (2009). *Punishing the poor: the neoliberal government of social insecurity*. Durham, NC: Duke University Press.

Wacquant, L. (2010). Crafting the neoliberal state: workfare, prisonfare, and social insecurity. *Sociological Forum*, 25(2), 197–220.

Wallis, J., & Gregory, R. (2009). Leadership, accountability and public value: resolving a problem in 'new governance'? *International Journal of Public Administration*, 32(3–4), 250–73. http://doi.org/10.1080/01900690902732608.

Wanna, J., Ryan, C. & Ng, C. (2001). *From accounting to accountability: a centenary history of the Australian National Audit Office*. Crows Nest, NSW: Allen & Unwin.

Watson, D. (1997). Quality, standards and institutional reciprocity. In J. Brennan, P. de Vries & R. Williams (eds), *Standards and quality in higher education* (pp. 131–45). London: Jessica Kingsley.

Watson, D., & Bowden, R. (2007). The fate of the Dearing recommendations: policy and performance in UK HE, 1997–2007. In D. Watson & M. Amoah (eds), *The Dearing Report ten years on: Bedford Way papers*. London: Institute of Education, University of London.

Weber, E., & Khademian, A. (2008). Wicked problems, knowledge challenges, and collaborative capacity builders in network settings. *Public Administration Review*, 68(2). Retrieved from http://onlinelibrary.wiley.com/doi/10.1111/j.1540-6210.2007.00866.x/full.

Weber, M. (1922). *Gesammelte Aufsätze zur Wissenschaftslehre*. Tübingen: Mohr.

Weber, M. (1948a). Politics as a vocation. In H. H. Gerth & C. Wright Mills (eds), *From Max Weber: essays in sociology* (pp. 77–127). London: Routledge.

Weber, M. (1948b). Science as a vocation. In H. H. Gerth & C. Wright Mills (eds), *From Max Weber: essays in sociology* (pp. 129–156). London: Routledge.

Weber, M. (1949). *The methodology of the social sciences*. New York: Free Press.

Weber, M. (1978). *Economy and society Vols 1 & 2*. Berkeley: University of California Press.

Weiss, C., Murphy-Graham, E., Petrosino, A. & Gandhi, A. G. (2008). The fairy godmother and her warts: making the dream of evidence-based policy come true. *American Journal of Evaluation*, 29(1), 29–47.

Wettenhall, R. (2005). Agencies and non-departmental public bodies. *Public Management Review*, 7(4), 615–35. http://doi.org/10.1080/14719030500362827.

Wildavsky, A. (1986). *Speaking truth to power: the art and craft of policy analysis* (2nd edition). New Brunswick: Transaction.

Williams, P. (2012). *Collaboration in public policy and practice: perspectives on boundary spanners*. Bristol: Policy Press.

Wise, L. (1996). Internal labour markets. In A. J. G. M. Bekke, J. L. Perry & T. A.

J. Toonen (eds), *Civil service systems in a comparative perspective*. Bloomington: Indiana University Press.

Wiseman, A. W. (2013). Policy responses to PISA in comparative perspective. In H. D. Meyer & A. Benavot (eds), *PISA, power and policy* (pp. 303–21). Oxford: Symposium Books.

Wolff, S. (2015). EU budget support as a transnational policy instrument: above and beyond the state? *Public Administration*, 93(4), 922–39. http://doi.org/10.1111/padm.12177.

Woolgar, S., & Latour, B. (1986). *Laboratory life: the construction of scientific facts*. Princeton: Princeton University Press.

Wright, W. E., & Dixon, M. C. (1977). Community prevention and treatment of juvenile delinquency: a review of evaluation studies 1. *Journal of Research in Crime and Delinquency*, 14 (1), 35–67. http://doi.org/10.1177/002242787701400104.

Wuttke, J. (2008). Uncertainty and bias in PISA. In R. Hopmann, G. Brinek & M. Retzl (ed.), *PISA according to PISA: does PISA keep what it promises?* (pp. 241–63). Vienna: SSRN.

Zheng, L., & Warner, M. (2010). Business incentive use among US local governments: a story of accountability and policy learning. *Economic Development Quarterly*, 24(4), 325–36.

Zittoun, P., & Demongeot, B. (2010). Debates in French policy studies: from cognitive to discursive approaches. *Critical Policy Studies*, 3(3–4), 391–406. http://doi.org/10.1080/19460171003619816.

Index